MW00958744

THE ETERNAL BLUEPRINT

The Eternal Blueprint

Bryan Kessler

Lifeschool International
Marietta, Georgia, U.S.A.
http://www.LifeschoolInternational.org

The Eternal Blueprint
Copyright © 2019 by Bryan Kessler.

Published by:

Lifeschool International
P.O. Box 671063
Marietta, GA 30066-0136
http://www.LifeschoolInternational.org

Printed and bound in the United States of America. All rights reserved. Written permission must be secured from the publisher to use or reproduce any part of this book, except for brief quotations in critical reviews or articles.
Italics in biblical quotes indicate emphasis added.

Unless otherwise noted, Scripture quotations are from the New American Standard Updated (NASU) Edition. Copyright © 1960, 1962, 1963, 1968, 1971, 1972, 1973, 1975, 1977, 1995 by the Lockman Foundation. Used by permission.

Scripture quotations marked NKJV are taken from the Holy Bible, New King James Version, © 1982 by Thomas Nelson, Inc.

Scripture quotations marked NIV are taken from the Holy Bible, New International Version, © 1973, 1978, 1984 by International Bible Society. Used by permission of Zondervan Publishing House.

Scripture quotations marked (NLT) are taken from the Holy Bible, New Living Translation, copyright © 1996, 2004, 2007. Used by permission of Tyndale House Publishers Inc., Carol Stream, Illinois 60188. All rights reserved.

Scripture quotations marked KJV are taken from the King James Version of the Bible. Scripture quotations marked ASV are taken from the American Standard Version of the Bible. Scripture quotations marked YLT are taken from the Young's Literal Translation of the Bible.

Editor: Elizabeth Dondiego Cossick
Cover Design: Lisa Hainline (http://www.lisahainline.com)
ISBN: 978-1073724437
Printed by Kindle Direct Publishing

Acknowledgements

I want to express my great appreciation to Noel Mann, who was truly a forerunner to forerunners. Noel, who went to be with the Lord in 2016, was a great friend and a spiritual father to me. The twenty years that Noel poured into my life helped prepare me to write this book. I know this book would not exist without Noel's influence.

I also want to thank Terry Bennett, who first made me aware that God had an eternal purpose. This book is truly the fruit of Terry's mentoring, training, and teaching. I am eternally grateful that Terry is a friend and a spiritual father to me. This book was birthed through Terry's prophetic teachings.

In addition, I want to thank my prayer team who labored in prayer for me to write this book. This was definitely a hard book to write as I attempted to make deep, complex subjects simple to read and easy to understand. It was my faithful team of intercessors that prayed me through to completion.

Furthermore, I want to thank my mom and dad (Donna and Ken) who are both my natural parents *and* spiritual parents. Your pure devotion to the Lord and faithful intercession for me and our family has shaped me into who I am today. I am forever grateful for your tireless prayers and your loving, non-religious expression of Jesus Christ. This book would not exist without you.

Additionally, I want to thank Sue Woods, Janie Wicker (my mother-in-law), Elizabeth Cossick (my editor) and my dad for reviewing this book and dramatically improving it with your insight, wisdom, and spiritual perception. You definitely made this book much better.

Finally, I want to thank my beautiful, sweet, and godly wife, Angie. Thank you so much for all that you do. I really appreciate you releasing me to bury myself in my computer for a year to write this book. Your encouragement, prayers, and support throughout this project sustained me and helped me complete this. Thank you for enduring through the spiritual warfare that was associated with bringing this manuscript to light. You showed much grace, patience, love, and endurance. I so appreciate you and love you!

Oh, I can't forget my funny and fun young daughter, Anna. I'll never forget the time when I was discouraged and wanted to quit writing this book. I woke up one morning with the theme song from *Zootopia*, "Try Everything," bouncing around in my head. When I told Anna about it, she had the wisdom of the Lord, saying, "Maybe the Lord is speaking to you about your book." When I looked up the lyrics, I realized that she was right. Here's an excerpt from the song:

> *I won't give up, no I won't give in*
> *Till I reach the end*
> *And then I'll start again*
> *Though I'm on the lead*
> *I wanna try everything*
> *I wanna try even though I could fail*
> *I won't give up, no I won't give in*
> *Till I reach the end*
> *And then I'll start again*

Thanks, Anna, for allowing the Lord to use you to speak encouragement to me when I was discouraged and ready to quit!

Contents

Introduction

Epic moments usually start with humble beginnings. For me, my life-changing moment was in the lobby of an Econo Lodge.

Early one morning in 2017, while attending a ministry-training event, I began reading through the book of Ephesians. But this morning, I can only say that the Holy Spirit opened my eyes as I read. For the first time, I realized that Paul wrote this book to unveil God's "eternal purpose" that was established "before the foundation of the world" (Eph. 3:11; Eph. 1:4). Suddenly, a light of revelation flooded my heart and truths that I had learned during my twenty-five-year pursuit of Christ converged. It was like the moment when you find the key missing piece to a puzzle and snap it into place, the picture becoming suddenly complete.

Discovering this missing piece gave me a clearer picture of God's grand master plan and of His heavenly perspective. God's eternal thoughts, desires, and will are no longer a blurry, ethereal, mysterious concept. Subsequently, my focus has shifted more from myself to God. As I have begun to see through His eyes, I've realized my own selfishness. Everything truly is "from Him and through Him and to Him" (Rom. 11:36). This revelation was the catalyst for an internal rewiring that paved the way for a greater infilling of Christ, releasing me from shallowness, self-centeredness, and "striving after wind" (Ecc. 1:14).

It may be helpful to share that, before this moment, I had spent the past twenty-five years pursuing the Lord with all of my heart. When it comes to the Christian experience, I have been there, done that, and bought the t-shirt. I have been in the traditional church and have also witnessed the good, the bad, and the ugly in the Charismatic movement. I've studied the end times extensively, engaged in prayer and spiritual warfare, and, though I can't clap on beat, went deep into the worship movement. I have studied theology and doctrine, reading all the must-have books in Christendom. I've served as an elder and now as a senior pastor of a local church.

I know how to hear the voice of God and minister in the gifts of the Spirit. I have been on and led mission trips to many nations, including traveling to Israel twice. And I currently co-lead a global missions organization that has trained over 2,000 senior pastors in East and South Africa. So if there's a t-shirt, I've got it.

Yet still . . . I knew there was more. Much more. Like many of you, my soul still hungered and thirsted for something greater than I had known—a more fulfilling purpose than I had experienced.

Perhaps you can relate. Maybe you, like me, have become weary of event-driven churches that entertain the soul but leave the spirit wanting. Or perhaps you, like me, are nauseated by rock-star, celebrity Christianity that eclipses Jesus. Or maybe you have been wounded by the rough edges of religion. Having tasted of the wine from the modern-day church, many of us have walked away thinking, "Is this all there is? Did Jesus save us for this? Do I have to wait until I die and go to heaven to experience the glorious reality for which I was created?"

If you are tired of the event-driven, man-centered, religious expression we call *church*, then I have good news for you: *There is more.*

And this longing for more is satisfied by God's ageless purpose—a purpose that was established before time and creation. A purpose that will leave you stunned, overwhelmed, and undone. A purpose so grand and majestic that you will forever be praising "the glory of His grace" (Eph. 1:6).

If you think about it, aren't we all searching for purpose and meaning in life? Because God created us in His image, the need for purpose and meaning has been wired into our DNA. Imperceptibly, however, we often try to meet this divinely-given desire with shallow substitutes, such as success, influence, prosperity, adventure, and worldly pleasures.

It doesn't take long to discover that none of these aspirations satisfies the intense longings of our hearts. Just as we were made for far more than the modern church experience, we were created for a purpose far beyond the American Dream. Our destiny is far greater than "living our best life now." The Lord has far more for us than being healthy, wealthy, and wise. When God's eternal purpose is revealed, we discover our ultimate purpose and our hearts find true satisfaction.

But here's the problem. Most believers are unaware that God even has an eternal purpose that drives everything He does. Ask most Christians, "What is God's ultimate intention? Why did God create the universe and humanity?" and you will likely hear many different responses, including "to save us," "to glorify Himself," "to feed the poor," or "to make disciples of Jesus in the nations." But what if there was something deeper? What if God had a grand master plan, a blueprint that He operates from, that has been hidden from many believers for centuries? What would happen if we rediscovered this?

That morning in the Econo Lodge the mystery that Paul unveiled some 2,000 years ago in Ephesians flipped my worldview on its head and transformed me from the inside out. It also helped me understand why we have such a shallow, man-centered, event-driven, celebrity-oriented church. We are operating from a blueprint that doesn't have its origins in God. It is a man-centered blueprint that views salvation as God's ultimate intention.

Stick with me on this for a minute. If the fall had not occurred, most of the issues that preoccupy the church wouldn't exist. There would be no human flaws requiring forgiveness or a need to establish justice and end oppression. There would be no suffering to alleviate or equality to establish. There would be no poverty to eradicate or disease to cure. The save-the-world manifesto that drives the majority of the church's activities, though vital now, would be unnecessary. My point is that we are preoccupied with patching up the effects of the fall. We are driven by purposes that are far below God's ultimate intention.

So what was God's original intention? God designed the human heart for something deeper, something richer, something more satisfying than merely receiving forgiveness from our sins and then wearying ourselves serving in the church for the rest of our lives. The passion that has burned within God's heart for all eternity is to put His very life into us. Jesus didn't just come to save us from our sins, but to release His life in fullness within our hearts and souls, inviting us into deep fellowship with God the Father, God the Son, and God the Holy Spirit. God is not merely tolerating us in our failures and shortcomings. He has marked us to *be* His inheritance, what Paul called "His inheritance in the saints" (Eph. 1:18).

We are invited to become mature, Christlike sons and daughters of the Father, who are a representation of *the* Son. We are destined to become the bride of Christ, who partners with Jesus for all eternity. We are called to become the Holy Spirit's temple, body, and spiritual house, whom He fills unto fullness. And finally, we are offered to sit with Jesus on His throne, from where we will rule the nations with a rod of iron. The Father, the Son, and the Holy Spirit have a glorious inheritance in us and we have a staggering and breathtaking inheritance in Christ.

Your destiny is far greater than going to church once a week, striving with gritted teeth to live a moral life free from sin, and then, when you die, to strum a harp on the clouds of heaven for the endless ages of eternity. Rather, the invitation is to experience an unending, ever-deepening relationship with the Godhead and to expand His kingdom into the vastness of creation forever and ever.

If you hunger for more than today's best-life-now gospel, where God's primary goal is to bless us with success, prosperity, health, favor, and influence, then this book is for you. If you desire more of God, to break free from the bondage of shallow religion and to experience a deeper, more fulfilling relationship with Christ, then keep reading. If you want to discover your true purpose and destiny, it's found in *The Eternal Blueprint*.

When your eyes are opened to God's eternal purpose—a purpose that drives everything that He does—you will realize why God created you. And having this understanding will transform your life, bring rest to your soul, and finally satisfy the intense longings of your heart. You and I were made for so much more.

Why I Wrote This Book

The great tragedy of our time is that God's eternal purpose is hardly mentioned anymore. Of the books and teachings that talk about God's ultimate intention, many of the authors are no longer living.

Think about this for a minute. If God established a blueprint before time and creation that drives everything that He does and the church is ignorant of this, what does this say about how far we have drifted from the gospel handed down to us by the apostles? Unfortunately, the mystery that Paul unveiled throughout his writings has become a mystery once again. This is an indictment against us. This explains why the church is man-centered, selfish, shallow, and ineffective.

When I think about my journey into eternal purpose—how my life and ministry have been greatly impacted by discovering it and yet how long it took for me to even realize God had an eternal purpose, it underscores the true state of the church.

At the age of 19, when I rededicated my life to Christ after a season of rebellion, I ran hard after the Lord. I pursued Him with everything in my heart. I read books by the great men of God of our time and by those from the past. I went to many conferences, events, and church services. I heard messages by the greatest preachers and teachers of our day. Yet it took me over twenty-five years to hear about God's eternal purpose, the blueprint that drives everything that God does.

I am so grateful for my friend Terry Bennett, whose entire message and ministry resonates with God's eternal purpose. Terry has great insight into God's eternal purpose, and if it wasn't for his teaching and ministry, this book would not exist. So, I thank God for Terry and the insight given to him.

Because God's eternal purpose is rarely mentioned today—even though thousands of Christian books are published every year—I decided to write *The Eternal Blueprint*. My hope and prayer is that this perspective will transform your life as it has mine.

OVERVIEW

In writing this book, one of my goals is to take a somewhat complicated subject and make it easy to understand. To accomplish this, I have broken the book into eight parts.

Part 1 – The Blueprint
To truly understand God's eternal purpose and our purpose in Him, we need a God-centered approach. This requires the proper starting point. We must begin in eternity past when it was only God. Part 1 focuses on the blueprint from eternity, established in a heavenly council of the Godhead, that determined God's master plan for the ages.

Part 2 – The Son Is God's Ultimate Intention
The first priority of God's eternal purpose is the supreme exaltation of His Son. God's ultimate intention is for the Son to have pre-eminence in everything. Part 2 examines the Son at the center of everything that God does.

Part 3 – The Purpose of the Ages
God's driving purpose for the ages is to gather everything in heaven and on earth under the headship of Jesus Christ. Part 3 focuses on how the Lord accomplishes this objective by establishing His kingdom in the different ages revealed in Scripture.

Part 4 – The Gospel and Ultimate Intention
Most gospel presentations are disconnected from God's ultimate intention. Part 4 looks at how the work of the cross and the way of the cross restore us back to God's purpose for the ages.

Part 5 – The Father's Inheritance in the Saints
Before the foundation of the world, the Father decided that He would conform men and women into the image of His Son and

thus have a family of sons patterned after His beloved Son. Part 5 focuses on God's predetermined plan to adopt us as His sons (Eph. 1:5).

Part 6 – The Son's Inheritance in the Saints
In eternity past, the Father determined to give His Son a beloved who would love Him like the Father (John 17:26). Part 6 examines God's eternal purpose to give His Son an equally yoked bride who will partner with Him throughout the endless ages of eternity.

Part 7 – The Spirit's Inheritance in the Saints
Before time and creation, God determined to place the Spirit of His Son into His people. Part 7 looks at the Holy Spirit's inheritance, which is a temple that He fills, a house in which He dwells, and a body that He possesses and brings to Christ-like maturity.

Part 8 – Our Inheritance in Christ
God's ultimate intention is to give His people eternal intimacy, eternal authority, and eternal glory. Jesus described this in His promises to the overcomers in Revelation 2-3. Part 8 explores the details of our future inheritance.

How to Read This Book

During my Christian journey, one of the main ways the Lord has trained me is through books. I love to read. I especially love to read books by men and women of God who have experienced the Lord in ways that I haven't. Some of my greatest revelations have come by reading Scripture-saturated books early in the morning.

Here's a suggestion for how to read this book. Don't try to speed race through it. Read a chapter per day and meditate upon it throughout the day. Read for revelation rather than for information. Read to transform your heart, not just to put information into your head.

Most books don't transform us because we are too driven to finish. We race from chapter to chapter without stopping to ponder, meditate, and pray through what we have read. As a result, we might gain knowledge, but we don't receive revelation. And it's only revelation that can transform us.

To get the most from this book, I encourage you to read only one chapter per day. I have tried to make the chapters short enough so that each chapter can be read in about 15 to 20 minutes.

Take your best time of the day—whether early in the morning, around lunchtime, or before bed—and read a chapter. Ask the Father to illuminate your heart and mind through the Holy Spirit. Take time to think deeply about what you read and to pray through areas that the Holy Spirit highlights.

View this thirty-one-chapter book as a journey to find your life purpose in relation to God's eternal purpose. My hope is that the information and revelation in this book will impact and transform you in the same way it has me.

A Good Comparison

One final thought before you get started. Perhaps you have read through a menu at a restaurant and wanted to order ten different entrees. That seems to be my experience often. Well, now there are tapas restaurants where you order appetizers as your main meal. Rather than just read about the mouth-watering dishes, you get to sample them. This helps you know what to order as your main dish the next time you eat there.

This book is similar to eating at a tapas restaurant. You get to sample what is on the menu of God's eternal purpose. But there are many details that I couldn't cover in depth.

If I were to cover all the components of God's eternal purpose in detail, this book would have easily been over one-thousand pages. So, view this book as sampling all that is on the menu of God's blueprint from eternity—a tapas selection of God's ultimate intention.

In the future, my hope is to write other books that dive deeper into various parts of God's eternal purpose.

PART 1

THE BLUEPRINT

If we truly want to understand God's eternal purpose and our purpose in Him, then we need a God-centered approach. This requires the proper starting point. We must begin in eternity past when it was only God. Part 1 focuses on the blueprint from eternity, established in a heavenly council of the Godhead before time and creation, which determined God's master plan for the ages.

CHAPTER 1

BEFORE THE FOUNDATION
OF THE WORLD

The Bucket List debuted in 2007. This movie popularized the idea of doing and achieving certain things before you "kick the bucket" (an English idiom for dying).

In the movie, billionaire Edward Cole (Jack Nicholson) and car mechanic Carter Chambers (Morgan Freeman) are terminally ill patients who are placed into the same hospital room. Faced with certain death, these two men vow to spend their last days fulfilling their life's dreams.

One of my bucket list items was fulfilled in 2015 when I went on a safari in Maasai Mara, Kenya.

You might have seen Maasai Mara in documentaries. This national reserve in southwest Kenya, along the Tanzanian border, is famous for its wildebeest migration. Twice a year, as the wildebeest migrate from the Serengeti to Maasai Mara and back, they must cross the Masa River. Lurking underneath the waters are large and fierce crocodiles that devour unfortunate wildebeests. Though we didn't witness this migration, we did see a lion, lionesses, elephants, giraffes, hippos, zebras, rhinos, and water buffalo. It was truly an amazing experience.

Seeing the wonder of God's creation in Maasai Mara—from the majestic animals to the expansive savannah, and from the breathtaking sunsets to thousands of stars glittering in the midnight sky—left me in awe of God. It made me ponder God's transcendence. It stirred my heart to question, "In all of creation, what does God really want from *me*? Am I fulfilling the purpose for which I was created?"

Perhaps you've had a similar experience. Maybe it was while hiking up a mountain to breathe in a panoramic view, or while exploring a far-off town that had previously only lived in books and dreams—and all of a sudden, in these bucket-list moments, you suddenly realize God's transcendence and that you are a speck of dust in the vast universe. Like me, you ponder, "What is God's purpose for my life? Am I fulfilling the purpose for which I was created? Do I even know what God's ultimate purpose is?"

A God-Centered Worldview

To find life's ultimate meaning in today's culture, we're told to chase our dreams. Build a legacy that will outlast you. Stand for something and make a difference. Become the person you've always wanted to be. Become the best version of yourself. Seek happiness and pleasure. Fulfill your destiny. Leave the world a better place than you found it. End suffering and create equality. Challenge oppression and bring justice. Accept, tolerate, and forgive human flaws. Help as many people as possible have a better life.

Unfortunately, these notions all fall flat. "Why?" you might ask. "What's wrong with these aspirations? Aren't these ambitions good and noble?"

The problem is that they are inherently selfish. They are humanistic. Look again, and you'll realize that God is not even factored into the equation. Which brings me to one of my main points.

If we want to understand the meaning of life and discover our purpose, God must be our starting point. Not ourselves. We must shift from a man-centered worldview to a God-centered worldview. We must begin with God Himself.

Discovering God's Ultimate Intention

A truly God-centered perspective, where we see the world through God's eyes, is the only way we can discover our true purpose, meaning, significance, and destiny. Only when we understand God's eternal purpose can we unravel and discern *our* life purpose.

Nevertheless, one pitfall that ensnares many believers is that they over-emphasize certain areas of Scripture, ignoring God's original intention before time and creation.

Here are some examples.

End-Time Prophecy

Many students of end-time prophecy have become so engrossed in understanding the end times that they overlook God's ultimate intention. They focus on the identity of the antichrist, where he will come from, when the Lord will return, and when the rapture will take place. They obsess over blood moons, the latest technology that could become the mark of the beast, and news headlines that confirm prophetic Scriptures.

Please don't misunderstand what I'm saying. All the end-time events recorded in the Scriptures will certainly take place, and we should diligently study these passages. We should also proclaim and long for the second coming of Christ, paying close attention to the signs pointing to His return. Like Jesus said, we are to watch and be ready (Matt. 24:42-44).

Nevertheless, we can't allow the unfolding of biblical prophecy to distract us from God's ultimate intention for creating the world. We have to be careful that end-time events don't eclipse the eternal purpose in God's heart.

Revival and Miracles

Reading through the book of Acts is awe-inspiring and breathtaking. I love hearing about the Holy Spirit baptizing the apostles with resurrection power. My heart is stirred when I read of the sick being miraculously healed. The lame leaping for joy. Thousands born again and baptized. Dreams, visions, trances, angelic visitations, translations from location to location, preaching that inspired true repentance, church growth, a multiplication of disciples, and a sense of awe and wonder as heaven invaded earth.

There has never been such a mighty move of the Holy Spirit as what is described in the book of Acts. And I believe, before the

Lord returns, there will be a final move of God that will surpass the accounts in Acts. Nevertheless, outward demonstrations of power are not God's ultimate intention. Signs, wonders, and miracles are not God's highest destiny for mankind.

As much as I hope for a Third Great Awakening in America, revival is not the ultimate goal in God's heart, either. Today, many are so focused on revival (which I'm certainly in favor of) that it has overshadowed God's ultimate intention. As wonderful as God's miracle-working power and revival are, there is a deeper purpose that we must discover.

Social Justice

Many who read the gospels, especially Jesus' teachings in the Sermon on the Mount and His emphasis on loving our neighbor as ourselves, focus on making the world a better place. The assumption is that God's ultimate aim is to liberate the captive, to deliver the oppressed, to heal the sick, to end cycles of poverty, to build water wells, to take care of orphans, to help the marginalized, to rescue the victimized, and to take the gospel to the ends of the earth.

Obviously, all of these are important to the Lord and His ultimate objective.

But if you think about it, without the fall, there would be no poverty to eradicate, human suffering to eliminate, and broken people who need to be restored. My point is that God's ultimate intention transcends social justice, compassion, and missions. God's original plan trumps even these noble acts of social justice.

The Restoration of Israel

The prophecies of Isaiah, Jeremiah, Ezekiel, Daniel, Zechariah, Zephaniah, and others point to a glorious time in the future when Israel becomes the praise of the earth and the nations stream to it. Words fail to describe how glorious this golden age of prosperity, righteousness, peace, and utopia will be.

The nations will lay down their weapons of war, and even the animal kingdom will be in harmony. The anti-Semitic nations who once hated Israel will bow down and kiss the feet of the Jewish people.

Though the restoration of Israel will be a glorious time, God's ultimate intention for creating the world was not to make Israel a praise in the earth. There is a higher purpose that we must find—a purpose that transcends what most assume is God's ultimate goal.

The Jewish Roots of Christianity

The story of the Exodus, when God miraculously delivered the Hebrews from Egyptian captivity and buried their armies on the floor of the Red Sea, is fascinating. Seeing how the Lord came down upon Mount Horeb in blazing glory and gave Moses the Law stuns us. All the types and shadows of Christ in the feasts and sacrifices display God's meticulous attention to detail.

Nevertheless, neither the Law, the feasts of Israel, nor the Torah were God's ultimate intention. Unfortunately, we are witnessing a growing trend in Christianity where Gentiles are trying to become Jews. Some, in their devotion to the Torah, have even renounced Jesus Christ.

Though we are thankful for the Jewish roots of Christianity, there is an eternal purpose that is much greater than the Torah.

The Blessings of Abraham

The Abrahamic Covenant contains some of the greatest blessings in history. God promised to bless Abraham, to make his name great, to give him the land of Israel, and to bless him with prosperity, health, destiny, a great family, success, protection from enemy attacks, and a joyful heart.[1] Paul said that all who are in Christ are heirs to the blessing of Abraham (Gal. 3:9-16).

Though God enjoys blessing His New Covenant children, a blessed life is not God's ultimate intention.

Sadly, many leaders in the prosperity gospel movement have become so focused on receiving God's blessings that they have drifted far from God's ultimate intention.

In East Africa, where we have a Bible-training program that trains pastors and leaders, our thirty-five-member leadership team testifies that about eighty percent of East African churches have fully embraced the prosperity gospel. According to them, many church services are focused solely on how you can be blessed and prosper. For example, if you give your tithe and offering to the man of God, then God will bless you with healing, prosperity, favor, and a fulfilling destiny.

Whether we are focused on our "best life now" or have been carried away by the extremes of the prosperity gospel, God's blessings are not His ultimate purpose for His people.

Advance the Kingdom

Some look at Genesis 1:28 as the Scripture that best defines God's ultimate intention. They believe that God's command to be fruitful, to multiply, and to take dominion over the earth is the reason why God created the world.

These emphasize God's governmental rule and authority, focusing on extending His kingdom into every sphere of society, including religion, family, education, government, business, media, arts, and entertainment.

Again, please don't misunderstand what I'm saying. Advancing the kingdom of God is certainly important. We are called to influence the culture as salt and light, to reign in life, and to occupy until He comes. Nevertheless, God's eternal purpose is greater than even this.

Salvation

Undoubtedly, salvation is the most common answer given to define God's ultimate intention. Many denominations, movements, and ministries only look to Adam's sin when defining God's eternal purpose.

When the fall is the starting point, salvation, grace, forgiveness, and redemption become the end for which God created the world. The finished work of the cross becomes the ultimate aim in preaching, teaching, ministry, missions, and church planting. To even suggest that God's original intention transcends salvation seems heretical.

Nevertheless, when God created the world, His intention was not for man to fall. Therefore, his foremost intention was not to bring redemption. The Lord's aim was for Adam to partake of the tree of life and to eventually have God's life released in fullness within him.

Obviously, salvation, grace, forgiveness, and redemption are now essential, for apart from the finished work of the cross, we are lost, dead in our sin, and hell-bound. But salvation was never God's ultimate intention. Rather, salvation is the means God uses to *restore* us to His eternal purpose.

Starting with Eternity Past

If you think about it, most of these focuses would be unnecessary if Adam had eaten from the tree of life and not from the tree of the knowledge of good and evil. God's life would have been imparted into him and his descendants, eventually filling them with the fullness of God's life. Subsequent generations would also have had God's life imparted into them. Ultimately, the earth would have been covered with men and women who were filled with the fullness of God's life.

This would have eliminated the need for salvation, revival, end-time prophecy, social justice, the Great Commission, the Jewish roots of Christianity, and the restoration of Israel—things which consume the majority of the church today.

If we hunger and thirst for more than patching up the effects of the fall—if we want to know God's original intention—then we need a starting point that is further back than the book of Genesis. Our starting point must be eternity *past*. Before humanity. Before the creation of the universe. Even before the angels, heaven, and the throne.

If we step backwards into eternity—back to the beginning when it was just God the Father, God the Son, and God the Holy Spirit dwelling together in unapproachable light in deep fellowship and intimacy—then we can discern God's eternal purpose.

DeVern Fromke, in his excellent book *Ultimate Intention*, wrote,

Let us go back in time—back into God's heart before He began creating anything, back before redemption was even necessary. Let us go back to the "blueprint" stage of His planning. What was God's intention then, before He began any of His activity on earth or in heaven? When we start reading in Genesis, "in the beginning," we see God's creative work. But the Apostle Paul takes us back "before the foundation (beginning) of the world." What was God's deep desire and intention in that great "before"? What was on the "white paper sheet" of His heart before He began creating the universe?[2]

Going back to God's "blueprint stage of His planning" takes us beyond the "in the beginning" of Genesis 1:1 and into eternity past. Jesus and Paul both described it as "before the foundation of the world" (John 17:24; Eph. 1:4).

If we could go back to this time, all we would see was "unapproachable light" (1 Tim. 6:16). A light so intense that nothing could penetrate it. A light so bright that the sun would pale in comparison. A light so powerful, it would make the present heaven and earth flee in utter terror.[3] Yet this light was not some cosmic force or celestial object. This light was a Person. John said that "God is Light, and in Him there is no darkness at all" (1 John 1:5). Hidden behind the curtain of this unapproachable light, we would find the eternal Son dwelling in "the Father's heart" in deep fellowship and intimacy (John 1:18, NLT).

THE ETERNAL FELLOWSHIP OF THE TRINITY

Here, in eternity past, there was no humanity, no sin, no need for salvation, no world, no angels, no heaven, and no throne. It was God and God alone dwelling in unapproachable light in the fellowship of the Trinity.

Within the radiance of this unapproachable light, the eternal Father, the eternal Son, and the eternal Spirit dwelt in unbroken union, joyful fellowship, and deep intimacy for billions and billions of years.[4]

During this pre-creation period, the Father's heart was filled with ecstatic pleasure, deep delight, and unbroken satisfaction in His beloved Son. Jesus mentioned this when He said to His Father, "You loved Me before the foundation of the world" (John 17:24).

Throughout eternity past, the Son was the object of His Father's affection and love. The two were bound together in perfect union. Human language fails to articulate the intimacy, deep conversations, and unending communion between the Father and the Son through the Spirit. The euphoric love that God has for God is beyond words!

In our ignorance, we might look at this and think, "How boring! For billions of years the Father and the Son just looked at each other, talked to each other, and loved each other? They had nothing to entertain them—no sports, no movies, no video games, no social media? How boring!"

Yet, we can say with certainty that the Father and the Son were never bored. Never lonely. Never needy. Rather, they had billions of years of unbroken joy, pleasure, and delight in the fellowship of the Trinity. Like David said, "In Your presence is fullness of joy" and "pleasures forever" (Psa. 16:11).

In our broken and fallen condition, we simply can't comprehend the ecstatic joy that existed in the fellowship of the Godhead in eternity past. We can't fathom the depth of the Father's boundless, passionate, affectionate, and ardent love for His beloved, eternal, uncreated Son. The Father's love for His Son never had a beginning.

As you will see in coming chapters, the Father's love for His Son is the catalyst for God's eternal purpose. It's out of this deep, abiding, eternal love relationship that the Godhead determined to create mankind and invite us into His purpose for the ages—a purpose that was established in a heavenly council before time and creation. In this mysterious meeting of the Godhead, the eternal blueprint was designed.

CHAPTER 2

THE BLUEPRINT FROM ETERNITY

If you have kids, you know that no matter how tired they are, when it's time for bed, it's like they just drank a cup of espresso. Kids will do anything to fight going to sleep.

One night, as we were putting our ten-year-old daughter, Anna, to bed, she pulled out a prayer box. She had taken an old shoebox and cut a slit into the top. Then she would write prayer requests on slips of paper and insert them into the prayer box. Whenever it came time for bed, she would empty her prayer requests and pray through each one-by-one.

I had mixed emotions about this. On the one hand, I was proud that she came up with this thoughtful idea. But on the other hand, I wondered if, deep down, she had a hidden motive to prolong her bedtime as long as possible.

Well, on this particular night, my wife, Angie, and I were both very tired and just wanted to get Anna to sleep so that we could go to bed. Anna, of course, wanted to squeeze out every last second.

So, as we started to say our prayers, Anna dumped her prayer box onto her bed, and to my disbelief, something like thirty slips of paper fell out—*as in thirty prayer requests we were going to have to listen to before we could relax, unwind, and go to sleep.*

As Anna started praying through her list, one of her prayer requests was for President Trump.

Anna prayed, "God, please help Donald Trump's back."

After she prayed this, I stopped her and asked, "What's wrong with his back?"

Anna, in the most innocent and sweet voice, said, "Someone stabbed him in the back."

With a grin on my face, suspecting that Anna had read the tabloids at the grocery store, I asked her, "How do you know that Donald Trump was stabbed in the back?"

She responded, "I saw a magazine at Wal-Mart that said Donald Trump was stabbed in the back."

Once we explained to Anna that Donald Trump was not literally stabbed in the back, but betrayed by someone, the three of us had a great laugh at Anna's cute misunderstanding.

God's Predetermined Plan

I tell this story because there's been a critical misinterpretation in the book of Ephesians. Just like my daughter thought Donald Trump was literally stabbed in the back, many have misunderstood the word translated as *predestined* in most Bibles. This misunderstanding has blurred God's eternal purpose for centuries. As a result, the mystery of God's eternal purpose that Paul revealed in the first century is a mystery once again.

Paul said, "Before the foundation of the world . . . He *predestined* us to adoption as sons through Jesus Christ to Himself" (Eph. 1:4-5, emphasis mine).

Throughout the centuries, many Christians have interpreted this verse to mean something like this:

> Before the foundation of the world, God preselected certain individuals to be saved. Those whom God had mercy upon, He revealed Himself to, saved, and adopted them as His very own children.

There are two fundamental flaws in this understanding. First, adoption is viewed through a twenty-first-century lens rather than a first-century lens. Adoptions in the first-century related to a mature son, whether natural born or from another family, being placed over a father's inheritance. I will explain this more thoroughly in a later chapter.

The second flaw is a misunderstanding of the Greek word translated as *predestined*. Let me pause for a moment and make an important statement. If digging into Greek words sounds boring, please consider this. If we don't examine what a Greek word means, then we are at the mercy of Bible translators. History has proven that many Bible translators have subtly interjected their doctrinal beliefs into various translations of the Bible. I'm not saying you have to be a Greek or Hebrew scholar to understand the Scriptures. But in certain situations, it is important to analyze the original Hebrew or Greek word meaning. Such is the case with Ephesians 1:5.

The word translated *predestined* is the Greek word *proorizō*. This is a compound word comprised of *pro* (before) and *horizō*. The English word *horizon* originated from the Greek word *horizō*. As we know, a horizon is the line where the earth appears to meet the sky. It's also the limit or the range of something, such as one's knowledge, experience, or interest.

Horizō means "to define" or "to mark out the boundaries or limits (of any place or thing)."[1] For example, a nation has clearly defined borders; a house has clearly defined boundaries. Once the boundaries or limits have been clearly established, *horizō* can then carry the further meaning of "to determine" or "appoint."[2]

Putting all of this together, *proorizō* means to define the boundaries or limits of any place or thing, and from these boundaries, to determine beforehand.

Here's an example to clarify. I live in the suburbs of Atlanta. In 2017, Mercedes-Benz Stadium opened its doors. This stadium is the home of the Atlanta Falcons football team and the Atlanta United soccer team. As of this writing, Mercedes-Benz Stadium is one of the most beautiful stadiums in the country, if not the world.

Like any building, before construction began on Mercedes-Benz Stadium, architects likely spent months drafting the blueprint. They established boundaries for the field, the seats, the concession stands, the bathrooms, and the locker rooms. They decided how the stadium's roof would open and close. Every detail was meticulously established before any construction began. When the blueprint was finalized, the architects had determined beforehand what would be built.

This is what *proorizō* means. *Proorizō* is a word that describes a blueprint. In other words, *the blueprint from eternity.*

Now, when you see the word *predestined* in the New Testament, rather than thinking of some mysterious choice that God made of who would be saved and who wouldn't, think instead of His predetermined plan. Think of the blueprint He established before the foundation of the world. Think of the details of His eternal purpose rather than some ethereal decision the Godhead made of who would go to heaven and who would spend eternity in hell. It was God's *plan* that was predetermined. Not who would be saved and who wouldn't. *What* was predetermined, not *who*.

Now, when you read, "He *predestined* us to adoption as sons through Jesus Christ to Himself," think, "He established a blueprint before the foundation of the world and therefore determined beforehand to adopt us as sons" (Eph. 1:5, emphasis mine).

Now, when you read, "We have obtained an inheritance, having been *predestined* according to His purpose," think, "He established a blueprint before the foundation of the world and therefore determined beforehand to give us an inheritance" (Eph. 1:11, emphasis mine).

Now, when you read, "Whom He . . . also *predestined* [to become] conformed to the image of His Son," think, "He established a blueprint before the foundation of the world and therefore determined beforehand to conform us into the image of Christ" (Rom. 8:29, emphasis mine).

It was God's *plan* for those in Christ that was predetermined. Not who would be saved and who would be damned. Not who would be adopted and who wouldn't. Not who would be conformed into the image of Christ and who wouldn't.

Later, I will explain in greater detail what this predetermined plan entails. But for now, let's begin looking at God's eternal purpose in the book of Ephesians.

AN OVERVIEW OF EPHESIANS 1

Ephesians 1 is one of the richest chapters in the Bible. I encourage you to pause now and read it for yourself. Paul exhausted human language trying to articulate the grandeur of God's eternal purpose. Almost every sentence should end with an exclamation point. Here we see Paul, a prisoner in chains under house arrest in Rome, overflowing with joy, excitement, passion, and awe as he contemplates God's ultimate intention.

Each verse in this chapter could be turned into a book. Each statement makes you want to "praise . . . the glory of His grace" (Eph. 1:6). Paul's writing style in this chapter is a hybrid of teaching, praise, and prayer. He could only write a few sentences before he broke out into spontaneous praise. He had to stop at key moments and intercede, so that his insight would become the Ephesians' personal revelation (Eph. 1:17-18).

Whenever you read different books of the Bible, it's always important to discern the main subject of the book. Once you discover the main theme, it helps you connect all the other dots, giving you the ability to understand what the author was trying to convey.

Reading Ephesians 1, you see phrases such as "before the foundation of the world," "predestined" (determined beforehand), "the mystery of His will", "the counsel of His will," and "the hope of His calling" (Eph. 1:4-5,11,18). It's clear from the first chapter that Paul wants to bring us onto heavenly ground and give us God-centered perspective so that we align our lives with the Lord.

When Paul wrote the book of Ephesians, one of his main objectives was to explain that:

> God's eternal purpose, established in the heavenly council of the Godhead in eternity past, is the blueprint that drives everything that God has done or will ever do.

How did Paul know this? Most likely, when Paul was caught up to heaven, the Lord revealed to him the eternal council of the Godhead before time and creation (2 Cor. 12:2-7). Because no other created being existed then, direct revelation is the only way that anyone could have insight into this mystery.

With this in mind, let's unravel what Paul was revealing in Ephesians.

1. *Paul was revealing God's eternal purpose.*
   Paul wrote, "The mystery of His will . . . which He purposed

in Him" (Eph. 1:9, emphasis mine). A few verses later, Paul stated, "Having been predestined according to His purpose" (Eph. 1:11, emphasis mine). This purpose is God's "eternal purpose" in Christ (Eph. 3:11). It is God's ultimate intention that would be accomplished with or without the fall.

2. *God's eternal purpose was determined by a heavenly council of the Godhead.*

In Ephesians 1:11, Paul wrote, "Having been predestined according to His purpose who works all things after the counsel of His will." Notice the connection between "His purpose" and "the counsel of His will." God's eternal purpose is connected to what was established by the "counsel of His will." What does this mean?

The Greek word for *counsel* is *boulē* and it's derived "from a root meaning 'a will,' hence 'a counsel, a piece of advice" that "is the result of determination."[3] When used outside the New Testament, *boulē* conveyed the result of a process of deliberation in which something was determined.[4]

As a cross-reference, consider Jeremiah 23:18-22. This verse states, "But who has stood in the *council* of the LORD, that he should see and hear His word? Who has given heed to His word and listened? . . . But if they had stood in My *council*, then they would have announced My words to My people, and would have turned them back from their evil way and from the evil of their deeds" (emphasis mine). Comparing Ephesians 1:11 with Jeremiah 23:18-22, we see that the Lord works through heavenly *councils* whereby the Father, the Son, and the Holy Spirit give their *counsel* for the purpose of making decisions and establishing plans.

Just so we are clear, a *council* is a group of people who gather for the purpose of giving advice, making decisions, and establishing plans. To *counsel*, on the other hand, is a verb meaning to give advice for the purpose of making decisions and formulating plans. When a *council* meets, they share their *counsel* about different topics in order to make the best decisions and plans given all of the known information.

Putting together Ephesians 1:11, Jeremiah 23:18-22, and the

meaning of *counsel*, it becomes clear that Paul was describing a heavenly council in which the Godhead deliberated and determined their eternal purpose. In this eternal council, the Father, the Son, and the Holy Spirit determined their purpose for creation, the reason why they would create the world, and the intention for their prized creation—humanity.

This heavenly council was vastly different from an earthly council where various people voice their opinions and offer advice. This was the Trinity determining their will and purpose for eternity.

3. *The heavenly council produced a blueprint that drives everything God does.*

Paul said that God "works all things after the counsel of His will" (Eph. 1:11). Notice the phrase "all things." That means everything that God has done or will ever do is driven by what the Godhead established in the heavenly council in eternity past.

In summary, Paul wrote the book of Ephesians to unveil the heavenly council of the Godhead where the Father, Son, and Holy Spirit consulted with each other (Eph. 1:9-11). This council produced God's eternal purpose and His predetermined plan (blueprint) that established His will (Eph. 1:9-11; 3:11). It's this will that drives everything that the Lord does (Eph. 1:11).

Knowing God's Eternal Purpose

In addition to holding leadership roles in my church and helping run a missions organization, my day job over the past twenty years has been as a software developer. For the first ten years, however, I didn't realize the importance of planning before coding. As a result, many of my software projects could have been much better.

I discovered the hard way that it's much easier to change a design document than it is to change code. After learning this valuable lesson, I spend much more time planning and designing before writing code. Now, if a project will take four to six months to develop, I usually will spend at least a month designing how the screens will look and function, the requirements for the data, and how the system will interact with other systems. When I'm finished planning, my design serves as a blueprint that drives all my subsequent work.

In a similar way, God's eternal purpose is the blueprint that drives all that He does. And the Lord does not deviate from what He established as His ultimate intention in the eternal council of the Godhead.

Imagine that a homebuilder was hired to build a house by a certain blueprint, yet used a different blueprint once construction began. The result would be a disaster. Yet, this is what much of the church is doing today. We're trying to build His church with a different blueprint. We are copying what the church down the street is doing and hoping that God will bless it. That's why studying the blueprint of God's eternal purpose is so important. We want to make sure that what we build is what God really wants.

Paul said to, "Find out what pleases the Lord" (Eph. 5:10, NIV). Don't assume that you already know what pleases the Lord because the church down the street has a formula that has resulted in growth.

As a wise master builder, Paul had tremendous insight into God's blueprint (1 Cor. 3:10-11). He had revelation and understanding of God's ultimate intention and could therefore build the church in a way that pleased the Lord. Without this same understanding, we will not build what pleases the Lord and makes an eternal impact. There simply is no substitute for knowing God's ultimate intention.

God's Measurement for Success

Not only is God's eternal purpose the blueprint that drives all that He does, but it's also the plumb line by which He measures success. In biblical times, plumb lines were commonly used (and still are) when constructing walls and other important structures.

A plumb line is a simple tool, consisting of a weight that dangles at the end of cord. Due to the force of gravity, the cord is pulled tight and helps establish a vertical point of reference for construction.

Just as plumb lines judge the verticality of a wall, God judges success by His plumb line, which is His eternal blueprint. God measures success by whether or not His eternal purpose is being accomplished in our lives, in our churches, in our ministries, and in the global body of Christ.

In the church today, many measure success much differently than the Lord. Many measure success by buildings, budgets, bishops, and baptisms. The bigger the building, the bigger the budget, the bigger influence of the bishop, and the bigger the baptisms, the more successful we are. Despite this skewed measurement, the Lord never deviates from His standard for measuring success, which is His eternal purpose.

God's ultimate intention will always be the plumb line that determines whether or not our work was right, justified, and centered.

Studying God's Eternal Purpose

Because God's eternal purpose drives all that God does and is the plumb line that measures success, I want to encourage you: Think deeply about God's eternal blueprint *before you build*.

If you are a church planter, this will help you build a church that fulfills God's eternal purpose. If you are an intercessor, this will help you give birth to God's ultimate intention. If you are a messenger, this will help you proclaim God's eternal thought, will, and desire. If you are a missionary, this will help you bring the unreached onto heavenly ground. Whether you are a business person or stay-at-home mom, an entrepreneur or a retiree, this truth will help you align your life to God's deepest desires.

Just as a homebuilder would study the details of a blueprint before building a house, studying the elaborate details of God's eternal blueprint will help us align our lives with God's eternal purpose and find true meaning in life.

So, what, exactly, is God's mysterious blueprint? Let's dive into the Scriptures that unveil that exact mystery, now.

CHAPTER 3

DISCOVERING GOD'S
ULTIMATE INTENTION

God's eternal purpose is the blueprint that drives everything He does. The Lord simply doesn't deviate from what He established as His ultimate intention in the heavenly council of the Godhead in eternity past. Paul emphatically said that God "works all things" based upon the decisions and plans that were established in this heavenly council (Eph. 1:11). That is why it's so important to discover the details of God's eternal purpose.

So, what is God's ultimate intention? And where do we find it in Scripture?

Keep in mind, when I use the term "ultimate intention," "original intention," or "eternal purpose" throughout this book, I'm referring to what God intended if the fall had not happened and salvation was unnecessary.

GOD'S ETERNAL PURPOSE IN THE SCRIPTURES

Before we answer, "What is God's ultimate intention?", we must first determine how to find it in the Scriptures. In studying God's eternal purpose, I haven't found one specific place in Scripture that lists all the aspects of God's ultimate intention. Instead, I've found it to be more like assembling a complex puzzle.

For example, imagine that you have a five-hundred-piece jigsaw puzzle scattered upon a coffee table. As you start putting it together, you can't find the box showcasing the finished product. This makes your task much more difficult. Now you are forced to carefully examine the colors and shapes of each puzzle piece. You must group similar pieces together and then assemble smaller segments of the puzzle. Following this process, you assemble the puzzle in stages until finally the puzzle comes together and you see the finished product.

This is similar to finding God's eternal purpose in the Scriptures. Different passages reveal God's ultimate intention, but you have to carefully examine the context and see where it fits together with other Scriptures. You have to look for keywords such as "before the foundation of the world," "predestined," "mystery," or "the mystery of His will."

Because the Scriptures do not always say "this was established in the eternal council," it's helpful to remember that God "works all things after the counsel of His will" (Eph. 1:11). That means both His original intention and His redemptive plan were established in eternity past in His heavenly council.

With this in mind, if we look at the Scriptures and extract out what was necessary because of the fall—such as the covenants, the finished work of the cross, justification, forgiveness, redemption, and restoration—we can safely determine God's original intention. We can see what would have happened if Adam had eaten from the tree of life instead of the tree of the knowledge of good and evil.

From my study, God's eternal purpose is most clearly revealed in the two trees in the garden (Gen. 3), John 17, the books of Ephesians, Colossians, and Hebrews, Philippians 3, Romans 8, Revelation 2-3, and Revelation 21-22. When you put these different passages together, you arrive at God's ultimate intention.

Let's get started by looking at John 17, the books of Colossians and Ephesians, Romans 8, and Revelation 2-3. We will extract key points of God's eternal purpose in this chapter and then summarize it in the next chapter.

God's Eternal Purpose in John 17

John 17, known also as the *High Priestly Prayer*, contains some of the most profound revelation in Scripture. Facing death, Jesus poured out His heart to the Father, expressing His deepest desires.

Carefully examining His words, it's clear Jesus was focused upon His relationship with the Father "before the world was" and "before the foundation of the world" (John 17:5, 24). Jesus was re-membering the love, intimacy, and fellowship that He shared with His Father before creation. He recalled the Father's love for Him and reminisced about the intimacy and union they enjoyed in eter-nity past (John 17:21-22, 24).

As you meditate upon John 17, you begin to see God's original intention unfold. Namely, you discover that God purposed that we would:

- Be with the Son in glory (John 17:21, 24);

- Have the Son in us (John 17:26);

- Be in union with the Father, the Son, and with one another (John 17:21-22);

- Know that the Father loves us like He loves the Son (John 17:23);

- Love the Son like the Father has since eternity past (John 17:24, 26).

In summary, Jesus' *High Priestly Prayer* details God's eternal purpose to bring humanity into the unceasing fellowship, love, and intimacy that the Father and the Son have enjoyed for all eternity. We're called to have the same relationship with the Father that Je-sus has. This relationship is both individual and corporate. Before time and creation, we were destined to enjoy God in the same way the Father and the Son through the Spirit have forever enjoyed one another.

God's Eternal Purpose in Colossians

Toward the end of his life, while under house arrest in Rome, Paul wrote the books of Colossians and Ephesians to unveil God's eter-nal purpose. These books help comprise what scholars call *The Prison Epistles.*[1] Some commentators have rightly stated that Co-lossians focuses on God's eternal purpose for Christ the head while

Ephesians focuses on God's eternal purpose for Christ the body. For example, F.F. Bruce writes,

> Ephesians provides the logical sequel to Colossians, expounding the cosmic role of the church, the body of Christ, as Colossians expounds the cosmic role of Christ, who is head of his body, the church, and at the same time "head of every principality and power."[2]

Studying Paul's revelation in these two books is essential to understanding God's eternal purpose. Let's start with the book of Colossians.

Colossians focuses on God's eternal purpose for His beloved Son—the head of the church. Christ is the preeminent One in whom God's eternal purpose revolves. God's eternal purpose is for Christ "to have first place in everything" (Col. 1:18).

In Colossians 1-2, Paul unveiled Christ as the centerpiece of God's eternal purpose. Specifically, he revealed Christ as:

- The image of the invisible God (Col. 1:15);

- The Creator of everything in heaven and on earth, both visible and invisible, including all thrones, dominions, rulers, and authorities (Col. 1:16);

- The One before all things and the One who holds all things together (Col. 1:17);

- The head of the body, the church (Col. 1:18);

- The embodiment of the fullness of deity (Col. 1:19; 2:9);

- A treasure chest of all wisdom and knowledge (Col. 2:3);

- The head over all rule and authority (Col. 2:10).

Colossians 1-2 is a breathtaking depiction of the beauty of Christ. Only John's vision of Christ in the book of Revelation compares.

Years before Paul wrote Colossians, he had been caught up to heaven. He had seen Christ exalted and enthroned. He saw the beauty and glory of Christ unveiled. His eyes beheld the centerpiece of God's ultimate intention. From this experience, Paul wrote the book of Colossians from a position of authority and true revelation.

As Paul unveiled the majesty and glory of Christ in Chapter 1, he penned one of the greatest statements about God's eternal purpose. He said, "The mystery which has been hidden from the past ages and generations, but has now been manifested to His saints . . . which is Christ in you, the hope of glory" (Col. 1:27).

What an amazing statement! God's grand eternal purpose has always been for the glorious Man, the One whom Paul just described, to be in His people through the Person of the Holy Spirit. Christ in you—the hope of glory.

Because "Christ is all, and in all" of His people, we are a new creation. We have a "new self who is being renewed to a true knowledge according to the image of the One who created him" (Col. 3:9-10). As a new creation with Christ dwelling in us, "there is no distinction between Greek and Jew, circumcised and uncircumcised, barbarian, Scythian, slave and freeman" (Col. 3:11).

This new creation, both individual and corporate, is central to God's ultimate intention. Humanity was destined, in the heavenly council of eternity past, to be the only creation to have God dwelling in them. This is "the mystery which has been hidden from ages and from generations" that has now "been revealed" (Col. 1:26, NKJV).

God's Eternal Purpose in Ephesians

Whereas Colossians reveals God's eternal purpose for Christ the head, Ephesians unveils God's eternal purpose for Christ's body. In fact, "church" is mentioned nine times in this book, underscoring Paul's focus upon the body of Christ.[3]

Specifically, God's eternal purpose is that the church would become:

- The Godhead's own inheritance, a people He fully possesses (Eph. 1:18);

- A mature man, a corporate expression of Christ's life in fullness (Eph. 1:23; 2:15; 4:13);

- A holy and blameless bride for Christ (Eph. 1:4; 5:27);

- The adopted sons of God placed into Christ's eternal inheritance, the Holy Spirit being the down payment (Eph. 1:5; Eph. 1:11-14);

- A spiritual house of living stones who are fit together as a dwelling place of God in the Spirit (Eph. 2:19-22);

- A new creation, having the fullness of Christ dwelling in them, able to do exceedingly more than what we can ask, think, or imagine (Eph. 3:14-21; 4:22-24).

Paul made it clear that God's "eternal purpose" is "in Christ Jesus our Lord" (Eph. 3:11; 1:9). Therefore, everything in the universe will be brought under the headship of the Lord Jesus Christ (Eph. 1:10). This includes everything "in the heavens" and "on the earth" (Eph. 1:10).

In summary, the book of Ephesians reveals God's eternal purpose to place the Spirit of Christ into a people who would become the Godhead's inheritance and possession. Specifically, the Father will have a family of Christ-like sons who are placed into the eternal inheritance of Christ. The Son will have an equally yoked bride who partners with Him for all eternity. And the Spirit will have a temple, house, and body that He fills and possesses.

GOD'S ETERNAL PURPOSE IN ROMANS 8

Romans 8 is one of my favorite chapters in the Bible. I could read it every day and never get bored.

In this pinnacle chapter of this glorious book, Paul revealed God's ultimate intention for us to become mature representations of Jesus Christ. Paul said, "He also predestined [us] to become conformed to the image of His Son, so that He would be the firstborn among many brethren" (Rom. 8:29, emphasis).

From the previous chapter, we know that *predestined* means to establish the boundaries and to determine a plan beforehand. Based on this definition, here's my paraphrase of Romans 8:29: "God established a blueprint before the foundation of the world and therefore determined beforehand to conform us into the image of Christ."

God's blueprint from eternity involves conforming those in Christ into the glorious image of His Son.

Having brought us from salvation (Romans 4-7) onto eternal ground (Romans 8), Paul revealed God's ultimate intention to make us mature representations of Christ. As we will see later in this book, this applies to us first individually. But the Lord's ultimate aim is to have a corporate representation of His Son, what Paul termed "a mature man" (Eph. 4:13).

With this in mind, as we read through Romans 8, we can extract God's ultimate intention from His plan of redemption. Seeing through God's eyes, we see His original aim to have "sons of God" who are "being led by the Spirit" (Rom. 8:14). As I will discuss later, the word for "sons" can mean a mature son. This means those who live by the indwelling Spirit of the Son of God are the mature, Christ-like sons of God. It's these mature, Christ-like sons that "creation waits eagerly for," the "revealing of the sons of God" who will set it free from "slavery" and "corruption" (Rom. 8:19-22).

Staying on eternal ground, we also see God's ultimate intention to make us "heirs of God and fellow heirs with Christ" (Rom. 8:17). This inheritance is not something that we possess at the moment, though we received a down payment of it through the indwelling Spirit (Eph. 1:14). This is an inheritance that comes to those who "suffer with Him so that we may also be glorified with Him" (Rom. 8:17). This is the eternal inheritance of Jesus Christ into which the Father will place His mature sons when our adoption is finalized (Rom. 8:23).

God's Eternal Purpose in Revelation 2-3

What is the eternal inheritance of Jesus Christ, exactly? The answer is found in the promises Jesus made to the overcomers in Revelation 2-3. Because Part 8 expounds upon this in great detail, I'll just summarize it here.

At the end of the book of Revelation, the Father says, "He who overcomes will inherit these things" (Rev. 21:7). If you read the entire book of Revelation, you realize that "he who overcomes" refers to Jesus' exhortations to the seven churches. He exhorts them—and us—to overcome such things as losing your first love, Jezebel, apathy, complacency, and lukewarmness. Each exhortation is accompanied by a promise, ranging from eating from the tree of life to dining with the Lord to sitting down on His throne. The Father was referring to these promises when He said the overcomers "will inherit these things."

In short, our eternal inheritance is revealed in Jesus' promises to the overcomers. Summarizing these promises, God's eternal purpose is to give us *eternal intimacy*, *eternal authority*, and *eternal glory*.

Eternal Intimacy

We are invited into the same intimacy, communion, fellowship, and love that the Father and the Son shared through the Holy Spirit in eternity past. This becomes clear when we understand Jesus' promises to eat from the tree of life, to feast upon hidden manna, to receive a white stone with a new name written on it, to be adorned with white wedding garments, to have the Father and the Son's names inscribed upon us, and to dine with Jesus (Rev. 2:7,17; Rev. 3:4-5, 12, 20).

Decoding these promises, we realize that God's eternal purpose is for us to experience greater measures of Christ's life within us for the endless ages of eternity, to feast upon Jesus' words in the heavenly holy of holies, to be His eternal wife in a deep, intimate, face-to-face relationship with Him, to become the Father and the Son's own inheritance and possession, and to enjoy the same relationship with the Father that Christ has had for all eternity.[4]

Eternal Authority

Furthermore, we are invited to exercise kingdom authority throughout eternity. We are called to expand the kingdom of God into all creation in the endless ages to come (Rev. 22:5). This becomes clear when we understand Jesus' promises to receive the crown of life, to have authority over the nations, and to sit down with Jesus on His throne (Rev. 2:10, 26-27; Rev. 3:21).

God's eternal purpose is for us to rule and reign with Jesus as His wife. We are invited to have authority over the nations, bringing justice and righteousness into the sphere of authority entrusted to us. We are destined for the throne. We are offered a position of judicial responsibility and kingly oversight in the most powerful royal family in history. For the endless ages of eternity, we are called to expand God's kingdom throughout the universe, so that His government will continually increase (Isa. 9:7).

Eternal Glory

Finally, we are invited to experience the depths of God's glory in the heavenly holy of holies for all eternity. We are called to shine forth God's glory like the sun in its strength. This becomes clear when we understand Jesus' promises to become a pillar in the temple, to have the new city Jerusalem inscribed upon us, and to shine like the sun in the kingdom of our Father (Rev. 3:12; Matt. 13:43).

God's eternal purpose is for us to dwell in heaven's throne room, to minister to the Father and the Son as priests, to have the capacity to see God's face without being incinerated, to experience perpetual pleasure in His presence, and to radiate God's glory like the sun on a cloudless summer day.

To Be Continued . . .

What an amazing God we serve! His eternal purpose is breathtaking. Seeing His ultimate intention ruins us for anything less.

As you can see from this chapter, there are many pieces to God's eternal-purpose puzzle. In the next chapter, we will put all of these pieces together so that God's master plan becomes more clear.

CHAPTER 4

Five Components of the Eternal Blueprint

The last chapter extracted key pieces of the eternal-purpose puzzle from Scripture. Together, these summarize the big picture of God's original intent for the world and His creation. So, building on this scriptural foundation, let's look at the five components of God's eternal blueprint. These are:

1. The Son will be at the center of everything in heaven and on earth.

2. The Father will have a family of Christ-like sons.

3. The Son will have an equally yoked bride.

4. The Holy Spirit will have a temple, house, and body that He fully possesses and fills.

5. Believers have been invited into eternal intimacy, eternal authority, and eternal glory.

Let's look at this briefly now. In later chapters, I will expound upon these components in much greater detail.

1. The Son will be at the center of everything.

In eternity past, before time and creation, the Father gazed into the face of His beloved Son. The Father's heart was filled with passion, joy, and delight as He beheld the Son's manifold perfections of beauty. Overflowing from the Father's deep love for His Son, the Father established His eternal purpose—a purpose that revolves around His Son (John 17:24). Indeed, the Father's love for His Son was the very catalyst for His creation.

Paul said, "He made known to us the mystery of His will . . . which *He purposed in Him*" (Eph. 1:9, emphasis mine). God's "eternal purpose" is "carried out in Christ Jesus our Lord" (Eph. 3:11). Jesus Christ establishes the boundaries of God's eternal purpose (Acts 17:31). He is the horizon, limits, and borders of the Godhead's blueprint from eternity. Bringing all of creation under the headship of the eternal Son is God's ultimate intention. The Godhead has predetermined that Jesus Christ will have the preeminence in everything (Col. 1:18).

As we saw in the books of Colossians and Ephesians, the eternal Son is the first priority of God's eternal purpose. The Godhead has laser-like focus on the Son's supreme exaltation. No king, president, or nation will stop this. No conspiracy, cabal, cartel, or coalition will thwart this. No demon, principality, or demonic world-ruler can derail God's predetermined purpose to place the Son at the center of everything. The entire universe will be brought under the headship of the Lord Jesus Christ (Eph. 1:10).

In the heavenly council, the Godhead established the Son as the creator, the only way to the Father, the truth, the life who would be placed within humanity, the pattern to which humanity would be conformed, the seed who would multiply into a harvest of sons, the Bridegroom who would be married to His people, and the King of kings and Lord of lords.[1] Everything truly is "from him and through him and for him" (Rom. 11:36, NIV).

In Part 2, we will go into great detail about the Father's desire to exalt the Son and to place Him at the center of His eternal purpose.

2. The Father will have a family of Christ-like sons.

As the Father looked upon the Son's glorious face in eternity past, He decided to multiply His pleasure by having a family of sons patterned after His beloved Son (Eph. 1:5). The Father determined to increase His eternal joy and delight by having a corporate son, comprised of millions of men and women, who would be conformed into His image and likeness.

Paul revealed the mystery of this corporate son when he wrote of God's predetermined plan to adopt us as sons to Himself (Eph.

1:5).

As I mentioned previously, adoption in the first-century was vastly different than the twenty-first century. In the first-century, adoption was about placing a mature, adult son, whether natural born or brought in from another family, over a father's inheritance.

Just like first-century Roman adoption, our adoption is accomplished in three phases. Phase one is placement into God's family. Phase two is placing us under the Holy Spirit's child training. And phase three is a corporate adoption at the second coming of Christ, when those who have been conformed into Christ's image are placed into the Son's eternal inheritance.

In Part 5, we will look in much greater detail at God's eternal purpose to give the Father an inheritance of Christ-like sons.

One quick note before moving on. The Scriptures refer to both men and women as sons of God and the bride of Christ. These identities are not related to our gender but to how we, both men and women, relate to God. When referring to us as sons, this means both men and women have a relationship with the Father, are becoming representations of the Son, and will be placed into the Son's eternal inheritance as a firstborn son with the highest privileges. When referring to us as the bride of Christ, this means we, both men and women, have an intimate relationship with Jesus and will partner with Him to advance the kingdom for all eternity.

3. The Son will have an equally yoked bride.

From the overflow of the Father's passionate love for His Son, He determined to provide Him with an equally yoked bride. A beloved whom the Son could pour out upon the passion of His being. A corporate bride made of millions of men and women who, joined together, would love the Son just like the Father.

In this highly specific sense, God the Son was like Adam, having no counterpart or beloved of His own. The eternal Son yearned to be the source of love to a beloved but there was no "helper suitable for him" (Gen. 2:18).

This is why the Godhead determined to give the Son a bride. In this relationship, the Son would be the source of love, and His bride would be the recipient and responder. The Son would pour out all the passion of His heart and soul upon her, and in return, His beloved bride would reciprocate His love back to Him, loving Him just like the Father (John 15:9; 17:26).

Paul unveiled this mystery when he wrote, "For this reason a man will leave his father and mother and be united to his wife, and the two will become one flesh. This is a profound mystery—but I am talking about Christ and the church" (Eph. 5:31-32, NIV). Marriage is but a foreshadow of God's eternal purpose to give the Son a beloved of His own.

The Lord has woven this eternal purpose into the fabric of Scripture. That's why the Bible starts with a wedding and ends with a wedding! Far beyond being a historical account, far and away more than just a book of law and principles, and infinitely greater than a rote guidebook of wisdom, the Scriptures are the ultimate romance novel between Christ and His church.

This mysterious romance—where believers are betrothed as a bride to Jesus Christ and married to Him for all eternity—is God's ultimate intention.

Through the finished work of the cross, we are like pure virgins in His eyes. Our heavenly Bridegroom cherishes, nourishes, and sanctifies us. Jesus is our lover, and we are His beloved. In response to Jesus' overwhelming love, we are to make ourselves ready by allowing the indwelling Spirit to live His life through us.

Make no mistake about it—the Father will provide Jesus with a pure, spotless, holy, and worthy bride who loves Him just like the Father (Eph. 1:4; 5:27). The Father will provide His Son with an equally yoked bride.

And what, exactly, is an "equally yoked bride"? Paul said that Christ would "present to Himself the church in all her glory, having no spot or wrinkle or any such thing; but that she would be holy and blameless" (Eph. 5:27). The sanctification process that makes the bride holy and blameless takes place before Jesus returns, not after we die and go to heaven. How do we know that? Because in the prior verse, Paul said, "That He might sanctify her, having cleansed her by the washing of water with the word" (Eph. 5:26). This type of sanctification is part of the salvation process (2 Thess. 2:13).

This means that, as the bride resolves to make herself ready, the Lord will respond by doing a deep work of sanctification in her, transforming her by the Spirit into a glorious, holy, pure, and blameless lover of Christ (Rev. 19:7). She will be transformed by the Spirit, from glory to glory, into the image and likeness of Jesus (2 Cor. 3:18). She will be conformed into a mature representation of the Son before He returns. She will become His equally yoked bride.

As I explain in Chapter 21, I'm not talking about pristine perfection but maturity. The bride will not be perfect, for only Christ is perfect. But she will be conformed into a mature representation of Christ prior to her marriage to Him. The "marriage of the Lamb" will not take place until the "bride has made herself ready" (Rev. 19:7).

In Part 6, we will dive further into God's eternal purpose to give the Son an equally yoked bride—an inheritance whom He can love and who would love Him back with the Father's very own love.

4. The Spirit will have a temple, house, and body.

The church, the *ekklēsia*, was conceived in the eternal council of the Godhead. Before time and creation, God purposed to place the Spirit of His Son into a unique creation. Humanity would be the only creation God designed to have the Spirit of the Son within them.

Paul unveiled this secret when he wrote, "The mystery which has been hidden from ages and from generations, but now has been revealed to His saints" (Col. 1:26, NKJV). What is this mystery? Paul said it's "Christ in you" (Col. 1:27).

What a beautiful plan! In the ageless past, the Father and the Son determined to create man and woman—you and me—and to place the Spirit of His Son within us. The angels must look at awe upon us. To think that the One they worship in awestruck wonder, undone by His indescribable beauty and glory, has chosen to make us His dwelling place!

God's eternal purpose is to give the Holy Spirit a temple, house, and body that He possesses and brings to full maturity. In the mysterious council of eternity past, the Trinity determined to make us a new creation that would have the indwelling life of Christ.

This new creation was never meant to be isolated and independent. God's ultimate intention was to have a corporate son and a corporate bride: individuals filled with the life of Christ, joined together as one new man (Eph. 2:15). Thus, God's ageless purpose is to have a corporate new creation—living stones filled with the fullness of the Spirit fit together to form God's spiritual house (1 Pet. 2:5). The Lord's ultimate intention is to have a people who've become a corporate dwelling place of the Spirit (Eph. 2:22).

This means—listen closely—that the church is not a building we go to nor a service we attend. The church is the very body of Jesus Christ. It is the corporate expression of individuals who have surrendered to the lordship of the Son and are allowing the indwelling Spirit to possess them in an ever-increasing measure. God's aim is for this corporate expression of Christ's indwelling life to become a "mature man," which Paul said is "the measure of the stature which belongs to the fullness of Christ" (Eph. 4:13).

In Part 7, we will unravel God's eternal purpose to give the Holy Spirit an inheritance—a people whom He can fill, possess, and bring to maturity.

5. **The believer's inheritance will be intimacy, authority, and glory.**

So, the Father's inheritance is a family of Christ-list sons. The Son's inheritance is an equally yoked bride, and the Spirit's inheritance is an eternal dwelling place within a mature body of believers. In God's infinite goodness, He also purposed to place us, as Christlike sons, into Jesus' eternal inheritance. As we saw in Revelation, God offers us an inheritance of eternal intimacy, eternal authority, and eternal glory (Rev. 2-3).

Incredibly, God's ultimate intention is to give us eternal intimacy with the Godhead. Don't miss this: we are offered the same relationship of communion, fellowship, intimacy, and love that the Father and the Son shared through the Holy Spirit in eternity past.

Jesus invites us to feast upon His words in the holy of holies in a deep, intimate relationship with Him. We have been called into the same relationship with the Father that Jesus has enjoyed forever!

As if that were not enough, God's ultimate intention is also to give us eternal authority. We are destined for the throne (Rev. 3:21). We are invited to exercise kingdom authority throughout the endless ages of eternity (Rev. 2:26). We are called to expand the kingdom of God into all creation forever. We are offered the rod of iron and the scepter of authority—to rule and reign with Jesus as His bride in the ages to come. We are invited to sit on the throne of Christ and to have judicial responsibility and kingly oversight. Throughout the endless ages of eternity, we are called to bring justice and righteousness into the sphere of authority entrusted to us.

Furthermore, God's ultimate intention is to give us eternal glory. That doesn't mean we will become gods, be worshiped in heaven, or usurp the glory that's due to God alone. I'm talking about a resurrected body that will shine forth God's glory like the sun (Matt. 13:43; 1 Cor. 15:41). And having this new glorified body, we will have the capacity to see God's face and not be incinerated as we worship Him and enjoy the fellowship of the Godhead in the holy of holies for all eternity (Rev. 22:4).[2] The Lord, in His goodness, invites us to minister to Him as priests in the new city Jerusalem for the eternal ages.

These words on a page—these frail human words—fail to accurately describe our eternal inheritance. What a glorious invitation to humanity! Like Paul said, we will forever be praising "the glory of His grace, which He freely bestowed on us in the Beloved" (Eph. 1:6).

As "fellow heirs with Christ," the Father has now placed us under the governmental hand of the Holy Spirit, our personal teacher and trainer. The Spirit is now working to prepare us for our inheritance, conforming us into the image of Jesus Christ. T. Austin Sparks referred to this as "the school of sonship unto adoption."[3]

As our personal trainer, the Holy Spirit disciplines, corrects, crucifies, circumcises, and instructs us. He works relentlessly to conform us to the pattern of the Son of God. He is training us for reigning. He is preparing us for the throne by immersing us into the ways, purposes, and nature of our heavenly Father. He is shaping our character and growing us up so that we can handle our inheritance. He is forming Christ's meekness, humility, and sacrificial love within us so that we don't squander our inheritance with childish and immature behavior.

We will go even deeper into the awe-inspiring purpose of God to place us as His corporate son into Christ's inheritance of eternal intimacy, eternal authority, and eternal glory in Part 8.

Destined for Indescribably More . . .

Simply put, God's eternal purpose is to bring us into the same relationship that the Father, the Son, and the Holy Spirit have forever enjoyed. We are invited to experience the same love, intimacy, joy, pleasure, delight, and fellowship of the Godhead. This relationship will be centered in the holy of holies, where the Father and Son dwell in indescribable glory. It's here, in the breathtaking throne room of God, that we will see Him face-to-face and minister to Him forever.

From the Father's perspective, we are to become a corporate son, a mature man, conformed into Christ's image and likeness. This begins individually, when we are adopted into God's family as His very own child. But it doesn't end individually. The Father wants one corporate son made of many individuals who have been conformed into a representation of His beloved Son. It will be this corporate son who will experience the same relationship with the Father that the Son has forever enjoyed.

From the Son's perspective, we are to become a corporate bride who has made herself ready. Jesus is the lover, and we are His beloved. From the overflow of experiencing His love for us, we love Him in return. The corporate bride of Christ will love the Son just like the Father. As the wife of the Lamb, we will be given the royal crown, the scepter of authority, and we will sit down with Him on His throne. Throughout the endless ages of eternity, we will partner with Him to expand His rule and reign throughout creation.

From the Spirit's perspective, we are to become the temple, house, and body that He possesses and fills. As a new creation—the only creation in the created order with God's indwelling life—the Holy Spirit is jealous to have all of us. He wants to possess and fill our hearts, souls, and bodies. As we allow Him to do this in us individually, He will then connect us to other like-minded living stones. Together, we will become the body of Christ, conformed into the image of the Son. This corporate man, this mature reflection of the Son, will dwell forever in God's throne room, ministering to Him face-to-face as His very own priesthood.

Before moving on, let me clarify an important point. Sometimes, people get confused about whether the Father's, the Son's, and the Spirit's inheritance are the same people. For example, they wonder if the bride of Christ differs from the mature sons of God or the Spirit's corporate temple. The answer is simple: These are the same people. The people who comprise the Son's equally yoked bride are the same people who make up the Father's corporate Son and the Spirit's corporate temple.

Moving On

As we conclude Part 1, let's quickly review. Having the proper starting point when determining God's ultimate intention is critical. We must begin in eternity past when it was only God. Out of the Godhead's eternally-satisfying relationship, God established a blueprint that drives everything that He does.

The five components of this blueprint are:

1. The Son will be at the center of everything in heaven and on earth.

2. The Father will have a family of Christ-like sons.

3. The Son will have an equally yoked bride.

4. The Holy Spirit will have a temple, house, and body that He fully possesses and fills.

5. Believers have been invited into eternal intimacy, eternal authority, and eternal glory.

In short, God will have what He has always wanted—a people that He fully possesses as His own inheritance.

We will look in much greater detail at these five components throughout this book. In Part 2, we will focus on the first component—the Son at the center of God's eternal blueprint.

PART 2

THE SON IS GOD'S
ULTIMATE INTENTION

The first priority of God's eternal purpose is the supreme exaltation of His Son. God's ultimate intention is for the Son to have pre-eminence in everything and to be the center of all He does. As His bride, it is critical for us to understand the role of Jesus Christ in God's ultimate purpose—and to embrace how we, too, can exalt Jesus here and now.

CHAPTER 5

CHRIST AT THE CENTER

Growing up in a denominational church, I was unfamiliar with the gifts of the Spirit. So, when I realized that I could hear the voice of God, operate in power, heal the sick, and cast out demons, I got really excited. I became a "conference hopper," going from conference to conference in order to learn all I could about the gifts of the Spirit.

Seriously, my dream back then was to hear God's voice so clearly that I could tell people the deepest secrets of their heart. I wanted to prophesy to strangers the conversations they just had with their spouses. I was eager to tell people whom I had never met their names, phone numbers, and addresses. I wanted to reveal secrets that only God knew so that people could see how real God is. I was always trying to one-up my last word, pressing in for greater details to reveal. I could tell many stories about my pursuit of the gifts of the Spirit, but I'll spare you the gory details.

Though I believe that we should pursue spiritual gifts, especially the gift of prophecy, my focus was on pursuing *gifts* rather than pursuing the *giver*—namely, the Son (1 Cor. 14:1).

To my amazement, the Lord honored my desire and gave me the ability to prophesy accurately. Almost every time I prayed for someone, the Lord gave me a word for them. Guess who people started coming to for a word? Guess who started to be exalted? Guess who liked it? Me.

Focusing on the gifts ultimately placed me at the center and brought glory and honor to myself rather than to Jesus Christ.

Thankfully, the Lord interrupted my out-of-priority pursuit in 1997 through a dream that I'll explain in the next chapter and brought me back to a love relationship with Jesus Christ. This encounter was the catalyst that led me to put my roots deep into the

Son of God. I spent the next two years intently focused on Christ and getting to know Him better.

A Deep Dive (and a Train Ride) into Eschatology

Back in my early days, I became desperately hungry for the person of Jesus Christ. This inspired me to pray continually for a deeper revelation of Him. Ultimately, this led me to the book of Revelation, which is "the revelation of Jesus Christ" (Rev. 1:1). As I read this book, I experienced the blessing that comes to those who read, hear, and obey this prophecy (Rev. 1:3). This was unlike any other previous spiritual experience. I was hooked.

This put a desire in my heart to become a scholar of the book of Revelation. My dream shifted from wanting to prophesy people's deepest secrets to becoming an end-times expert. One of my favorite things was to read commentaries on the book of Revelation. The most extensive commentary I purchased was a two-volume set, together weighing five pounds and exceeding one-thousand pages.

I'll never forget the time in 2002, when my wife, Angie, and I went on an extensive vacation in England and Scotland, and I brought volume two of this commentary. First of all, I carried it in my backpack, which, given its weight, was not a good idea. My back didn't forgive me for days. But the most memorable moment was on the train from London to Edinburgh. Angie pulled out *The English Garden* magazine to look at beautiful pictures of the English countryside, and I hauled out that three-pound commentary on the book of Revelation. Angie was enjoying cottages and flowers, while I was reading about the great red dragon and the seductive harlot. It's funny now, but this train ride made me realize that I might want to turn down my zeal a notch or two.

In any case, I dove deep into eschatology, a fancy word for the study of the end times. I devoured commentary after commentary on the books of Daniel, Isaiah, and Revelation. I searched incessantly for the identity of the antichrist, the harlot Babylon of Revelation 17-18, what nations would invade Israel during the war of Gog and Magog, the meaning and timing of Daniel's Seventy Week prophecy, and what the Millennial Kingdom would be like. I studied the rapture and when it would take place. And I loved getting together with people and letting them know how much I knew about the end times.

For ten years, I studied every nuance of end-time prophecy. I learned every argument for and against various positions. Studying eschatology became my passion. I loved preaching about it and writing about it.

The problem was, I got distracted once again from the person at centerstage of end-time prophecy. By focusing on the end times, the person of Christ was placed on the backstage of my heart. Imperceptibly, my focus slowly shifted from the person of Christ to the *things* of Christ, from knowing Him to knowing *about* Him.

Obsessed with Israel

My fascination with the end times also led to an obsession with anything related to Israel.

It began around the year 2000, when I had a dream about two Orthodox Jews. Dressed in black, they were coming out of a bookstore carrying two very large books. One of the books was titled *Matthew 24* and the other was titled *Zechariah 8*. Both of these portions of Scripture contain significant prophetic promises concerning the Jewish people and their end-time destiny.

As I think about this dream today, I realize that God was awakening a desire within me to understand Israel's prophetic destiny and to know God's heart for the Jewish people.

This dream inspired me to study the destiny of Israel in the Scriptures. I became an advocate against Replacement Theology (and still am). My blood would boil anytime I heard a preacher or teacher take an Old Testament prophecy, written to the nation of Israel and the Jewish people, and replace Israel with the church.

I spent an entire year slowly reading through the book of Isaiah. I also read a five-hundred-page commentary on Isaiah. My heart burned within me as I discovered Israel's prophetic destiny. After going to Israel in 2002 and 2004, I was filled with even more zeal for Israel.

I devoured book after book about Israel and the Jewish people. I even wrote a book about Israel. Eventually, I came close to committing an even more grievous error than Replacement Theology. *Replacing Christ with the Jews.* Thankfully, I woke up before I went too far down that path.

Christ or the Things of Christ?

I had similar experiences with Christian doctrine and theology, spiritual warfare, praise and worship, and God's blessings. All of these things of God are important. They're just not nearly as important as the Son of God. We can never let the things of Christ eclipse Christ Himself.

Looking back, the Lord led me to pursue the gifts, to learn about Israel and the end times, and to study Christian doctrine and theology. The Spirit taught me about praise and worship, spiritual warfare, and God's blessings. The problem wasn't learning about these things. It was that I allowed these things of Christ to surpass the person of Christ.

You see, spiritual gifts are a *thing*. The end times are a *thing*. Israel is a *thing*. Christian theology is a *thing*. Spiritual warfare is a *thing*. Praise and worship is a *thing*. God's blessings are a *thing*.

What I discovered—and still am discovering—is that I don't need a *thing*. I need *Him*. I need the person of Christ far more than I need the things of Christ.

And so do you.

Jesus Christ is everything we will ever need. He is the horizon of God's eternal purpose. He is the center of God's ultimate intention. He is the sun around which our lives are designed to orbit. He is everything. As Paul said, "Christ is all, and in all" (Col. 3:11).

When I have Christ at the center of my life, then spiritual gifts operate naturally. When I have Christ at the center of my life, then the end times, Israel, and theology find their proper balance. When I have Christ at the center of my life, God's blessings, spiritual warfare, and the thousand other things of Christ come into proper alignment.

Paul said that Christ "became to us wisdom from God, and righteousness and sanctification, and redemption" (1 Cor. 1:30). The Father doesn't want to give us things. He wants to give us Christ, for He is the *embodiment* of every spiritual thing.

Jesus Christ is righteousness. Jesus Christ is power. Jesus Christ is Israel. Jesus Christ is holiness, wisdom, and knowledge. Jesus Christ is the incarnation of God's eternal Word.

The Father doesn't give us salvation. He gives us Christ, who is salvation within us. He doesn't give us righteousness. He gives us Christ, who is righteousness within us. He doesn't give us love, joy, or peace. He gives us Christ, who is love, joy, and peace within us.

Christ doesn't just show us the way. He is the Way. Christ doesn't just teach us truth. He is the Truth. And Christ doesn't just give us life. He is the Life.

This means maturity is not about learning more doctrine, having greater understanding of theology, or reading more of the Bible. Maturity is not measured by how high we jump during worship or how loud we shout during praise. Maturity is not measured by how much power we operate in or by the accuracy of our prophetic gifts. Maturity is not measured by how many demons we can discern or by the greatness of our faith.

At the end of the day, maturity is not how much we know, but Who we know.

Maturity is knowing Christ intimately and deeply—knowing His heart, His ways, and His whispers.

Maturity is having Christ formed within us and allowing Him to live instead of us (Gal. 4:19). The measure of Christ living in us is the measure of our maturity.

The Father wants to give us more of His Son. Not more things. Not more stuff. Not more knowledge, wisdom, gifts, grace, and virtues. The Father wants to unveil His Son to us and fascinate us with the beauty and glory of what has satisfied Him for all eternity.

Worshiping Miracles

As I previously mentioned, I help lead a missions organization named Lifeschool International. We train and equip senior pastors in East Africa.

In May of 2018, we gathered about thirty-five of our leaders from Kenya, Tanzania, Uganda, Malawi, the Congo, and Rwanda. We spent a week equipping them in God's eternal purpose so that they could multiply this message throughout their nations.

I'll never forget the word I had to share. Deep in my spirit, I knew I had to confront the idolization of signs, wonders, and miracles in the African church. To quote Terry Bennett, this would surely "go down like a rat sandwich."

Much of the African church is like the idolatrous Israelites, who worshiped the bronze serpent. As the story goes, the Lord used a bronze serpent to heal the Israelites from poisonous snake bites in the days of Moses (Num. 21:9). Whenever a person was bit by a snake, they could look to the bronze serpent and be healed. Hundreds of years later, this miraculous move of God had become an idol. The sons of Israel were burning incense to this miracle-working snake (2 Kings 18:4).

A similar form of idolatry has crept into the African church. Men of God, who "perform" signs, wonders, and miracles, are virtually idolized by gullible churchgoers. These innocent sheep are then duped into giving the "man of God" their tithes and offerings in exchange for a miracle. In reality, their ancestral witchcraft practices have been mixed into their Christianity. Rather than going to the witchdoctor for healing, they now flock to the "man of God," who has the power to heal them and pronounce blessings upon whoever will sow a financial seed.

Though this prosperity gospel heresy has varying degrees in Africa, most believers in Africa have embraced this mindset: A preacher is godly and anointed to the degree that the power of God flows through him. The pastors who preach Christ and the undiluted gospel, not obsessing over miracles, run the risk of losing members to the church down the road where the "anointed man of God" performs signs and wonders every Sunday. In short, many African pastors feel tremendous pressure to conform to this prosperity-gospel culture and "perform" for the people.

With this background established, you can imagine how well my message was received. I was confronting the sacred cow of Africa. My words were like a hammer that was demolishing their most beloved idol.

When I finished, the message hit such a raw nerve that many of our leaders wondered if I even believed that God still performed miracles. One of our Lifeschool leaders spoke afterwards, assuring everyone that I still believed in miracles.

My point wasn't to diminish the need for God's power, but to redirect their focus to the person of Jesus Christ. My goal was to see Christ placed back at the center of the African church, for Christ to become the primary message. Just like the apostles in the book of Acts, who preached Christ and not the things of Christ, I encouraged them that miracles would naturally flow as Christ was exalted and lifted up.

Thankfully, the response to this message ended up overwhelmingly positive.

THE CHURCH HAS REPLACED CHRIST IN GOD'S HOUSE

In Colossians 2, Paul faced a similar situation that we are faced with today. In the church at Colossae, the believers were being seduced away from Christ by human wisdom, the traditions of men, religion, the Law, and by an excessive focus on the supernatural. To be more specific, some of the snares he listed were "philosophy" (literally "the love of wisdom"), "empty deception," "the tradition of men," "the elementary principles of the world," the "shadow[s]" in the Law, "self-made religion" that delighted in "self-abasement," "severe treatment of the body," abstaining from touching and tasting certain foods, and an obsession with the supernatural, including "the worship of the angels" and soulish visions (Col. 2:8-23, emphasis mine).

To curtail this deception, Paul brought Christ back into the center of the conversation, exhorting the Colossians to attain to "all the wealth that comes from the full assurance of understanding, resulting in a true knowledge of God's mystery, that is, Christ Himself, in whom are hidden all the treasures of wisdom and knowledge" (Col. 2:2-3).

Paul contrasted the emptiness of human wisdom, soulish religion, and supernatural fixations to the infinite treasures of Christ. He showed that in Christ "all the fullness of Deity dwells in bodily form" (Col. 2:9). He revealed Christ as "the image of the invisible God" and the Creator of everything "in the heavens and on earth, both visible and invisible, whether thrones or dominions or rulers or authorities" (Col. 1:15-16). He unveiled Christ as the One "before all things" and in whom "all things hold together" (Col. 1:17). He showcased Christ as "the head over all rule and authority" and the "head of the body, the church" (Col. 2:10; 1:18). And he expounded upon Christ's central role in our redemption through His finished work on the cross (Col. 2:9-15).

In short, Paul wanted to lead the Colossians away from the things of Christ back to the person of Christ. He wanted to place Christ back at the center of the church, so that He might have the "first place in everything" (Col. 1:18).

What we see in Colossians is repeating itself today. Sadly, the church has replaced Christ in God's house. We have exalted the things of Christ above the person of Christ. We've made Jesus into a doctrine and have elevated events, revival, evangelism, miracles, God's blessings, doctrines, spiritual gifts, leadership principles, cultural relevance, end-time prophecy, social justice, church growth, missions, discipleship, and Israel above Jesus Christ. Unfortunately, church leaders use the name of Jesus Christ and the doctrine about Jesus Christ to advance their own selfish agendas—often without even realizing they're doing it.

What I have discovered is that the person of Jesus Christ is vastly different from the religion bearing His name. It's time, then, to place Christ back at the center of His church. It's time to make Him the King once again in His own house.

The Revelation of Christ

Jesus asked Peter, "Who do you say that I am?" (Matt. 16:15). After Peter responded that Jesus is the Christ, the Son of the living God, Jesus made it clear that this was a revelation from the Father (Matt. 16:17).

By looking at Jesus of Nazareth in the flesh, Peter never would have been able to know that He was the uncreated Son of God. Jesus didn't have a halo around His head. He wasn't glowing with heavenly light. He looked like an ordinary Jewish man. Revelation was the only way Peter could have known that Jesus was God's Son.

Jesus' response was profound. He said to him, "You are Peter, and upon this rock I will build My church" (Matt. 16:18). My apology to Catholicism, but Jesus did not mean that Peter is the rock upon which the church is built. Rather, the unshakable foundation of the church is Peter's revelation of the true identity of Jesus. Not *revelations*, but *the revelation* of Jesus Christ.

Somehow the church has missed this vital truth. We think the church is built upon charisma, talent, spiritual gifts, leadership principles, and church-growth schemes. We think the church is built upon knowledge, information, manifestation, human wisdom, creative eloquence, technology, and the latest trends in social media. And if all that fails, just combine stage lights and fog machines.

Hopefully, sooner rather than later, we will realize that Jesus doesn't need our help building His church. He is quite capable of building it Himself, just like He said. He does this by revealing Himself. There is simply no other way He builds it.

When the splendor and glory of Christ is revealed, and we see Him as He truly is, it changes everything. If we were able to see Him like Paul did, we, too, would count our greatest accomplishments as animal manure compared to the treasure of knowing Him (Phil. 3:8). He is simply that beautiful and glorious.

When Christ is revealed to us and in us, He will have preeminence in everything.

And what I've discovered is that, when Christ is the center of my life, family, and church, He brings everything into balance.

Christ at the center brings balance to spiritual gifts, doctrines, praise and worship, spiritual warfare, eschatology, Israel, revival, and blessings. Christ at the center aligns missions, church growth, evangelism, faith, and theology into their proper order.

Jesus builds His church by the unfolding revelation of Himself. And as He does this, the kingdom of God is established within us because the King of kings is revealed to us.

The revelation of Jesus Christ is how God begins to fulfill His eternal purpose to place His Son at the center of everything, for the Son is God's ultimate intention. He is the One to whom all of Scripture points, and the Father will bring everything in heaven and on earth under His headship.

So, what is God's motivation for establishing Christ as the center? As we will see next, it is the Father's passionate love for His Son.

CHAPTER 6

The Father Loves the Son

In 1997, at the age of twenty-five, the Lord brought me into a fiery season of testing. I found myself on the backside of the wilderness. I was single, virtually friendless, and lonely. The Lord was breaking me and stripping me of every rival. He was rewiring me from the inside out. It was an awful but necessary time.

During this season, I had a dream that changed my life, which I mentioned in the previous chapter. It was the beginning of my journey into God's eternal purpose.

In the dream, John the Baptist was talking to me about his forerunner ministry. John looked completely different from the movies. He was not an angry man, dressed in a hairy outfit, eating locusts, and screaming to the masses. He was like an old sage. He was like a spiritual father giving me critical advice for my ministry.

John was incredibly passionate. Not the kind of passion that leads to fanaticism. His passion was graceful and poised, completely under control. I could tell he had something very important to tell me.

Resolute and focused, he looked me straight in the eyes and said, "The Father loves the Son." That was all he said. Five simple words.

Yet intuitively, I knew this revelation fueled his forerunner ministry. John's insight into the Father's burning love for His Son empowered him to prepare the way for the Lord's first coming.

Later that day, during my lunch break, I was reflecting on this dream. I was relatively new to walking with the Lord and had never studied John the Baptist. Curious whether John had ever spoken these words, I pulled out my Bible. Flipping through John the Baptist's statements in the gospels, I landed in John 3. To my utter amazement, I read these words spoken by John the Baptist to His disciples: "*The Father loves the Son* and has given all things into His hand" (John 3:35, emphasis mine).

What John the Baptist said in my dream was exactly what he said to his disciples! I was stunned. I had just heard God's voice from the throne. A ray of heavenly sunlight broke into the darkness of my soul. I had just encountered the living God in an unmistakable, irrefutable, life-changing way.

Still pondering this dream, I was in a Christian bookstore a few days later. Scanning the bookshelves, I saw John Piper's book *The Pleasures of God*. Immediately, I knew that I had to buy this book. I must have read the first chapter, *The Pleasure of God in His Son*, ten times. Every sentence resonated deep in my spirit, setting off an avalanche of revelation. I spent the next two to three years focused upon the Father's love for His Son.

Little did I realize then, but the Lord was drawing me into His eternal purpose. He was unveiling the catalyst of His ultimate intention. He was revealing the driving force behind His eternal blueprint. The Father's love for His Son is the energetic force of His ageless plan.

This simple revelation was my entry into God's eternal purpose.

The Father and Son in Eternity Past

If we want to understand God's ultimate intention to place His Son at the center of everything, then we need to be grounded in the Father and Son's eternal relationship. To understand their intimate bond, let's travel back in time to eternity past, before the uncreated Son became Jesus of Nazareth.

Journey with me for a moment to the dateless past, when it was God and God alone.

No one else and nothing else existed. The universe was but a thought in the mind of the Godhead. Earth and humanity were but a distant dream. Heaven, the angels, and the throne were still on the drawing board.

In this state of timelessness, the Father, the Son, and the Holy Spirit dwelt in unapproachable light (1 Tim. 6:16). A light so intense that it would make the sun seem like a faint star in comparison. A light so intolerable that nothing could penetrate it.

"God is Light," wrote the apostle John, alerting us that this light was not some celestial object or cosmic force (1 John 1:5). This light was a Person. This light *was* God.

Hidden inside of this bright light was the eternal Son, before He became Joseph and Mary's baby boy. To be more specific, the eternal Son was hidden in "the Father's heart" in deep fellowship and intimacy (John 1:18, NLT).

The eternal Son was not merely a holy man whom God created and brought into the light of His presence. John tells us that the eternal Son "was in the beginning with God" and is Himself fully God (John 1:1-2). Being without a beginning, the Son "is the beginning" of all things (Col. 1:18).

Like the Father, the uncreated Son always existed. That's why Jesus, during His earthly ministry, could tell the Pharisees, "Before Abraham was born, I am" (John 8:58).[1] It's why, over seven-hundred years before the incarnation, Isaiah saw the eternal Son enthroned, radiating the Father's glory (John 12:41; Isa. 6:1).

The eternal Son has always been an exact representation of His Father. He is the Father's perfect reflection and radiance (Col. 1:15; Heb. 1:3). He has always embodied, expressed, and exuded the Father's glory. "The light of the knowledge of the glory of God," wrote the apostle Paul, is in "the face of Christ" (2 Cor. 4:6). Jesus could honestly tell Philip, "He who has seen Me has seen the Father" (John 14:9).

John Piper said, "From all eternity God has beheld the panorama of his own perfections in the face of his Son. All that he is he sees reflected fully and perfectly in the countenance of his Son. And in this he rejoices with infinite joy."[2]

The Son of God is not less than the Father, but is coequal with the Father's essence, nature, glory, and beauty. He has always "existed in the form of God" and has always been "equal with God" (Phil. 2:6, NASB and NKJV).

Hidden within the Son are "all the treasures of wisdom and knowledge" (Col 2:2-3). He has never been informed of anything.

He has never learned anything. He has no need to seek understanding or consultation. Even if all the brilliant minds since the creation of the world gathered together, it would be impossible to tell the Son something He didn't already know (Isa. 40:13-14).

The Eternal Son Is the Creator

Out of the intimate love relationship of the Godhead, the Father determined that the Son would be the creator and sustainer of all things. This would place the Son at the center of everything and give Him the preeminence that the Father earnestly desired.

Speaking of the eternal Son, Paul said, "For by Him all things were created, both in the heavens and on earth, visible and invisible, whether thrones or dominions or rulers or authorities—all things have been created through Him and for Him" (Col. 1:16).

Consider the complexity and order of the universe. Ponder the infinitesimal atom to the far-reaching stretches of the solar systems. Reflect upon the humble sand gnat to the majestic Himalayas peaking over 24,000 feet into the South Asia skies. Contemplate the complex food chain that nourishes and sustains animals and humans. Consider the miracle of childbirth. The uncreated Son of God created all of this with just a few words.

Think about the human body and brain coordinating perfectly to produce speech and motion, thought and invention. Ponder the number of hours doctors have studied the human body for thousands of years, and yet they still have only scratched the surface of biological understanding.

Contemplate the complexity of creation. Ponder those things that we now take for granted. As John Piper described, things such as the "redness of the rising sun, and the roundness of the moon, and the whiteness of the snow, the wetness of rain, the blueness of the sky, the buzzing of bumble bees, the stitching of crickets, the invisibility of wind, the unconscious constancy of heart and diaphragm, the weirdness of noses and ears, the number of the grains of sand on a thousand beaches, the never-ceasing crash crash crash of countless waves, and ten million kingly-clad flowers flourishing and withering in woods and mountain valleys where no one sees but God."[3]

The Son of God created all of this with just a few small phrases: "Let there be light," "let the earth sprout vegetation," "let the waters teem with swarms of living creatures," and "let birds fly above the earth" (Gen. 1:3-20). For ages, humanity has been studying the intricacies of what took the Son but a moment to create. When you consider this—and that creation is but "the mere edges of His ways" (Job 26:14)—just who is He?

"In these last days [God] has spoken to us in His Son," wrote the author of Hebrews, "through whom also He made the world. . . . and [He] upholds all things by the word of His power" (Heb. 1:2-3, emphasis mine). By the Son's word, the sun and earth remain at the perfect distance from one another, keeping us from incinerating or freezing (Heb. 1:3). By the Son's word, the earth continues rotating at a tilt of 23.5 degrees, allowing the seasons, its associated fluctuations in weather, and the maximum amount of farmable land. By the Son's word, as Paul said, "All things hold together" (Col. 1:17).

Thus, the eternal Son is one with the Father in essence, power, and glory. Nevertheless, the Son is "distinct in personhood" so that the Father and Son "have had a personal relationship for all eternity."[4]

THE FATHER AND SON'S ETERNAL RELATIONSHIP

Jesus said, "I and the Father are one" (John 10:30). This union didn't occur after the incarnation. Reading through John 17, you see that the Father and the Son's inseparable relationship never had a beginning (John 17:10, 21-22, 24).

Throughout eternity past, the Father and Son shared an intimacy with each other that is beyond words. The two were bound together in perfect union by the Holy Spirit. Human language fails to articulate the intimacy, deep conversations, and unending communion the Father and Son shared through the Holy Spirit.

For billions of years, without external entertainment, the Father and the Son were delighted, joyful, and eternally satisfied in the fellowship of the Trinity. Never bored or needy, the Father and Son experienced unending pleasure in unbroken union.

Jesus said, "The Father loves the Son, and shows Him all things that He Himself is doing" (John 5:20). In response, "Whatever the Father does, these things the Son also does in like manner" (John 5:19). What beautiful, unbreakable intimacy that the Father and the Son have always shared.

Jesus said, "All things have been handed over to Me by My Father; and no one knows the Son except the Father; nor does anyone know the Father except the Son, and anyone to whom the Son wills to reveal Him" (Matt. 11:27).

The Father and the Son's eternal intimacy and union was manifested and revealed throughout Jesus' earthly ministry. That's why Jesus could say, "The Father abiding in Me does His works. . . . In that day you will know that I am in My Father" (John 14:10,20).

Simply, words fail to describe the Father and the Son's eternal union and inseparable bond. No relationship rivals theirs. It is utterly unique, incomparable, ineffable, and transcendent.

The Father Loves the Son

Just prior to His crucifixion, Jesus said to His Father, "You loved Me before the foundation of the world" (John 17:24). The Son was the object of the Father's affection and love throughout eternity past. He has always been the "beloved Son" or "the Son of His love" (Col. 1:13, NASB and NKJV).

Before time and creation, the Father burned with affection, rejoiced with ecstatic joy, overflowed with pleasure, and delighted deeply in His Son. Jonathan Edwards said, "The infinite happiness of the Father consists in the enjoyment of His Son."[5] John Piper said, "God's pleasure is first and foremost a pleasure in his Son."[6] God's euphoric love for His Son cannot be overstated.

As the Father gazed upon His Son in eternity past and beheld the excellencies of His beauty, glory, and nature, we can imagine the Father erupting with shouts of joy, "This is My beloved Son in whom I am well-pleased."[7]

What is it about the Son that fills the Father with such joy and delight? It's His perfect balance of infinite majesty and transcendent meekness. His radiant glory and servant-like humility. His exacting justice and unmerited grace. His uncompromising righteousness and tender mercies. His fear of God and equality with God. His submission to the Father and His absolute dominion. His self-sufficiency and utter reliance upon God.

The Father's love for His Son "come[s] not just from his majesty, nor just from his meekness, but from the way these mingle in perfect proportion."[8] The Son is the Lion of Judah who will shake the heavens and the earth when He unleashes the events of the last days (Rev. 5:5). But this is only half the picture. The Son is worthy of this role because He is the Lamb who was slain (Rev. 5:6). What seems utterly incompatible in one person is perfectly balanced in the Son. As A.W. Tozer said, God "never suspends one of His attributes in order to exercise another."[9] The eternal Son is the Lion of Judah and the slain Lamb, interwoven. And this makes Him glorious and beautiful to the Father.

When the Scriptures describe the Father's love for His Son, it's not speaking of a self-denying, sacrificial love. It's not a love rooted in mercy or compassion. The Father is not lowering His standards to love one who is unworthy. As John Piper said,

> When we say that God loves the Son . . . we are talking about a love of delight and pleasure. God is not stooping to pity the undeserving when he loves the Son. He is well-pleased with his Son. His soul delights in the Son! When he looks at his Son he enjoys and admires and cherishes and prizes and relishes what he sees. The first great pleasure of God is his pleasure in the Son.[10]

Overflowing from this fiery, passionate love, the Godhead established their purpose for the ages. A purpose that revolves around the Son of God. A purpose, as we will see in the next chapter, that was for God's good pleasure.

CHAPTER 7

THE GOOD PLEASURE OF HIS WILL

In Ephesians 1, Paul said that God's mysterious eternal purpose was established "according to His good pleasure" (Eph. 1:5, 9, NKJV). The NASB translates this as "the kind intention of His will." Based on this rendering, some mistakenly believe that God's eternal purpose was motivated by His compassion for people, His benevolence toward the needs of humanity.

In today's self-centered church culture, we define God's goodness by His blessings. We think *God is good because He blesses us with prosperity, healing, favor, influence, and destiny.* Thankfully, the Lord does bless us this way. But this is not the ultimate expression of His goodness. Contrary to popular opinion, God is not good because He blesses us. God is good because He gives us Himself.

Though God is unbelievably kind, wants the best for us, and blesses us immensely, the eternal blueprint was established for the good pleasure of the Godhead. It was designed to bring pleasure to the Father, Son, and Holy Spirit. The Godhead established their ultimate intention from the overflow of the Father's eternal pleasure in His Son.

The Father, Son, and Holy Spirit were so happy in their eternally satisfying fellowship that they wanted to share this with a creation. For their good pleasure, they wanted to invite men and women to experience the bliss of their joyful relationship.

The Father wanted to multiply His pleasure in His Son by having a multitude of Christ-like sons. This corporate son would then experience the same relationship with the Father that the Son has enjoyed for all eternity.

The Son wanted to be the source of love to a beloved. From the overflow of the Son's love, this corporate bride would return His love back to Him, loving the Son with the Father's very own love and passion.

The Holy Spirit wanted to possess a people with His indestructible life. He wanted to fill a creation with the fullness of Himself.

God's eternal purpose to bring a creation into the fellowship of the Trinity overflowed from the good pleasure of God's love for God.

This brings me to a very important point. *God is supremely relational.* For centuries, the church has missed this simple but essential truth. We have become so preoccupied with revival, spiritual gifts, theological doctrines, religious rules, social justice, cutting-edge events, and the latest and greatest technologies that we have missed the most important reason for our existence.

God created us so that we could enjoy the same relationship that the Father and the Son have enjoyed for all eternity. God's eternal purpose is for us to be in a heart-satisfying relationship with Him.

But here's a vital truth we need to understand. The Father decreed that His Son would be the only way humanity could be brought into the eternal fellowship of the Godhead. The purpose of the ages can only be fulfilled in the Son. There is no other way.

God's Eternal Purpose Is in Christ

In the heavenly council of eternity past, the Son of God was established as the Way (John 14:6). No matter how good, righteous, or holy someone might be, they simply cannot come into a relationship with the Father but through the Son. No amount of human compassion, human goodness, charity, self-deprecation, good works, sacrifice, or prayer can bring a person to the Father. God determined to relate to creation through His Son.

Terry Bennett describes this dynamic in his book, *Within the Circle of the Throne*, stating,

> We have been called to the fellowship of His Son. What does that mean? That means the eternal relationship that God the Son has had with the Father. We have been invited into that relation-

ship. It is not our own relationship with the Father. We have been brought into the Son (and the Son into us) to have the very relationship that the Son has eternally had with the Father.[1]

The eternal Son is the only Way to the Father. He is the only One who can bring us into the eternal fellowship that the Trinity has enjoyed forever.

Just as the earth orbits the sun, God's eternal purpose revolves around the eternal Son. This means that the good pleasure of God's will can only be accomplished in the Son. Paul revealed this when he said, "In accordance with the eternal purpose which He carried out in Christ Jesus our Lord" (Eph. 3:11). The Father "purposed" to do everything "in Him" (Eph. 1:9). In the heavenly council of eternity past, the Son of God was forever established as the boundaries of the eternal blueprint (Acts 17:31). He is the horizon and limit of God's ageless purpose.

Everything that God does is from, through, and for His beloved Son (Rom. 11:36; Col. 1:18). So, for the Father, the Son, and the Holy Spirit to have what they desire in a creation, the Son was not only established as the way into a relationship with the Trinity, but He was also established as the life who would be imparted into humanity, the pattern and seed that would multiply the Father's pleasure in His Son as He brings many sons to glory, and the Bridegroom who would have a bride. This will become clear in a minute. But first, we need to see the utter importance of the Son becoming a Man.

THE MAN ON THE THRONE

For the Son to bring humanity into His relationship with the Father and accomplish the full spectrum of God's ageless purpose, there was a problem—even before sin entered heaven and earth through Lucifer and Adam.

The Godhead dwelt in unapproachable light. Even though God earnestly desired a relationship with creation, it was impossible because of His transcendence, majesty, and glory. Nothing and no one could penetrate the intensity of His light. It was like an impassable fortress. If any creation attempted to draw near, they would collapse at a cellular level at the outer fringes of His impenetrable glory. Unless God acted, creation would be kept at a distance forever.

But God, being supremely relational, wanted more. He had to have more. He burned with desire for intimacy with a creation. He wanted to draw near to His prized creation to come—to draw near to us.

Paul said, "It was the Father's good pleasure for all the fullness [of Deity] to dwell in Him [in bodily form]" (Col. 1:19; 2:9, emphasis mine). To draw near to creation, the eternal Son would become a Man. Unapproachable light would dwell in fullness in the Son's body.

The Greek word for *good pleasure* was frequently used in legal documents in biblical times. According to the *Theological Dictionary of the New Testament*, this means that God *resolved* or *decreed* with pleasure that the fullness of deity should dwell in the body of Christ.[2] This decree, that the eternal Son would become a Man, was made in the heavenly council in eternity past. God would relate to creation through the Man Christ Jesus. The eternal Son would become the Way that the Godhead would bring humanity into a deep, eternal relationship.

Consider this mystery. Close to six-hundred years before the eternal Son became a Man in Jesus of Nazareth, Ezekiel was escorted into heaven's throne room (Ezek. 1). There he beheld the breathtaking glory and beauty of God. At the pinnacle of this experience, after encountering living beings and a mysterious whirling wheel, Ezekiel looks up and sees "something resembling a throne" (Ezek. 1:26). Sitting upon the throne "was a figure with the appearance of a man" (Ezek. 1:26). Who was this mysterious man, enthroned at the pinnacle of heaven, some six-hundred years before Jesus of Nazareth?

It would be hard to argue against this Man being the preincarnate Christ, the eternal Son in whom the fullness of deity dwelt in bodily form.

For creation to draw near, God transfigured Himself into a Man. He clothed His impenetrable light in a body.

Now let's look at Jacob's mysterious wrestling match. All alone at night, "a man wrestled with him until daybreak" (Gen. 32:24). Notice that Jacob wrestled with a man. Yet this was not just any ordinary man, for after the contest, the man told him, "You have striven with God . . . and have prevailed" (Gen. 32:28). After this encounter, Jacob testified, "I have seen God face to face, yet my life has been preserved" (Gen. 32:30).

Jacob's opponent was none other than the God-Man—the pre-incarnate Christ. The One who clothed His unapproachable light in a body so that He could draw near to creation.

The Godhead has such a desire to draw near to us. What amazing love!

THE SON IS LIFE

To bring humanity near, the Son was not only established as the Way, but also as the Life who would be imparted into humanity. Jesus didn't become the Life when He was incarnated. He's been the Life for eternity.

John said, "What was from the beginning, what we have heard, what we have seen with our eyes, what we have looked at and touched with our hands, concerning *the Word of Life*—and the life was manifested, and we have seen and testify and proclaim to you the eternal life, which was with the Father and was manifested to us" (1 John 1:1-2).

Notice that "the life was manifested." That means the Son, who has always been the Life, was incarnated in human flesh. He is the "Word of Life" that came "down out of heaven, and gives life to the world" (John 6:33).

The Son has always been the Life, but in the eternal council, it was established that the Son would be the Life who would be imparted into humanity. The importance of this can't be overstated.

Unless humanity was filled and possessed by the Son's indwelling life, it would be impossible to have unending fellowship with

God in the holy of holies. In the eternal council, therefore, the Son was established as the One who would be imparted into men and women.

The eternal Son now manifests His life through the tree of life, the bread of life who gives His life to the world, the life-giving Spirit who dwells within a people, the light of life shining in the darkness, and the resurrection life who gives life to the dead (John 6:35; 1 Cor 15:45; John 8:12; John 11:25).

You can see God's eternal purpose clearly when Jesus said, "I came that they may have life, and have it abundantly" (John 10:10). Jesus clothed Himself with human flesh, endured the cross, and was resurrected so that His life-giving Spirit could dwell within us.

Jesus came to place His life within us. Not just in seed form, but so abundantly we would be a gushing river of life to the broken and needy world around us (John 7:38). God's ultimate intention is for us to be filled with the fullness of the Son's indestructible life. Like John said, "He who has the Son has the life" (1 John 5:12).

In the garden, God gave humanity the choice to eat from the tree of knowledge or the tree of life. If Adam had eaten from the tree of life, he would have partaken of Christ. The Son's life would have been implanted within him. Subsequently, this life would have multiplied throughout the human race.

The fall obviously affected this, but it did not deter God from His original intention to place the Son's life into humanity. This was an indispensable part of God's eternal purpose for humanity to enjoy the eternal relationship between the Father and the Son.

THE FATHER'S PLEASURE MULTIPLIED

The Father, wanting to multiply His pleasure in His Son, determined to have a family of sons patterned after His beloved Son. In the eternal council, therefore, the Son was established as the pattern to which humanity would be conformed, shaped, and molded. God's destiny for us is to become a mature representation of the Son.

Paul revealed this eternal purpose when he wrote, "He also predestined [us] to become conformed to the image of His Son" (Rom. 8:29, emphasis mine).

From eternity, the Father's burning desire has always been to form the Son's lamb-like nature in us. He wants to establish the Son's humility, meekness, tenderness, selflessness, generosity, and sacrificial love within our hearts and souls.

God's predetermined destiny, offered to all mankind in Christ, is to become a complete and mature representation of the Son.

"Learn of me," said Jesus, "For I am meek and lowly in heart" (Matt. 11:29, KJV).

Christ was not transformed into a meek and lowly Lamb through the incarnation. These traits have been inherent in His nature from eternity. The Son has always been the Lamb. He has always been humble, meek, gentle, selfless, and sacrificial. It's part of His eternal nature. These attributes have always been essential parts of His character.

God's eternal purpose is that we would have the Son's lamb-like nature formed within us. The Holy Spirit is working in accordance with God's eternal blueprint to transform us into mature representations of Christ. He is jealously shaping and molding us into humble, meek, tender, selfless, generous, and sacrificial men and women. He is urging us to embrace the cross-life as the way of life. His heart's desire is that we would be like the Lamb—continually laying ourselves down in sacrificial love, allowing death to work in us so that life can work in others.

The Son is also the seed for a harvest of sons. Paul said that He might be "the firstborn among many brethren" (Rom. 8:29). This doesn't mean that the Son was born, but that He is like a firstborn son with the highest privileges, inheritance, responsibilities, and authority.

Jesus said, "Unless a grain of wheat falls into the earth and dies, it remains alone; but if it dies, it bears much fruit" (John 12:24).

Jesus, the pattern Son of God and the seed for a harvest of sons, gave His life to multiply the Father's pleasure. He sacrificed Himself so that the Father's ultimate intention to bring "many sons to glory" could be realized (Heb. 2:10). Because Jesus planted His life into the ground like a seed, it guaranteed a harvest of sons who would be conformed into His image and nature. "Sons of the kingdom" who will shine like the sun in its strength and rule the nations with a rod of iron (Matt. 13:38; Rev. 2:27).

THE BRIDEGROOM GOD

As a prophet and seer, John the Baptist had the ability to peer beyond his cousin's Jewish heritage. He saw beyond the man from Galilee's outward appearance into the spirit. John knew his relative was no ordinary man. He was the eternal Son incarnated in human flesh. He was the Bridegroom who has a bride (John 3:29). John saw God's eternal purpose to give the Son a beloved who would one day love Him with the Father's very own love (John 17:26).

Jesus of Nazareth never married on earth. But one day He will have the greatest wedding in history. He will marry a bride who is like Him, who came forth from Him, and who is joined to Him Spirit-to-spirit. The marriage supper of the Lamb will be the pinnacle event of human history. The eternal Son of God will be married to His people forever.

In the eternal council, I imagine the Father telling His Son something like this:

> My Son, for all eternity, You have been My beloved. But now I am going to give You a unique creation that You will dwell within. This creation will be Your very own beloved. She will be a companion whom You can pour out upon the passion of Your being. You will be the source of love and she will return Your love back to You. She will love You just like I love You.
>
> She will be like You, will come forth from You, but will be distinct from You. She will dwell forever with us and will become Your very own inheritance.
>
> You will be the Bridegroom and this new creation will be Your bride.

Thus, in the eternal council, the Son was established as the Bridegroom who will have a bride burning with the Father's very own love for Him. Regardless of the fall, God's ultimate intention has always been to provide His Son an equally yoked bride. One who is filled with His life, conformed into His image, and is a mature representation of His nature.

It's no coincidence, as Paul unraveled the mystery of God's eternal purpose, that he revealed Jesus as the Bridegroom and the church as the bride (Eph. 5:22-33). As Paul Billheimer said in his classic book, *Destined for the Throne*, "Creation has no other aim. History has no other goal. From before the foundation of the world until the dawn of eternal ages God has been working toward one grand event, one supreme end—the glorious wedding of His Son, the marriage supper of the Lamb."[3]

The blueprint from eternity established the Son as a Bridegroom who will have a new creation joined to Him forever. She will be His beloved, aflame with the same passion the Father had for Him in eternity past.

When Jesus said, "The kingdom of heaven may be compared to a king who gave a wedding feast for his son," He was heralding the plan contained in the eternal blueprint (Matt. 22:2). And when the bride finally makes herself ready at the end of the age and "the marriage of the Lamb has come," what God purposed in eternity past will finally be realized (Rev. 19:7-9). The Bridegroom will have a worthy bride!

THE SON COMES FOR HIS BRIDE

For God to recover His ageless purpose from the effects of the fall, the eternal Son had to become a Man of flesh and blood. The Son had to become fully human to obtain His beloved bride.

The One who painted the night sky with stars, suspended the planets in orbit, fashioned earth's dazzling paradises, shaped the majestic mountains, wove the seasons into place, initiated the weather patterns, and designed and formed every species of insect and animal had to become a Man.

The One who created man with His breath of life, instilling the intricate and masterfully designed parts of our being, including our brain, heart, organs, soul, and spirit, had to become an embryo in the womb of Mary.

The Creator had to become a creature. The Author had to step into his own story, taking the role of a character in the world He created, welcomed by the stench of animals and manure.

The angels who worshiped Him from eternity past, in the words of Sam Storms, would watch "Mary change His diapers!"[4] The One once surrounded by the glorious praise of angels would be surrounded by the "lowing of cattle, the bleating of sheep, [and] the stammering of bewildered shepherds."[5] The One whose word upholds the solar systems would coo and cry, as He exchanged "the robes of eternal glory for the rags of swaddling clothes."[6]

God's redemptive plan, to restore us from the effects of the fall back to His ultimate intention, was also established in the eternal council (1 Peter 1:19-20). This required the eternal Son to assume human flesh without sacrificing any of His deity. This required the eternal Son to become the atoning sacrifice for our sins. And this required a Roman spear to pierce Jesus' side, for the second Adam's bride would come forth out of Him, as in the beginning (1 Cor. 15:45-47).

Like in Genesis, the bride was in the Man Christ Jesus. When the blood and water poured forth from Jesus' side, it laid the groundwork for a new creation. The blood provided atonement; the water foreshadowed the life-giving Spirit dwelling within His people (John 7:38). This new creation bride, taken from the Son's side, would become "bone of [His] bones, and flesh of [His] flesh," so to speak (Gen. 2:23).

This great mystery of mysteries, whereby God the Son became fully human without ceasing to be fully divine, reveals the extent to which the Bridegroom goes to redeem the bride He so loves. Seeing how He freely sacrificed Himself for us demonstrates His relentless pursuit to capture our hearts, for we are His beloved.

Entering the Joy of the Master

Those who are faithful in this life will "enter into the joy of [their] master" (Matt. 25:21, emphasis mine). What is this joy? It is the eternally-satisfying, blissful relationship of the Trinity.

For God's good pleasure, we were created and have been invited into the very relationship that has delighted God for all eternity. As we just saw, the full spectrum of God's ageless purpose revolves around the Son.

In the eternal council, the Godhead established the Son as the way into this fellowship. He was also established as the life to be imparted into humanity, the pattern to which we would be conformed, the seed for a future harvest of sons that would multiply the Father's pleasure in His Son, and the Bridegroom who would have a bride that would love Him like the Father.

God, being supremely relational, so desired fellowship with us that the eternal Son became a Man. Not only that, but as we will see next, the Son also yearned to be in us. What amazing love indeed!

CHAPTER 8

CHRIST THE LIFE

When death looms at your doorstep, what's most important in your heart has a way of surfacing. Facing imminent death, Jesus poured out His heart to the Father, reaching back to their relationship in eternity past.

"You loved Me before the foundation of the world," He said (John 17:24).

In this moment of intense grief, Jesus found great comfort in His Father's eternal affections. There was also *someone* who gave Him courage to embrace the cross. There was a "joy set before Him" by which "He endured the cross" (Heb. 12:2). Who was this *someone* and what was this *joy* that motivated Jesus to suffer such persecution, pain, rejection, and shame? The last words of His prayer answer this question.

With every ounce of His heart, Jesus prayed, "Father . . . I have made Your name known to them, and will make it known, so that the love with which You loved Me may be in them, and I in them" (John 17:25-26).

As the Lover in the romance of the ages, the eternal Son became a man of flesh and blood to win the heart of His beloved. Jesus endured the pain and shame of the cross so that He could have a bride, *someone* He could lavish with His unrelenting love. The Bridegroom willingly suffered at Golgotha so that He could have a beloved, *someone* who would receive His relentless love and love Him in return.

Jesus died on the cross so that He could have voluntary lovers who would choose Him and love Him with the Father's very own love. Thus, the love which Jesus experienced from His Father in eternity past would be multiplied through a corporate bride, one who came forth from His very own side.

But there's a precursor that can't be ignored. God's entire purpose for the ages hinges upon three simple words: "I in them."

Meditate upon this for a minute. Ponder the deep implications of this.

There is only one way for humanity to become the bride. Christ must dwell within her. The life-giving Spirit of the Son must be planted within the spirit of His beloved. Why? Because human life and divine life are incompatible. Only by possessing the divine life of the Son could humanity be conformed into His image and be fit to marry the King. Without divine life implanted within us, we could never have unending fellowship with God in the holy of holies. Drawing near would be as impossible as combining oil and water.

God loves us so much that He wants not only to be with us, but within us. Have you ever thought about that? Jesus burned with such a desire to live in us that He ended His most heartfelt prayer recorded in the Scriptures with this request.

This brings us to the story of the eternal Son, chosen in the eternal council, to be the Life who would be implanted into humanity.

Christ In You—The Hope of Glory

Paul adds profound insight to this story in his letter to the Colossians. Indeed, not many revelations in Scripture compare.

Reaching back into the ageless past, Paul unearthed one of the most important truths of the eternal blueprint:

> The mystery which has been hidden from the past ages and generations, but has now been manifested to His saints, to whom God willed to make known what is the riches of the glory of this mystery among the Gentiles, which is Christ in you, the hope of glory. (Col. 1:25-27)

This mystery—"Christ in you"—had been hidden inside of God's heart for millennia. Most of the great men and women of God in biblical history, however, had no concept of God dwelling within His people. This was a revelation that was hidden from Abraham, Moses, David, and many of the prophets. Even the angels were stunned at such an idea (1 Pet. 1:12). They couldn't comprehend that the One whom they worshipped in such glory and beauty would take up residence in the spirit of men and women.

Christ in you—the great eternal plan of God.

What a privilege we have. Humanity has the exclusive opportunity to become the dwelling place of the uncreated Creator. This is unique among God's created order. Neither the angels, the cherubim, nor the seraphim will ever have God's life within them. They can only relate to God externally, not internally. Only humanity was destined to have the life of the Son within them.

The Son Is Life

If you search the New Testament for the word *life*, you quickly realize how often the Scriptures refer to the Son as the Life.

He is the bread of *life*, the resurrection and the *life*, the Word of *life*, and the light of *life* (John 6:35; 11:25; 1 John 1:1). He is the *life-giving* Spirit imparted into all who believe in Him, giving *life* to their spirit, heart, soul, and body (1 Cor. 15:45).

The Son has *life* in Himself, He gives *life* to those who believe in Him, and He wants to release His *life* in fullness to those who yield wholly to Him (John 1:4; John 7:38; John 10:10). The Son's *life* is a well of water in us that springs up into rivers of living water, flowing outward to a dark and desperate world (John 4:14; 7:38).

The Son wants to become your *life*, where He lives His *life* in you and through you, empowering you to walk in newness of *life* (Col. 3:4; Gal. 2:20; Rom. 6:4). He wants to fully save our souls by the power of His indestructible *life* (Heb. 7:16). And as John said, "He who has the Son has the life" (1 John 5:12).

The Greek word for *life* in most of these passages is *zoe* (pronounced zō-ā'). When referring to God's life, *zoe* is the highest life, the superlative life. God's life is infinitely higher than animal life, human life, and angelic life. God's *zoe* is the uncreated, divine, indestructible, and eternal life that the Father and Son possess in themselves.

The eternal Son was not transformed into *zoe* in the incarnation. He has been this highest measure of life forever. But in the eternal council, the Son was established as the Life who would be implanted within humanity. This was the only way for the Son to have a bride who was like Him, from Him, and in love with Him. This was the only way that humanity could enjoy the eternal fellowship of the Trinity in the holy of holies.

ABUNDANT LIFE

Jesus said, "I came that they may have life, and have it abundantly" (John 10:10). Can you see God's ultimate intention in this statement? Because God's eternal purpose was for the Son's life to be implanted within humanity, the Father sent His Son to earth. The blueprint established in the eternal council, which decreed that the Son's life would be imparted into mankind, drove Jesus' coming to earth and motivated His entire ministry.

In Jesus' statement in John 10, we see two aspects of Jesus' life in us. First, we see the initial impartation of His life—"that they may have life." This life is imparted into our spirits the moment we are born again. Second, we see that God intends for the life of Christ in our spirits to blossom and mature until we "have it abundantly" in our hearts, souls, and bodies. Jesus wants His life to be released in us in fullness—without limits, without hindrances, and without measure.

This progression from the seed of Christ planted in us to the fullness of Christ blossoming within us is similar to Ezekiel's vision of the river in the temple. It begins as a trickle, increases to the ankles, rises to the knees, surges upward to the waist, and then overflows to such a degree that you can only swim in it (Ezek. 47).

God's predetermined plan is for the Son's life to be implanted within us in seed form and to progressively increase until we have it in an overflowing abundance. Paul described it as "the fullness of Christ" (Eph. 4:13).

What a beautiful plan that our loving Father decreed before the foundation of the world! Words fail to express the glory of this inconceivable idea. That humanity would have the life-giving Spirit of the Son within us—an internal intimacy and union with our Creator that is unique among all creation.

Christ in you, progressively released into your heart, soul, and body. His life increasing in you until His indestructible life fills and permeates every molecule of your being. Ultimately, you become a powerful, overflowing river of the very *zoe* of God, pouring out onto the needy world around you.

This has always been God's ultimate intention.

CREATION AND ULTIMATE INTENTION

Creation was not a random event. God didn't establish the galaxies, solar systems, and Earth because He was bored. Humanity wasn't fashioned for divine entertainment, as if the Trinity needed to add some spice to their life.

The eternal blueprint drove creation. God created male and female for His eternal purpose. Only humanity was destined, in the eternal council of the Godhead, to have the life of God within them. Nothing was random, nothing done by accident.

Executing their plan, the Father and Son said to one another, "Let Us make man in Our image, according to Our likeness" (Gen. 1:26).

We are not some arbitrary blob that has evolved over millions of years from apes. We are the one-and-only creation, among God's entire created order, to be offered the exclusive privilege of having the life-giving Spirit of the Son within us.

God created Adam and Eve—and all mankind thereafter—for the purpose of having God's indwelling life. The Lord fashioned us for internal intimacy and union with the Father, the Son, and the Holy Spirit.

When the Lord took the dust of the earth and released His breath into it, Adam was created as a "living soul" (1 Cor. 15:45). Innocent, pure, and childlike, but not holy, righteous, or godly. Adam still needed God's life within him.

Nevertheless, Adam was designed to become the habitation of God. The one-of-a-kind creation shaped for Spirit-to-spirit union with the eternal Son. Christ in you, the hope of glory, motivated God to create Adam and Eve.

The Scripture says, "And the LORD God formed man of the dust of the ground, and breathed into his nostrils the breath of life; and man became a living soul" (Gen. 2:7, KJV). The "dust of the ground" refers to Adam's body. The Lord's "breath of life" refers to the creation of Adam's spirit.[1] And it's clear from this Scripture that Adam "became a living soul." Thus, Adam—and all humanity— was created as a spirit, soul, and body (1 Thess. 5:23).

God created Adam's spirit with the innate ability to communicate in the spirit realm, to know God intuitively, and to have an awareness of Him. Adam's spirit had a sharp sensitivity to the Spirit of God, enabling him to quickly sense God's presence, discern His voice, and commune with Him. Adam's spirit made him God-conscious.

Adam's soul was comprised of his mind, will, and emotions. With his mind, Adam had thoughts, an intellect, wisdom, knowledge, reasoning, logic, ideas, and creativity. With his will, Adam had the power to make decisions. He could choose God's will or his own. He could live in submission to God or independently of Him. With his emotions, Adam had the ability to love or hate, to be happy or sad, to be fearful or depressed, and to be passionate or complacent. Adam's soul defined his personality and made him self-conscious.

Adam's body is how he communicated with the material world. Through his five senses of taste, touch, smell, sight, and sound, he interacted with the physical. Adam's body was driven by four primary desires: eating, sleeping, reproduction, and comfort. Adam's body made him world-conscious.

In God's original design, Adam's spirit was the most important part of his being. His spirit was designed exclusively for communion, union, and intimacy with God. The Lord fashioned his spirit for His ultimate intention of Spirit-to-spirit union with the indwelling life of the Son.

Created as a "living soul," Adam's self-life was in his soul. His intellect, emotions, and desires, uncorrupted by the fall, dictated how Adam lived. His soul was the power-source that drove him.

Though Adam's life was in his soul, where his self-life resided, God's intention was for Adam's spirit to become the leader that directed his soul and body. God's aim was for him to be spirit-oriented rather than soul-oriented.

The problem was that Adam's spirit was underdeveloped, for he did not have the indwelling Spirit of the Son. For that to happen, Adam would have to make a moral choice between self-rule (the tree of the knowledge of good and evil) or the lordship of Christ (the tree of life). Thus, the reason God placed two trees in the garden.

TWO TREES IN THE GARDEN

Today, when many think of the two trees in the garden, they view it as a fairytale. Something that you would read in a kid's book. One of those Sunday School stories that's cute for kids but isn't practical for adults. Unfortunately, some look at it with derision. They discredit those who believe it actually happened, mocking them as unintelligent, uninformed, and unenlightened.

Tragically, many Bible teachers, leaders, and pastors never discuss the importance of the tree of the knowledge of good and evil and the tree of life. Influenced by humanistic thought and the spirit of the age, they keep silent about the key event that has marked and shaped human history for thousands of years.

Oh, how the crafty serpent from the garden has worked overtime, undermining one of the most important events in history.

Imagine if we could travel back in time and see the two trees in the garden. Have you ever wondered what they would have looked like?

I suppose that the tree of knowledge would have been the most attractive. It undoubtedly had a seductive pull on the soul. A magnetic force that drew Adam and Eve's thoughts, emotions, and desires under the enchanting power of lust.

After all, the tree "was good for food," enticing the desires of the will. It was "a delight to the eyes," stirring the emotions. And it was "desirable to make one wise," stimulating the mind (Gen. 3:6).

The tree offered Adam and Eve freedom, liberty, independence, wisdom, knowledge, a self-governed life, and the ability to do what was right in their own eyes. They would no longer have to consult and rely upon God for every decision. They could become "as gods, knowing good and evil" (Gen. 3:5, KJV).

From what we know about God's ways, I imagine that the tree of life looked ordinary and unappealing.[2] More like a lowly vine than a luscious tree. Perhaps Jesus was referring to Himself as the tree of life when He said, "I am the vine" (John 15:5).

In any case, if you search the Bible for the "tree of life," you will discover it's mentioned in Genesis 2-3, but removed from the earth after the fall. Though mentioned four times metaphorically in Proverbs, the tree of life doesn't reappear until the last book of the Bible. In Revelation 2:7, Jesus offers the fruit from this tree to those who return to their first love. Following this, the tree of life once again has a prominent role as the eternal ages commence (Rev. 22:2,14,19).

What does this mean? Simply that the tree of life was part of God's original intention. He offered it to mankind in the beginning, He offers it to those who love Him now, and it will have a prominent role in the new Jerusalem throughout eternity.

Why is this tree so significant? Because the fruit from this tree contained the Son's indestructible life. You could even say that Jesus *is* the tree of life.

If Adam and Eve would have eaten its fruit, they would have partaken of Christ. God's divine nature would have been implanted within them. The Son's holiness, righteousness, humility, and love would have permeated their spirits. Their spiritual DNA would have been forever altered, transforming them into children of God who lived in moment-by-moment dependence upon their Father. The Son's indestructible life would have been deposited into the spirits of Adam and Eve, and they would have become the first dwelling place of God. The Father, the Son, and the Holy Spirit would have had their prized possession and inheritance in a race of men and women filled with the Son's life. The Godhead's ultimate intention would have been realized apart from the fall, the cross, salvation, and redemption.

From the beginning, however, the Lord wanted autonomous lovers, not pre-programmed robots. A beloved who freely chose Him and loved Him. A voluntarily lover who prized Him more than herself.

For such a high calling, Adam had to be tested. So God put two trees in the garden. Adam had to make a moral choice between self-governance or Spirit-reliance, self-rule or humble dependence upon God, the self-life or the life of Christ . . . the antichrist nature or the nature of the Lamb.

The tree of knowledge offered Adam self-rule, self-love, and self-deification. The tree of life offered humble reliance upon God as a true and authentic lover.

God would never make mankind His own possession and co-heirs with His Son without this test.

We know what Adam chose. But thankfully, God had a plan to restore us back to His original intention. (God's restoration plan is unwrapped in Part 4).

So, are you beginning to see the amazing plan of our Father to establish the Son as the Life who would be implanted within humanity? And that His indwelling Life is the only way we can possibly become God's inheritance? It's an amazing reality! There's yet another facet of the eternal Son for us to understand, though, which is progressively unveiled from Genesis to Revelation: the Son was also established as the Truth. Just what does it mean for the eternal Son to become the embodiment of God's word, His ways, and His wisdom? That's what we will answer next.

CHAPTER 9

THE GREATEST SERMON IN HISTORY

I would have loved hearing John Wesley and George Whitfield preach during the first Great Awakening—or hearing any of the great reformers preach during the Protestant Reformation. Just imagine hearing Martin Luther preach on justification by faith to an audience mired in dead religious works.

Likewise, what would it have been like to hear Paul preach at Mars Hill or to the church of Ephesus? What about hearing the fiery prophet clothed in camel's hair, John the Baptist, call the nation of Israel to repentance? Or hearing Elijah, who called down fire from heaven on Mount Carmel and then slayed the wicked prophets of Baal?

Imagine sitting on the hill on the northwestern shore of the Sea Galilee, between Capernaum and Gennesaret, and listening to Jesus teach the Sermon on the Mount.

But there's one sermon that tops all sermons. It's when the resurrected Christ preached Christ to His disciples on the road to Emmaus. Think about it for a minute. Jesus was just raised from the dead. Only a handful even know He's alive. Here's the Son of God in human flesh, resurrected after three days in the tomb.

Luke tells us that "beginning with Moses and with all the prophets, He explained to them the things concerning Himself in all the Scriptures" (Luke 24:27). Wow! This must have been an awesome experience.

As Christ revealed Himself in the Torah, I imagine He began something like this:

I am the One who said, "Let there be light," and there was light.
I am the One who said, "Let the waters below the heavens be gathered into one place, and let the dry land appear," and it hap-

pened. I am the One who spoke the vegetation and the animals into existence. And I am the One who formed Adam from the dust and breathed into Him the breath of life. I am the Creator of the earth, humanity, and the universe.

How could these disciples doubt His words? After all, the One who just predicted and fulfilled His own death and resurrection was standing right in front of them.

Continuing through Genesis, when He got to Abraham, perhaps Jesus said something like this:

Isaac was a type and a shadow of Me. I am the seed of Abraham. I am the One to whom God gave His oath. I am the One to whom the Father was ultimately looking toward when He spoke the blessings and promises over Abraham and his seed.

This must have sent shockwaves through their souls. Jesus of Nazareth, fresh nail marks in His hands and feet, just told them that He was the centerpiece of Israel's 2,000-year history. He is the One to whom the promises were made.

When He got to Exodus, Leviticus, Numbers, and Deuteronomy, maybe Jesus said something like this:

Just as a body cast a shadow in the bright sun, I am the One casting the shadows of the feasts and the sacrifices in the Law.

When our people just celebrated Passover, bringing their perfect lambs to Jerusalem to be examined and sacrificed by the priest, I too was being examined by the High Priest. When they sent Me to the cross, I was like the spotless and blameless lambs that are slaughtered during Passover. I am the ultimate Passover Lamb to whom this feast pointed.

Not only that, but when I rose from the dead three days later, I fulfilled the Feast of First-Fruits.

I am the One casting the shadows seen in the feasts of Passover, First-Fruits, Pentecost, and Tabernacles. I am the substance and fulfillment of every feast of Israel and the One casting the shadows of the Old Covenant priesthood, temple worship, and sacrifices. I am the One of whom the Law prophesied through its types and shadows.

I can't imagine what it would it would have been like when Jesus got to the book of Isaiah. Perhaps Jesus expounded upon this prophecy and told them something like this:[1]

I am the Branch of the Lord who will be beautiful and glorious when I return. I am the beautiful King, the majestic One, who will be a place of rivers and wide canals on which no mighty ship will pass. When I set up My throne upon Mount Zion, I will be the judge, lawgiver, and king over the entire earth.

I am the child born to Israel who now shoulders God's government. I am the Wonderful Counselor, Mighty God, Eternal Father, and Prince of Peace. I am the root and offspring of David, who sits on David's throne and reigns over His kingdom with justice and righteousness.

I am also the suffering servant of Isaiah 53. I am the One who suffered a substitutionary death on the cross that will now result in justification for many. This will produce a harvest of sons who will be conformed into My image and likeness.

I am the One in whom the Father delights, and I was divinely commissioned to bring justice to the nations, to become a covenant for the people, to be a light in the darkness, to liberate the captives, and to open blind eyes.

I was called from the womb, and My mouth is like a sharp sword. I am the select arrow that has been hidden within God's quiver. I will restore Israel and be the salvation that extends into the nations.

When I return and set up My kingdom on Mount Zion, Jerusalem will become the praise of the earth. I am Israel, the One to whom the promises were made and fulfilled.

Continuing with the other prophets, maybe Jesus said something like this:[2]

When Daniel saw the Son of Man before the Ancient of Days, it was Me that He saw. I am the Son of Man who has been given dominion, glory, and a kingdom. All the peoples, nations, and men of every language will serve Me. I am the stone of Daniel's prophecy that will crush the statue of man's kingdoms. My kingdom will become a great mountain that will fill the whole earth. As Jeremiah said, I am the Son of David who will reign as king, act wisely, and do justice and righteousness in the land. And as Haggai said, I am the Desire of All Nations to whom the tribes of the earth will flock when I return. Then, as Zechariah prophesied, I will be king over the entire earth.

When Jesus finished preaching this unrivaled sermon, the disciples' "hearts were burning within" them (Luke 24:32). Imagine seeing the resurrected Christ with your own eyes, then hearing Him unveil God's plan through the ages. Christ revealing Christ as the resurrected Christ! Words likely failed them.

THE SCRIPTURES POINT TO CHRIST

Jesus is the Word of God (John 1:1). He is the Truth in whom all of God's treasures of wisdom, knowledge, council, ways, purposes, and plans are fully embodied (Col. 2:2-3).

The entire Bible, from Genesis to Revelation, is a progressive revelation of the eternal Son. "The volume of the book," from beginning to end, "is written of" Him (Heb. 10:7).

Jesus told the most ardent biblical scholars of His day, "You search the Scriptures because you think that in them you have eternal life; it is these that testify about Me" (John 5:39). Keep in mind that these men spent most of their waking hours studying the Old Testament. Yet Jesus told them that the Scriptures ultimately point to Him—that He is life.

The Scriptures are not meant to be our god, but the compass that points us to the Son of God, who is the Word of God and the full embodiment of the truth. The Bible was not written to fill us with the knowledge of history or to recount the past displays of

God's power. It was inspired by the Holy Spirit to lead us to the eternal Son, of whom Genesis to Revelation testify.

Paul said that "Christ is all, and in all" (Col. 3:11). When you study the Scriptures, every revelation and inspiration ultimately points to the eternal Son, who is at the center of God's eternal purpose. The prophecies in the Old Testament are thoroughly Christ-centered, for Jesus is the horizon and boundaries of God's eternal plan. The types and the shadows of the Law point to Jesus, who is God's ultimate intention.

God's eternal blueprint placed His Son at the center of everything, and the Scriptures testify to this. From the beginning to the end, you see hints of the supremacy of Christ scattered throughout the pages of the Bible.

Seeing the Christ-centeredness of the Scriptures, it's time for Jesus to have the preeminence once again. This must begin in God's house, the church.

MOVING ON

As we bring Part 2 to a close, remember that Jesus Christ is God's ultimate intention. He is the Way who brings us into His eternal relationship with His Father. He's the Life chosen to be implanted within humanity, enabling us to become His bride. And He's the One to whom all of Scripture points. The eternal Son is the fulfillment of it all.

Moving on to Part 3, let me set the stage. One of God's primary purposes for this age is to bring His people completely under the headship of Jesus Christ. The Lord wants to establish His kingdom fully within us in this age, so that we can establish His kingdom fully throughout the earth in the age to come. This will be our focus in Part 3.

PART 3

THE PURPOSE OF THE AGES

God's driving purpose for the ages is to gather everything in heaven and on earth under the headship of Jesus Christ. Part 3 focuses on how the Lord accomplishes this objective in the various ages revealed in Scripture by establishing His kingdom.

CHAPTER 10

THE LORDSHIP OF JESUS CHRIST

If you step back and look at the scope of world history, you'll find that it can be viewed through the lens of two kingdoms: the kingdom of darkness and the kingdom of light.

After his fall, Lucifer morphed into Satan, the great red dragon described in Revelation 12. The dragon and his kingdom are characterized by pride, rebellion, independence, self-love, self-rule, lawlessness, lust, greed, and covetousness. Satan's kingdom is the empire of self.

The kingdom of God, however, reflects the nature of its King, the Lord Jesus Christ, who is the Lamb. The lamb-like nature of this kingdom is characterized by humility, meekness, obedience, selflessness, full submission to the lordship of Christ, self-control, generosity, and servanthood. Jesus' kingdom is the empire of sacrificial love.

Speaking about these two kingdoms, T. Austin Sparks wrote:

Anything and everything but the Lamb is in the present constitution of things. Everything that is a complete antithesis of the Lamb pervades this order of things, in its very constitution. You see the point. The whole constitution has got to be changed. Another constitution needs to be given to this universe and it must be the constitution of the Lamb. Yes, this universe has got to be reconstituted upon the basis of the Lamb-nature, and the wonderful thing is that all these tremendous forces—these simply terrific forces, in this universe, of iniquity, evil, wickedness, sin, hatred and malice—all these forces are gathered up, and the Bible tells how a Lamb can deal with the whole thing.[1]

So, basically, the two kingdoms—of Christ and of self—are like warring forces, with self ruling the current order. But, the "whole constitution" can be—*must* be—changed, and this change begins in the deepest recesses of the human heart. It is a reconstitution in our hearts, transforming our selfish natures into the "Lamb-nature."

Paul underscored this truth when he wrote, "He made known to us the mystery of His will, according to His kind intention which He purposed in Him with a view to an administration suitable to the fullness of the times, that is, the summing up of all things in Christ, things in the heavens and things on the earth" (Eph. 1:9-10).

This is a mouthful, so let me simplify. When you dig into the Greek, a simple way to say this is: God's eternal purpose is to bring everything in heaven and on the earth under the headship or lordship of Jesus Christ.[2]

This work has been underway since the fall. In every age of history, God has been working according to His eternal purpose to bring everything under the lordship of Jesus Christ. From Adam to Abraham to Moses to the birth of the church, even to this present day, the Lord has preserved a remnant of faithful men and women. In and through these individuals, the Lord works to progressively reconstitute the universe into the nature of the Lamb.

The Purpose of the Ages

The amazing thing is that God has been working to transform humanity and society to the Lamb's nature throughout history and will continue into the future. Paul confirmed this when he said, "This was in accordance with the eternal purpose which He carried out in Christ Jesus our Lord" (Eph. 3:11). The phrase "eternal purpose" actually means "the purpose of the ages." So, God's purpose has been and will continue to be achieved.

Digging deeper into Ephesians 3:11, the Greek word for *eternal* is *aiōn*, meaning "time viewed in relation to what takes place in the period."[3] According to *Vine's Expository Dictionary of New Testament Words*, the meaning of "eternal" here "is not so much that of the actual length of a period, but that of a period marked by spiritual or moral characteristics."[4]

Based on these definitions, *aiōn* or age, is an indeterminate period of time in which God has a specific "to-do" list. You've heard of a "honey-do list;" well, this is a "God-do list." Basically, history can be divided into periods of time marked by God's specific mission, objective, and mode of operation. In each "age" or period of time, God seeks to achieve unique goals.

When you consider this definition, it sheds new light on common Scriptures. For example, what we normally consider "the end of the world" is actually the end of this present age and God's current mode of operation (Matt. 24:3). Another example is Paul's great desire to be rescued "from this present evil age," which is characterized by the reign of sin and the rule of evil (Gal. 1:4). This is because Satan is still "the god of this age" (2 Cor. 4:4, NKJV).

And when Paul said, "To whom be the glory forevermore," the actual translation is "to whom be the glory from the ages to the ages" (Gal. 1:5). This shows there will likely be an infinite number of ages for eternity. In each of these unique ages, the Lord will accomplish a specific mission or task in His creation related to His original intention.

A similar example is found in Revelation 22:5, where John wrote, "The Lord God will illumine them; and they will reign forever and ever" (Rev. 22:5). Again, the literal translation is "they will reign from the ages to the ages," showing that the bride of the Lamb will have kingdom authority in each of the unique ages that spans from the Lord's return into eternity.

In summary, the Scriptures reveal that there are distinct ages in which God has a specific mission, unique goals, and a predefined objective that He seeks to accomplish. This divine initiative is in accordance with "the purpose of the ages" that was established in God's eternal council. This is the blueprint that drives all that God has done or will ever do. Thus, God's ultimate intention has driven every age thus far and will drive every subsequent age into eternity.

The Ages Revealed in Scripture

A detailed look at the ages in Scripture is beyond the scope of this book.[5] But to be brief, the ages can be summarized as follows:

- *The Age of the Gentiles*: Spanning from Adam to Abraham and characterized by unrestrained sin.

- *The Age of Israel*: Established by the Abrahamic Covenant, the Law, and the Prophets.

- *The Church Age*: Inaugurated by the New Covenant. One of the Lord's primary intents during the Church Age is to establish the kingdom of God within His people. (More on this in Chapter 12.)

- *The Kingdom Age*: Commences when Jesus returns, sets up His kingdom in Jerusalem, and rules over the nations for one-thousand years in partnership with His bride. (More on this in Chapter 13.)

- *The Eternal Ages*: After the Kingdom Age, the eternal ages begin with the creation of a new heaven, a new earth, and the new Jerusalem coming down from heaven to earth. Though we know there will be specific ages throughout eternity, each with a unique mission and objective, these ages are still a mystery.

Since the ages mentioned above are shaped by my view of Bible prophecy, you can read several online articles that I wrote detailing my position.[6] I will also address this topic in Chapter 13.

Here's the main point to take away: God's eternal purpose—to bring everything in heaven and on earth under the lordship of Jesus Christ—has driven every age of history and will drive every future age. God has determined to place His Son at the center of everything, and nothing will stop Him. He will reconstitute the entire universe into the nature of the Lamb.

This purpose will be accomplished first in a people during the Church Age, second in the earth during the Kingdom Age, and third throughout the universe for the endless ages of eternity.

God's Purpose for This Age

Have you ever wondered what God's primary purpose is for this age? Have you ever pondered what the Lord's specific mission, objective, and unique goals are, which can only be achieved in this time period? Though many answers could be given, one of God's primary purposes for this age is to bring us entirely under the headship of Jesus Christ. After all, how can we ever extend the kingdom of God into the nations if we are not submitted to King Jesus in our hearts, souls, and bodies?

Paul said that Christ is the "head of the body, the church" (Col. 1:18). And we, as Christ's body, are called to "grow up in all aspects into Him who is the head" (Eph. 4:15). This means that, as we mature, we become more submitted to the lordship of Jesus Christ in every facet of our lives: our deepest thoughts, motives, inclinations, desires, words, and actions.

Looking at the church today, can we honestly say that the majority of Christ's people are submitted entirely to Him? There's undoubtedly a remnant who are possessed by Him, but the majority of God's people are content with just having a free ticket to heaven and enjoying the journey in the meantime.

In Ephesians 4:15, the verse just quoted above, Paul is expounding upon us becoming "a mature man" (Eph. 4:13). If we want to mature into a corporate representation and reflection of the Son, we have to grow up.

It's interesting that God gave this assignment to His leaders, those called as apostles, prophets, evangelists, pastors, and teachers (Eph. 4:11). The Lord wants His leaders aligned to one of His primary purposes for this age—to see a corporate son conformed into the image and likeness of Jesus Christ.

That means apostles are called to do more than plant churches. They are also commissioned to prepare a mature man.

That means prophets are called to do more than give prophetic words and equip the saints to minister in the gifts. They also have a mandate to develop the body of Christ into a representation of the eternal Son.

That means evangelists are called to do more than win people to Christ. Their ultimate goal should be to see new converts become a true embodiment of the Lamb.

That means pastors are called to do more than shepherd the flock and take care of their needs. They should be working toward God's ultimate aim of having a corporate son that reflects the nature of Christ.

That means teachers are called to do more than expound upon the intricacies of the Word and keep us balanced in sound doctrines. Their teaching should help develop believers into vessels who embody the kingdom and the character of the King.

One of God's primary objectives in this age is to have a corporate representation of His Son, and for this to happen, the kingdom of God must be fully established within us. God must have a people who are internally reconstituted to the nature of the Lamb. This involves bringing your whole being—thoughts, motives, desires, words, and actions—under the lordship of Jesus Christ.

To more fully submit, it helps if we understand the present-day clash between the kingdom of darkness and the kingdom of God. This epic struggle for your very own heart is our next frontier to explore.

CHAPTER 11

The Tale of Two Kingdoms

To better understand God's eternal purpose to bring everything in heaven and on earth under the lordship of Jesus Christ, we need deeper insight into the origin of the kingdom of darkness, Adam's (and hence all of humanity's) alignment with Lucifer, and the clash between these two kingdoms throughout history.

Let's begin with Lucifer's fall from heaven.

After the Lord created the Garden of Eden but before the serpent tempted Adam and Eve, the kingdom of heaven was shaken (Gen. 2:8; 3:1). A rebellion took place, led by Lucifer, the anointed cherub (Ezek. 28:12-18).

Lucifer was breathtakingly beautiful. Every precious stone covered him. He had the seal of perfection and was full of wisdom. Lucifer had direct access to God on His holy mountain. He dwelt in the holy of holies right before God's throne, constantly surrounded by the fullness of God's glory.

Lucifer was also assigned to the earth. In the words of Ezekiel, he was "in Eden, the garden of God" (Ezek. 28:13). He was "anointed as a guardian cherub" (Ezek. 28:14, NIV). Lucifer was responsible to protect the Garden of Eden. Perhaps he assisted humanity with God's mandate to take dominion over the earth (Gen. 1:28). In any case, Lucifer had duel access to heaven and earth. He could traverse between God's throne in heaven and the Garden of Eden on the earth.

But one day in heaven, Lucifer turned from gazing upon the splendor of God's majesty to look upon himself. Tragically, Lucifer became enamored by his own splendor. In the words of Ezekiel, Lucifer's "heart was lifted up because of [his] beauty" (Ezek. 28:17, emphasis mine). Pride entered his heart and Lucifer's wisdom was corrupted. His judgment was compromised.

Lucifer boasted within, "*I will* ascend . . . *I will* raise my throne above . . . *I will* sit on the mount . . . *I will* ascend above the heights of the clouds; *I will* make myself like the Most High" (Isa. 14:12-14, emphasis mine). In brazen pride, Lucifer vowed five times, "I will." Independence had crystallized within him. There no was no turning back. He had crossed the line.

God's response was swift. His voice thundered to Lucifer, "You sinned; therefore I have cast you as profane from the mountain of God. . . . I cast you to the ground" (Ezek. 28:16-17). The loyal angels resonated with holy fear as they watched Lucifer fall like lightning from heaven to earth. All of heaven reverberated from the aftershock of God's voice.

Prior to this, there was no devil to tempt Lucifer into pride. There was no adversary to lure him into independence. There was no Satan to persuade him to lead a rebellion.

Self turned Lucifer into the devil.

Lucifer's own pride deluded him. He thought he could be like God. He believed he could be enthroned above the Most High. And he persuaded multitudes of angels to follow him (Jude 1:6). This insurgence created the kingdom of darkness. And Lucifer became the king of this evil empire.

The kingdom of darkness is the kingdom of self. Pride, independence, self-rule, and rebellion are at the heart of this dark domain.

So, how did Adam, Eve, and all humanity align with this dark empire?

The Tree of the Knowledge of Good and Evil

When God created the tree of the knowledge of good and evil, He already knew of Lucifer's insurgence. He knew that multitudes of angels would follow Lucifer's pride and rebellion to form the kingdom of darkness.

Since the Lord wanted voluntarily lovers rather than pre-programmed robots, He gave Adam the choice to follow the example of Lucifer.[1] He put two trees in the garden so that Adam could choose between self-rule or Spirit-reliance. He offered Adam the self-life that now characterized Lucifer or the sacrificial, meek and humble life of Christ.

We all know what happened. Adam ate the forbidden fruit and death pierced his spirit. Self-love was awakened, transforming him into a self-conscious and self-aware man (Gen. 3:6-7). His childlike innocence was replaced with prideful autonomy. Adam was now his own independent god, doing what was right in his own eyes. He was now his own king, governing according to his own thoughts and self-interests.

Now having the knowledge of good and evil, Adam gained his independence from God—a "freedom" that would forever forge the chains of mankind's bondage. Adam no longer had to wait in God's presence for solutions to problems. He no longer had to inquire of the Lord about what to do. He was liberated from his moment-by-moment reliance upon the Lord. Just as Satan had promised, this fruit changed Adam and Eve into their own "gods, knowing good and evil" (Gen. 3:5, KJV). Self-deification had entered the human race.

With Adam's spirit now darkened by death, his soul and body became the governing force of his life. Adam's five senses of taste, touch, smell, sight, and sound were coupled together with his mind, will, and emotions, forming what the Bible refers to as the flesh.

HUMANITY'S ALIGNMENT WITH LUCIFER

When God gave Adam the choice between the two trees, He was entering into a covenant with humanity (Hosea 6:7). This covenant was related to His ultimate intention. If Adam would have chosen the tree of life, God's ultimate intention would have been accomplished apart from the fall, the cross, salvation, and redemption. If Adam chose the tree of the knowledge of good and evil, God's ultimate intention would then require the finished work of the cross.

In biblical days, covenants were a common way to secure alliances, pacts, and treaties, serving as a formal, solemn, and binding agreement that joined two parties together as one. Covenants were often secured by a blood sacrifice, joining two parties together based upon a common agreement and often extending into future generations.

Whenever a covenant was made between two parties, a covenant representative was always selected on behalf of each group. These representatives entered the covenant on behalf of everyone in their party. They would bind the entire group to the expectations of the agreement. Everyone belonging to a particular party was considered to be "in" its representative. Thus, everything the representative did and agreed to in making the covenant would be imputed to each member of the group.

In the garden, Adam was the covenant representative of humanity. If Adam chose the tree of knowledge, then his sinful choice would be imputed to all humanity as if they had chosen the forbidden fruit as well. If Adam chose the tree of life, then his obedience would be imputed to all humanity as if they had obeyed God. The fate of mankind hinged upon Adam's decision.

Paul alluded to this covenant dynamic in Romans 5:12-14. He taught that we are sinners in Adam, not because we sinned like him, but because we sinned in him. We are not sinners because we imitated Adam's sin. Rather, we are sinners because his sin was imputed to us in the first covenant transaction. As the covenant representative of humanity, Adam's choice is transferred to all humanity, as if we made the same fateful decision.

Not only are we constituted sinners by imputation, but we are also sinners by impartation. That is, Adam's selfish, proud, independent, and antichrist nature was imparted into the DNA of all men and women after him, forever altering the nature of humanity's spirit, soul, and body. Jesus confirmed this when He said, "That which is born of the flesh is flesh" (John 3:6). The flesh is the coupling of the unredeemed body to the unrenewed soul. This nature characterizes the entire Adamic race.

Just looking at our own life and the world around us, we know this to be true. But have you ever thought about what would have happened if Adam chose the tree of life? Though Scripture is silent about this, I'll give you my opinion.

Seeing how covenants work in Scripture, logic tells us that the reverse would have also been true. That is, if Adam, as the covenant representative of humanity, had eaten from the tree of life, his obedience would have been imputed to the entire human race. Thus, subsequent generations would have been reckoned to have obeyed God "in" their covenant representative. Because of this, the life of the Son would have been imparted to all humanity thereafter, making Adam the federal head of a new creation of men and women filled with God's indestructible life.

Just as Adam's sin, selfishness, and death gradually spread throughout the human race, it's likely that the opposite would have transpired. That is, the life of Christ would have gradually increased in mankind's spirit, soul, and body, leading to the fullness of Christ released through Adam's lineage. This would have fulfilled God's ultimate intention apart from the finished work of the cross.

Unfortunately, this didn't happen, for Adam's choice to eat the forbidden fruit aligned him, and all humanity following him, with Lucifer and the kingdom of darkness.

A Tale of Two Kingdoms

With the two paths set before him, Adam chose to become his own god and to live independently of His Creator, aligning him with Satan's kingdom. Adam became the head of a race of people with a dead spirit, an evil heart, and a proud soul coupled together with a sinful body. All humanity after him were born into Lucifer's "domain of darkness," a kingdom characterized by self-love, pride, independence, and rebellion (Col. 1:13).

When Adam sinned, he forfeited his authority over the earth to Satan (Luke 4:6). Fallen Lucifer had now become the king of the earth, crowned "king over all the sons of pride" (Job. 41:34). The whole world was now under his authority and domain (1 John 5:19). The kingdom of darkness ruled the earth.

But hope was not lost.

"I will put enmity between you and the woman," the Lord told the serpent. "Between your seed and her seed" (Gen. 3:15).

Here we have the first prophecy in Scripture, foretelling an ongoing clash between two kingdoms. The unfolding of this prophecy runs from Genesis to Revelation and has defined human history for thousands of years.

If we could peer behind the veil, we would see the real battle. We would see the violent conflict between the kingdom of light and the kingdom of darkness. This war will escalate until "the kingdom of the world" becomes "the kingdom of our Lord and of His Christ" at the second coming (Rev. 11:15).

History is truly a tale of two kingdoms. It's the unfolding drama of the Lord preserving a seed from the woman, who would challenge the world aligned with Satan and the kingdom of darkness.[2]

The conflict between the two seeds started with the line of Seth, as the ancients partnered with God to see Genesis 3:15 fulfilled (Gen. 5). Then came Noah and his family, who were divinely sheltered from the flood that wiped out the hedonistic world.

Later came Abraham, Isaac, and Jacob, eventually leading to the nation of Israel. Through a faithful Jewish remnant, the Lord eventually brought forth the Messiah, the eternal Son of God who crushed the head of the serpent on the cross. Speaking of Jesus Christ, God told the serpent, "He shall bruise you on the head, and you shall bruise him on the heel" (Gen. 3:15).

Jesus would lay the first death blow to the serpent and his kingdom. But there would be another who would finish this work. Paul said, "The God of peace will soon crush Satan under your feet" (Rom. 16:20). The final seed of the woman is the church, the *ekklēsia*. This corporate Christ, the Lord's very own body, will enforce the finished work of the cross upon Satan and his angels, exercising the authority of the kingdom at the end of the age.[3]

With this foundation laid, we're now ready to look in more detail at one of God's primary purposes for this age—to have a corporate son who has the kingdom of God fully established within them.

CHAPTER 12

THE INTERNAL KINGDOM

Jesus rebuked the religious leaders of His day with these stinging words: "The kingdom of God will be taken away from you" (Matt. 21:43).

The great hope of the Jewish prophets, of God's kingdom coming to Israel, was now placed into the archives, waiting for a future age (Acts 1:6).

"The kingdom of God," Jesus continued, "will be . . . given to a people, producing the fruit of it" (Matt. 21:43).

A new age had dawned. The Church Age had arrived. God's primary mode of operation had shifted from the physical and the external to the spiritual and the internal. Jesus gave the kingdom of God to the church, both Jew and Gentile.

Jesus continued, "And he who falls on this stone will be broken to pieces; but on whomever it falls, it will scatter him like dust" (Matt. 21:44).

Jesus, who often quoted the prophet Daniel, was undoubtedly thinking about Daniel 2 and the prophecy of the stone, "cut out without hands," that would crush the kingdom of this world at the end of the age (Dan. 2:34). As the King of the kingdom of God, Jesus is the stone and His kingdom will become "a great mountain" that will fill "the whole earth" at His second coming (Dan. 2:35).

When Jesus addressed the Jewish leaders of His day, He described the operation of God's kingdom in two different ages: the present age and the age to come. In the present Church Age in which we live, God's kingdom rule is established through voluntary submission to the King. Jesus invites us all to fall "on this stone" and "be broken to pieces." In this age, we can willingly yield to Him and let His indwelling Spirit break our pride, independence, rebellion, lawlessness, greed, covetousness, and lust. We can fall upon the stone and let our self-rule be shattered and replaced by the internal reign of the Lamb. In this age, our response to the King and His kingdom is a choice.

The next age will be different. When Jesus returns, He will "set up a kingdom which will never be destroyed" (Dan. 2:44). His kingdom "will crush and put an end to all these kingdoms" and it will "endure forever" (Dan. 2:44). At the second coming, the kingdom of God is coming with such force that no one and nothing can stop it. "On whomever it falls," Jesus said, "it will scatter him like the dust."

Since the fall of Lucifver and his usurping of Adam's authority in the garden, the kingdom of darkness has had its heyday in the kingdoms of the world, including Babel, Egypt, Assyria, Babylon, Media-Persia, Greece, and Rome. Some of these kingdoms were mentioned in Daniel's prophecy of the statue and the beasts (Dan. 2, 7).

At the end of the age, Satan will unite the nations through a one-world government, a one-world economy, and a one-world religion (Rev. 13; 17-18). This is the kingdom that Jesus Christ will strike, crush, and shatter. When this happens, "the kingdom of the world" will "become the kingdom of our Lord and of His Christ" (Rev. 11:15). Christ the stone will fall upon the brittle empire of man and scatter it like the dust.

At His second coming, Jesus will gather His enemies, namely those "who did not want me to reign over them," and they will be slayed in His presence (Luke 19:27). The Lord will vanquish all who aligned themselves with the antichrist and his evil regime, including everyone who took the mark of the beast in order to buy and sell (Rev. 13:16-17). As Paul said, "These will pay the penalty of eternal destruction, away from the presence of the Lord and from the glory of His power" (2 Thess. 1:9).

Following this, Jesus' kingdom will become a great mountain that will fill the whole earth. Jesus and His bride will then rule the nations with a rod of iron (Rev. 2:26-27). During this age, resistance to His government will be futile. Every sphere of society, including the world's systems of government, economics, education, media, and business will be conquered by the returning King of kings and Lord of lords. God's mode of operation will no longer be voluntary submission, but mandated subjection. In this mode of operation, the Lord will destroy those aligned with the antichrist and his evil world system as He releases justice to the oppressed, marginalized, and persecuted.

During this time, as Paul said, "Every knee will bow, of those who are in heaven and on earth and under the earth, and . . . every tongue will confess that Jesus Christ is Lord, to the glory of God the Father" (Phil. 2:10-11). Every creature will bow to the lordship of Jesus Christ during the Kingdom Age.

However, before this glorious age takes place, when the entire earth is submitted to the lordship of Jesus Christ, the Holy Spirit must first establish His kingdom fully within His people. This is one of God's primary purposes for the Church Age. This purpose will be accomplished before the Lord returns, for God will have a corporate son who is a representation and reflection of the eternal Son, one who has come fully under internal dominion of the Lamb.

THE KINGDOM OF GOD WITHIN

A hotly debated subject among scholars, theologians, teachers, and preachers is what Jesus meant in Luke 17:21. The NASB translates this verse as "the kingdom of God is in your midst." But the NKJV version renders it as "the kingdom of God is within you."

Looking at twelve of today's popular translations, it's basically a split between some variation of the kingdom within versus the kingdom in your midst.[1] The bottom line: Really smart scholars can't agree on what Jesus meant.

Since translators are divided, we must look at the Greek to see if it's easier to decipher. The Greek word translated *within* or *in your midst* is *entos*. According to *Strong's*, this word means *inside*.[2] *Thayer's* defines it as *within* or *inside*.[3] *Vine's* adds that it can also mean *among*.[4]

Once again, we have a stalemate. *Entos* can mean within, inside, or among.

Now we need to see if *entos* is used in other verses. This might help us see how the ancient authors used this word in context.

Unfortunately, *entos* is only used in one other passage, when Jesus told the Pharisees to "clean the inside [*entos*] of the cup and of the dish, so that the outside of it may become clean also" (Matt. 23:26, emphasis mine). If you stopped here, you could conclude that *entos* should be translated "within you."

But wait! There's more to consider.

It was the proud, arrogant, and hypocritical Pharisees who questioned Jesus in the first place. They asked Him "when the kingdom of God was coming" (Luke 17:20). So, verse 21 is Jesus' answer.

This leads many to conclude that the verse must be translated "in your midst" because the Pharisees, who Jesus called sons of the devil, would never have the kingdom of God within them (John 8:44). This seems to make the translation "in your midst" more accurate.

But others push back on this idea, saying that Jesus could have taken the Pharisees' question and used it to teach His disciples, who were standing by His side. After all, if you read verse 21 and 22 together, it reads like this: "The kingdom of God is within you. And he said unto the disciples . . ." (Luke 17:21-22, KJV). The idea is that Jesus flowed from this statement about the kingdom of God straight into teaching His disciples. Therefore, Jesus could have taken the Pharisees' question and used it to teach His disciples about the nature of the kingdom.

Having said all of that, both translations are supported by other Scriptures. For example, when Jesus said that the kingdom of heaven was at hand, it meant that He embodies the kingdom (Matt. 4:17). Christ's earthly presence meant that the kingdom of God was among them.

On the other hand, when Paul taught the Romans that the kingdom of God is righteousness, peace, and joy in the Holy Spirit, this proved that the kingdom of God is also an internal kingdom (Rom. 14:17).

If Jesus was indeed answering the Pharisees' question and not teaching His disciples, His statement that the "kingdom of God is in your midst" makes the translation "the kingdom of God is within you" also true. Why? Because Christ embodies the kingdom, and Christ dwelling in His people means that the kingdom of God is within us.

So, both translations are valid. The NASB translation that "the kingdom of God is in your midst" makes the point that Christ embodies the kingdom, and the NKJV translation emphasizes that the kingdom is within you because Christ dwells in you.

The Kingdom of God and Eternal Purpose

So, why does it matter that the kingdom of God is embodied in Christ and is within the believer? Because the kingdom of God and God's eternal purpose are virtually synonymous.

Consider this profound realization from Frank Viola's book *Insurgence*:

> For the last two decades, my main focus, burden, and passion has been God's eternal purpose. . . . The eternal purpose of God is the grand narrative of the entire Bible.
>
> The kingdom of God is at the heart of God's eternal purpose. In fact, in recent years, I've come to realize that the kingdom of God is just another term for the eternal purpose.[5]

I couldn't agree more.

Jesus taught us to pray, "Your kingdom come. Your will be done" (Matt. 6:10). The kingdom is how God's will is accomplished in the earth. The Greek word for "will" is the same word used in Ephesians 1:11, where Paul said that God "works all things after the counsel of His will." As we know, "the counsel of His will" is God's eternal purpose. Thus, the kingdom of God is how the Lord's eternal purpose is accomplished.

Summarizing the Kingdom of God

Describing every nuance of the kingdom of God is far beyond the scope of this book. Nevertheless, since the kingdom is how God fulfills His eternal purpose, I will briefly highlight some important concepts.

We would all likely agree that the three components of any kingdom are a sovereign ruler; a people who are ruled; and a territory where this rule takes place.

God's kingdom is no different. First, Jesus is the authoritative ruler of the kingdom of God. He is the King of kings and Lord of lords. Wherever He is, there is His kingdom. Wherever Jesus' Spirit is welcomed and embraced, there the kingdom of God has been established.

During His earthly ministry, Jesus said, "Repent, for the kingdom of heaven is at hand" (Matt. 4:17). With this statement, Jesus revealed that He embodies the kingdom of God. In the body of Jesus of Nazareth was the fullness of God's kingdom. Wherever Jesus was, there was the kingdom of heaven. So, Jesus is the supreme ruler of the kingdom of God.

Second, the people who have been conquered are the church, God's own people who have voluntarily submitted to the lordship of Jesus Christ. Actually, a better way to say it is that we *are being* conquered, for it takes a lifetime to reconstitute our entire being into the nature of the Lamb. Until the day we meet the Lord face-to-face, the indwelling Spirit will be breaking our pride, independence, rebellion, and selfishness. Because of His jealous love for us, the Lord will not relent until our deepest motives, desires, thoughts, emotions, and inclinations are fully yielded to the Lamb. His work will continue until Christ is Lord of every part of our being. So, God's people, the church, are the ones voluntarily being conquered and brought into submission to the internal reign of the Lamb.

Third, the realm where this rule takes place begins in our spirits, hearts, and souls. Jesus said, "The kingdom of God is within you" (Luke 17:21, NKJV). Because of the "Christ in you" reality, the King dwells within us. Every part of our being, where we allow the Spirit to establish the reign of the Lamb, is where the kingdom of God resides. This means the kingdom of God begins internally within the hearts and souls of God's people.

Paul said that the "kingdom of God is not eating and drinking, but righteousness and peace and joy in the Holy Spirit" (Rom. 14:17). The indwelling Spirit, who is the Spirit of Christ, establishes the kingdom of God within our spirits, hearts, and souls. Thus, God's eternal purpose to bring heaven and earth under the headship of Jesus Christ begins within His people. The transformation of the universe into the nature of the Lamb begins internally as Christ becomes Lord of our thoughts, emotions, desires, choices, words, and actions.

As God's kingdom is established within us, His kingdom then flows like a mighty river out of us. We then function as salt and light in our culture, bringing the kingdom of God wherever we go (Matt. 5:13-16). We advance the kingdom of God through intercession, preaching the gospel of the kingdom, healing the sick, and casting out demons. Like Jesus told His disciples, "As you go, preach, saying, 'The kingdom of heaven is at hand.' Heal the sick, raise the dead, cleanse the lepers, cast out demons" (Matt. 10:7-8). Paul said, "The kingdom of God does not consist in words but in power" (1 Cor. 4:20). Operating in God's power is one way to advance the kingdom.

Whenever someone receives Christ and surrenders to His lordship, the kingdom of God expands. Whenever the gospel of the kingdom is warmly embraced, the kingdom of God advances.

In short, the kingdom of God is *entered* at salvation, *embodied* because we have Christ's indwelling life, *proclaimed* as we preach the gospel of the kingdom, *demonstrated* as we operate in God's resurrection power, and *advanced* through prayer, preaching, missions, ministering in power, and spiritual warfare.[6]

THE COMING KINGDOM OF GOD

George Eldon Ladd, a popular theologian from the last century, popularized the concept of God's kingdom being "already but not yet."

We have God's kingdom already because we have Christ the King dwelling within us. We have the kingdom already because we have power to heal the sick, cast out devils, and raise the dead. We have the kingdom already because the Lamb's reign is being established within our hearts and souls. But we don't yet have the fullness of God's kingdom. That won't happen until King Jesus returns in power and glory and He crushes, scatters, and vanquishes every other kingdom. The fullness of His kingdom will then pervade every sphere of society in all nations.

KEEPING IT SIMPLE

With all of this in mind, a simple way to summarize the kingdom of God is: *The realm where the person of Christ and His Spirit reign.*

This reign begins within the heart and soul of God's people, it flows outward from us wherever we go, it advances as others surrender to the lordship of Christ, and it will be fully established in every sphere of all nations when Jesus returns. As Isaiah said, "There will be no end to the increase of His government or of peace" (Isa. 9:7). God's kingdom will never stop expanding. Ever.

In summary, God's eternal purpose to bring heaven and earth under the headship of Jesus Christ is accomplished by the kingdom of God being established:

1. Within a people during the Church Age;

2. In every sphere of society in all nations through His people during the Kingdom Age;

3. Throughout the entire universe, as His government never stops expanding, for the endless ages of eternity.

Establishing the kingdom is how God accomplishes His ultimate intention to place His Son at the center of everything.

THE SERMON ON THE MOUNT AND THE KINGDOM WITHIN

What does it look like when the kingdom of God is established within His people? A simple answer is they will "follow the Lamb wherever He goes" (Rev. 14:5). They will be a people of humility, meekness, obedience, selflessness, and sacrificial love. Pride, presumption, and self-rule will be extracted out of their hearts and souls. Agreement with Satan and his kingdom of self will be broken. The Lamb's nature will be established fully within them.[7]

When I think about the kingdom of God being established within us, I always go back to the Sermon on the Mount, one of the greatest sermons in history (Matt. 5-7).

The Sermon on the Mount reveals the culture of the kingdom of God. It's also the kingdom's constitution, revealing in explicit detail the nature of Christ.

You see, when the kingdom of God is established within us, we will fully embody Jesus' teaching in the Sermon on the Mount. We will be a people who are humble, meek, hungry and thirsty for righteousness, merciful, pure in heart, peacemakers, and steadfast in persecution (Matt. 5:3-12). We will influence the world around us as salt and light (Matt. 5:13-16). Our hearts will be free from anger, bitterness, unforgiveness, and lust (Matt. 5:21-30). We will be a people of our word. Our yes will mean yes and our no will mean no (Matt. 5:34-37). We will be generous, sacrificial, and will go the extra mile for the sake of love (Matt. 5:39-42). We will love our enemies and pray for those who persecute us (Matt. 5:44-47).

When the Sermon on the Mount is fully established within us, we will not serve the Lord with an ulterior motive to be praised and honored by people (Matt. 6:1-5). Rather, we will be content before an audience of One, happy to be alone with the Lord in the secret place (Matt. 6:6).

Our hearts will be free from greed, covetousness, and the love of money (Matt. 6:24). Jesus will be our supreme treasure, and we will live for eternity rather than amassing treasures on earth (Matt. 5:19-21). We will not be overcome by the anxiety and pressures of this age but will fully trust the Lord to provide for our every need (Matt. 6:25-34).

Every form of unrighteous judgment—motivated by pride, hypocrisy, self-righteousness, criticism, envy, jealousy, and covetousness—will be removed from our hearts (Matt. 7:1-5). Having pure hearts, we will have the ability to appraise people and situations with righteous judgment.

Furthermore, we will treat people the way we want to be treated (Matt. 7:12). We will embrace the pressure and discomfort of walking the narrow path that leads to greater measures of Christ's life (Matt. 7:13-14). Our deepest desires, thoughts, emotions, and inclinations will be free from lawlessness (Matt. 7:21-23). And we will be wise, for we will fully obey every word in this sermon (Matt. 7:24-27).

When the kingdom of God is established within us, the Sermon on the Mount will be written on our hearts, rewiring us internally according to the culture of the kingdom. This is what it looks like to be brought under the headship of Jesus Christ in our hearts, souls, and bodies. This is what it looks like to be conformed into the image of Christ. And this is what it looks like for God's eternal purpose to be established within us.

Before Jesus returns in blazing glory to establish His kingdom in the nations, He will first establish His kingdom within us. Before the kingdom of the world becomes the kingdom of our Lord and of His Christ, the kingdom of self will be conquered.

Borrowing the words of Francois Fenelon, may Christ establish His throne upon the ruins of our self-love.[8]

This is one of God's primary objectives in this age and can only be accomplished by the indwelling Spirit.

CHAPTER 13

THE KING OF THE EARTH

If Jesus' Emmaus road sermon was the greatest in history, a close second were the sermons He gave prior to His ascension, which are recorded at the beginning of Acts.

The resurrected Son of God, having the ability to appear and disappear at will, "presented Himself alive after His suffering" to His disciples (Acts 1:3). Luke, the author of Acts, interviewed the eyewitnesses and stated that His appearings were with "many convincing proofs" (Acts 1:3).

Think about this for a minute. Every apostle except for John willingly died as a martyr. Utterly convinced that Jesus was exactly who He claimed to be, they paid the ultimate price for Him. I can't even imagine what these "convincing proofs" had been. But whatever Jesus showed them instilled unshakable confidence, inspiring them to testify of Him no matter the cost.

Luke tells us that Jesus appeared to them over a period of forty days. This language suggests that Jesus would suddenly be in their midst. Whenever He appeared, Luke said that Jesus spoke "of the things concerning the kingdom of God" (Acts 1:3).

A forty-day sermon series on the kingdom of God, straight from the lips of the resurrected King of kings and Lord of lords, is really hard to top!

After Jesus instructed the apostles and equipped them to be His witnesses, He gathered them together in Jerusalem and commanded them to wait for the outpouring of the Holy Spirit. With great anticipation, the apostles asked Him, "Lord, is it at this time You are restoring the kingdom to Israel?" (Acts 1:6).

I know the disciples did some dumb things, but it's unthinkable, after forty days of hearing about the kingdom of God straight from the lips of the resurrected King, that they would be confused about the future of Israel and the kingdom of God. This wasn't just Peter blurting out this question. Luke suggests that all of the apostles were asking this.

If God didn't have plans to restore the kingdom to Israel, Jesus would have undoubtedly corrected their misguided idea. But Jesus didn't. Instead, Jesus said, "It is not for you to know times or epochs which the Father has fixed by His own authority" (Acts 1:7).

When Jesus taught the apostles about the kingdom during these forty days, my hunch is that He opened up key passages about the kingdom of God from the Old Testament prophets, especially Isaiah, Daniel, Ezekiel, Jeremiah, and Zechariah. As He navigated through these Scriptures, Jesus revealed that He is the King that these prophecies spoke about.

Jesus, "the King of the Jews," likely taught them that the kingdom will one day be restored to Israel. After all, Jesus is Israel (Isa. 49:3). He is the One to whom all the promises to Israel were made and fulfilled (Gal. 3:16; 2 Cor. 1:20).

During these forty days, Jesus likely taught His disciples that God would one day restore the kingdom to Israel. That's why, when Jesus finished His teachings and was poised to ascend to heaven, the apostles immediately asked if He was restoring the kingdom to Israel right then.

Perhaps they were thinking something like this: "The Lord has been talking about restoring the kingdom to Israel. He just went through the Old Testament prophets and revealed that He is the King who would fulfill all of these promises. Now He has gathered us together and commanded us to wait in Jerusalem. Maybe everything He just taught is about to be fulfilled."

We know that didn't happen, but a day is coming when the kingdom of God *will* be restored to Israel.[1] This will mark the dawn of a new age, what many scholars refer to as the Kingdom Age. As we transition from the current Church Age to the Kingdom Age, everything that can be shaken will be shaken. This transition to the Kingdom Age is detailed in the book of Revelation.

During both the Kingdom Age and the transition leading up to it, Jesus Christ will be at the center. God will fulfill His eternal purpose to bring heaven and earth under the headship of Jesus Christ at the end of this age and throughout the next age, ensuring that His eternal Son has preeminence in both.

Four Views of Prophecy

Understanding how God will fulfill His eternal purpose in this age and the next is easier if we cut through the confusion and controversy that various interpretations of biblical prophecy have generated. Theologians have categorized these interpretations into the following four main views:

1. Preterism

This view interprets some or all biblical prophecies as events that have already occurred. According to this view, the prophecies of Daniel happened between the 7th century B.C. until 70 A.D., when the Romans destroyed Jerusalem and the temple. Full Preterists believe that Matthew 24 and the book of Revelation were fulfilled in 70 A.D. while Partial Preterists believe that only parts of Matthew 24 and the book of Revelation have been fulfilled. Both types of preterism believe that Israel finds its continuation or fulfillment in the church. To read why I disagree with this view, please see my online article *Why I Don't Believe in Preterism*.[2]

2. Postmillennialism

This view believes that Jesus Christ will return after the church has Christianized the world and has taken dominion over the world's systems of government, business, education, arts and entertainment, media, and religion. Postmillennialists believe that the preaching of the gospel will be so successful that it will usher in a Golden Age of Christianity. They foresee a time when the majority of the world becomes Christians, the nations of the earth obey the teachings of the Bible, and faith, righteousness, peace, and prosperity prevail. At some point during this utopian age, Jesus Christ will return and transition the earth to the eternal age. This view interprets the one-thousand-year reign of Christ happening through the church, before Jesus returns (Rev. 20:6). To read why I disagree with this view, please see my online article *Why I Don't Believe in Postmillennialism*.[3]

3. Amillennialism

As the "a" indicates, this view doesn't interpret Christ's one-thousand-year reign literally (Rev. 20:6). Amillennialists believe that the millennium, which is another term for the one-thousand-year reign of Christ on the earth, began at Christ's resurrection, will last until Christ returns, and is spiritual in nature. This view believes that Christ is presently reigning over the earth from heaven through His church. They also think that Satan has already been bound and is no longer able to deceive the nations. Some conservative Amillennialists, however, believe that Satan is only bound from launching Armageddon prematurely. After this present age has ended, Amillennialists believe that Christ will return and usher in the eternal state. To read why I disagree with this view, please see my online article *Why I Don't Believe in Amillennialism*.[4]

4. Premillennialism

This view interprets biblical prophecies literally, unless the context suggests otherwise. Premillennialists believe that Jesus Christ will physically return to the earth and will reign from the city of Jerusalem for a thousand-year period. Some Premillennialists debate whether this period is exactly a thousand years or represents a long but finite period of time prior to the eternal ages. This view also believes that all of Israel's covenant promises, which are scattered throughout the Old Testament prophets, will literally be fulfilled after the second coming of Christ. When His reign is fully established, Premillennialists believe that Jesus will hand the kingdom over to the Father and will then create a new heaven and new earth (1 Cor. 15:24; Rev. 21-22). To read why I hold to this view, please see my online article *Why I Believe in Premillennialism*.[5]

With this background established, let's look now at the transition from the Church Age to the Kingdom Age. Keep in mind that we are still looking at God's eternal purpose to bring everything in heaven and earth under the headship of Jesus Christ.

TRANSITIONING TO THE KINGDOM AGE

As previously stated, one of God's primary objectives during the Church Age is to fully establish the kingdom of God within His people. This is accomplished by the indwelling Spirit reconstituting our hearts and souls into the nature of the Lamb. He does this by inscribing the Sermon on the Mount upon our hearts, rewiring us internally according to the culture of the kingdom. He also accomplishes this by revealing Jesus Christ to us and in us. This is how Christ builds His church and fulfills God's eternal purpose to bring a people under the headship of Jesus Christ in this age.

When the Lord has fully established His government within a people, Jesus will return with these same people (His bride) to fully establish His government throughout the earth (Rev. 17:14; 19:14). During this age, resistance to His kingdom will be futile. The kingdom of God will penetrate every sphere of society, including the world's systems of government, economics, education, media, and business. God's mode of operation will no longer be voluntary submission, but mandated subjection. Every knee will bow and every tongue will confess that Jesus Christ is Lord.

THE REVELATION OF JESUS CHRIST

In all of Scripture, the book of Revelation contains the most details about the transition to the Kingdom Age. Though many are obsessed with the identity of the antichrist, the harlot Babylon, and the four horsemen of the apocalypse, few realize that this prophecy is "the revelation of Jesus Christ" (Rev. 1:1). This invaluable book contains the greatest revelation of Jesus in Scripture, and unless we dive deep into its pages, our knowledge of the Son will be limited.

The church is very familiar with the Jesus of Christmas, the Jesus of Easter, and the Jesus taught in Sunday School, but most believers don't know the Jesus revealed in the book of Revelation.

Jesus Christ is no longer a baby in the manger, the carpenter from Galilee, or even a broken man on the cross. He is the resurrected, glorified, and exalted Son of God.

When John saw Jesus, he fell down as a dead man (Rev. 1:17). Keep in mind that John was arguably closer to Jesus than anyone in history, referring to himself as "the disciple whom Jesus loved" several times in his gospel. Yet when he saw Jesus in His resurrected glory, he was so overwhelmed that he felt like he was going to die.

When John beheld Him, He saw Christ as He truly is, both fully human and fully divine. He beheld the eternal Son of God as a resurrected, ascended, enthroned, and glorified Jewish Man. John saw His face shining like the sun in its strength and His mouth like a sharp sword that will strike down the nations (Rev. 1:16; 19:15). He also saw Christ as the root and offspring of David, the Lion of the tribe of Judah, who is coming to take over the earth and rule the nations with a rod of iron (Rev. 5:1-5; 19:15; 22:16).

The book of Revelation reveals Jesus as a *righteous Judge* who will come to His church in judgment before He comes for His bride in glory (Rev. 2-3; 1 Peter 4:17). Jesus will purify His church with strong correction and discipline, so that the one He so loves will be made ready (Rev. 2-3; 19:7-9). As the righteous Judge, Jesus is the only One worthy to open the book containing God's redemptive plan for the earth (Rev. 5:5). When the Lamb breaks the seven seals of this book, it will unleash judgments against the kingdom of darkness, removing everything resisting God's kingdom from coming to the earth in fullness (Rev. 5:5; 16:10).

The book of Revelation also reveals Jesus as a *mighty Warrior* who will vanquish the antichrist—the cruelest, fiercest, most ruthless dictator in history—with the mere breath of His lips (Rev. 19:20-21; 2 Thess. 2:8). Jesus will wage war against the ungodly nations aligned with Satan and obliterate them (Rev. 19:11-16). Whoever refuses to fall upon the rock in this age and be broken to pieces might find themselves at war with the ultimate Warrior of the ages, who will return "in flaming fire" and take "vengeance on those who do not know God, and on those who do not obey the gospel" (2 Thess. 1:8, NKJV).

The book of Revelation also reveals Jesus as a *majestic King* who will take His great power and reign over the nations (Rev. 11:17; 19:16). We will witness the clash of two kingdoms at the end of the age. King Jesus will confront fallen Lucifer and his kingdom of darkness in the days just prior to His second coming.

Since the tower of Babel, Satan has been tirelessly working to have total control of the earth and to be worshiped by its inhabitants. In the final manifestation of Babel, fallen Lucifer will finally have the dream of his heart in end-time Babylon—a one-world religion, a one-world government, and a one-world economy (Rev. 13; 17-18). Through his wicked puppet, the antichrist, the kingdom of darkness will stretch to the ends of the earth and all the nations will give Lucifer the worship he's always craved (Rev. 13:8).

When Christ returns, He will overthrow the kingdom of darkness with violence. Every government, king, ruler, leader, and citizen who gave their allegiance to the antichrist and Satan will experience the fierce wrath of God Almighty as He takes His great power and begins to reign. "The kingdom of the world" will become "the kingdom of our Lord and of His Christ" and He will then "reign forever and ever" (Rev. 11:15).

Jesus Christ, who is the stone described by Daniel, will strike the brittle empire of man and crush every human kingdom aligned with the kingdom of darkness. Following this, the kingdom of God will become "a great mountain" that fills "the whole earth" (Dan. 2:35). Jesus will set up His kingdom in Jerusalem and will rule over the nations with justice and righteousness.

"The Lamb at the center of the throne" is the One at centerstage of end-time prophecy as God works to fulfill His ultimate intention to bring the nations under the lordship of Jesus Christ (Rev. 7:17, NIV).

THE KINGDOM OF GOD IS COMING IN FULLNESS

Jesus is returning to establish His kingdom on the earth in fullness. Scholars refer to this time as the Messianic Age, the Kingdom Age, or the Millennial Kingdom. This age is when Jesus reigns as King from Jerusalem for a thousand years (Zech. 14:16; Rev. 20:4).

Because Jesus Christ "will be king over all the earth," the Millennial Kingdom will be a time of unprecedented peace, prosperity, righteousness, and glory (Zech. 14:9; Isa. 60). Heaven will invade earth. All of God's enemies will be defeated. And Satan will be bound for a thousand years (Rev. 20:2-3).

"In that day," wrote Zechariah, "the Lord will be the only one, and His name the only one" (Zech. 14:9). What a glorious day this will be!

When Jesus Christ is enthroned as King of the earth and the kingdom of God comes to the earth in fullness, the world will be transformed into a lush paradise, harmony will be restored between humanity and creation, and worship will fill the planet as the glory of God covers the earth like the waters cover the sea (Isa. 11:6-10).

Revelation 20:6 states that "Christ . . . will reign . . . for a thousand years." Whether this period is exactly a thousand years or represents a long but finite period of time prior to the eternal ages is debatable. The main point is that the kingdom of God is coming in fullness and will penetrate every sphere of life, including politics, agriculture, economics, education, law enforcement, family dynamics, media, the arts, technology, and every social institution. This will result in a period of unprecedented blessing for the whole earth as Jesus establishes righteousness and prosperity, and restores the agriculture, atmosphere, and animal life to conditions similar to the Garden of Eden.[6]

During the Millennial Kingdom, there will be worldwide justice, the abolition of war, unprecedented peace, fullness of joy, healing, longevity of life, the swift punishment of sin, and economic prosperity.[7]

Jesus, who is the King of the Jews, will make Jerusalem the capital city of the kingdom of God (Isa. 2:1-4). From Jerusalem, God's kingdom will go forth in fullness into every Gentile nation on the earth.

Jesus called Jerusalem "the city of the Great King" (Matt. 5:35). Jeremiah declared, "At that time they will call Jerusalem 'The Throne of the Lord,' and all the nations will be gathered to it, to

Jerusalem, for the name of the Lord" (Jer. 3:17). Zechariah prophesied, "I will return to Zion and will dwell in the midst of Jerusalem. Then Jerusalem will be called the City of Truth, and the mountain of the LORD of hosts will be called the Holy Mountain" (Zech. 8:3). Isaiah described Jerusalem as the place where justice, peace, divine decrees, instruction, and the Word of God will go forth into the nations (Isa. 2:2-4).

From Jerusalem, Jesus will reign as King over the earth, serve as judge of the nations, and administer God's word (Isa. 33:20-22; Zech. 14:9). Kings, queens, presidents, and statesmen will come to Jerusalem to meet with King Jesus, seeking His wisdom, guidance, blessing, and favor (Isa. 2:1-4).

God will also showcase the glory of His Son to the nations from Jerusalem. Isaiah prophesied, "For the LORD has redeemed Jacob and in Israel He shows forth His glory" (Isa. 44:23). Isaiah said further, "You are My Servant, Israel, in whom I will show My glory" (Isa. 49:3). Both of these promises will be completely fulfilled in the Millennial Kingdom when Jesus Christ reigns as King from Jerusalem, making this city the praise of the earth (Isa. 62:6-7).

God's Eternal Purpose During the Kingdom Age

T. Austin Sparks said, "Another constitution needs to be given to this universe and it must be the constitution of the Lamb."[8] This is God's eternal purpose. He wants to reconstitute the universe into the nature of the Lamb and bring everything in heaven and earth under the lordship of Jesus Christ.

As we have seen, this will be accomplished first within a people, and then, through these same people, it will be accomplished throughout the earth. In the Sermon on the Mount, Jesus said that the "meek . . . shall inherit the earth" (Matt. 5:5, NKJV). The meek are the ones who have allowed the kingdom of God to be fully established within them. Jesus said that these are the ones who will inherit the earth. Many scholars believe Jesus was referring to the Millennial Kingdom.

The people who have allowed the kingdom of God to be fully

established within them are the same people, alongside Christ, who will establish the kingdom of God fully upon the earth during the Kingdom Age (Rev. 17:14; 19:14).

This brings us to an important point: Many who teach about Israel in the Millennial Kingdom make a grave mistake. They focus so much on Israel that the eternal Son of God is eclipsed by the Jews. Let me be clear: Jerusalem will only become the praise of the earth during the Kingdom Age because Jesus Christ dwells there.

Another common mistake is failing to view the Millennial Kingdom through the lens of God's eternal purpose. The very reason for the Millennial Kingdom is to fulfill God's eternal purpose to place the Son of God at centerstage of the earth. Jerusalem just happens to be the place God has chosen as the epicenter of this work.

When the Father fulfills His eternal purpose in the Kingdom Age, Jesus Christ will be king over all the earth.

MOVING ON

Simply put, God's eternal purpose—to bring everything in heaven and on earth under the lordship of Jesus Christ—has driven every age of history and will drive every future age.

God has determined to place His Son at the center of everything and nothing will stop Him. He will reshape the entire universe into the nature of the Lamb. This purpose will be accomplished first in a people during the Church Age, second in the earth during the Kingdom Age, and third throughout the universe for the endless ages of eternity.

PART 4

THE GOSPEL AND
ULTIMATE INTENTION

The work of the cross is the cornerstone of most gospel presentations—and rightfully so. However, believers commonly fail to connect the gospel back to God's ultimate intention. Part 4 looks at how the work of the cross and the way of the cross restore us back to God's purpose for the ages.

CHAPTER 14

Seeing Through God's Eyes

During our first year of marriage, Angie and I often bumped heads. It seemed that we argued about everything. One of the greatest sources of contention revolved around the way I drive.

Angie could have been a logistics planner for a package delivery company. She loves finding the optimal route to take, even if that means winding through dozens of backroads to shave off two minutes of drivetime. That's not me. I often zone out into deep thought, oblivious to potential shortcuts.

Angie also loves to weave through a parking lot, searching for the perfect space that will optimize her exit. I hate navigating through parking lots, so I usually park in the first open space I find. This often means a little extra walking.

Whenever it rains, even if it's a sprinkle, I turn the windshield wipers on full speed. Because I start thinking about something else, I usually forget to turn the wipers off, causing them to screech against the windshield. This drives Angie crazy.

So, driving together has been a source of contention from the start, especially during that first tumultuous year. And I humbly admit that this was my fault *because I desperately needed glasses.*

Whenever we would drive, especially on the highway, I would brake hard whenever I was thirty feet from a car. Because my eyesight was so poor, I couldn't judge the distance of the car in front of me. Not only was this annoying to Angie, but it was also dangerous.

Angie kept telling me that I needed to get glasses, but I was stubborn and resisted her counsel. Finally, after putting her through much anxiety, she insisted and I complied.

I'll never forget what it was like to wear glasses for the first time. Everything that was blurry was now sharp, crisp, and clear. Many things that I hadn't noticed before caught my attention. It was quite dramatic.

And I have to say, glasses might just have saved my marriage—not to mention our lives.

An Eternal-Purpose Worldview

Just as glasses transformed my perspective, we need a new lens through which we view the world. We need to view life through the lens of God's eternal purpose. We need an eternal-purpose worldview.

What exactly is a worldview? It's a framework from which we make sense of life. It's a particular philosophy of life or conception of the world that shapes and drives our beliefs and actions. It's the way we think about the world. It's our overall perspective from which we see and interpret everything around us.

For example, an atheist believes that the material world is all that exists and that each person establishes their own morality. A Muslim believes that the Koran, Shira law, and Allah shape the world. And, closer to home for all parents, every two-year old believes they are the center of the universe.

Everyone has a worldview, whether consciously or not. And your worldview dictates all that you believe to be true, driving your thinking, emotions, decisions, and actions. As a result, your worldview affects your perspective about everything, including philosophy, science, politics, economics, entertainment, sports, family, and religion.

Essentially, our worldview influences everything about us.

If we want to see the world through God's eyes, then our worldview needs to be rooted in God's eternal purpose. The blueprint from eternity needs to be our "glasses," shaping our overall perspective of how we interpret and interact with the world around us—bringing everything into sharp focus.

I have discovered that an eternal-purpose worldview transforms everything. Now, when I read the Scriptures through the lens of God's ultimate intention, the biblical narrative comes alive. Everything from Genesis to Revelation begins to make sense. The

Lord has been working from a blueprint that transcends human wisdom. He is working everything to accomplish His ultimate intention, in spite of the fall.

Unfortunately, most Christians don't view the world through the lens of God's eternal purpose. Most believers don't even know that God has an eternal purpose. They view the world from a starting point that doesn't originate in eternity, before time and creation.

Most believers think God's ultimate intention is to save us. Once that is accomplished and we're heaven bound, our purpose is then just to be good and do good.

SAVED TO SERVE

As I mentioned in an earlier chapter, I grew up in a traditional denominational church. I would describe it as moderately fundamental.

I went to church on Sunday morning, Sunday night, and Wednesday night. Thankfully, I heard the simple gospel message repeatedly. During a Sunday night service when I was ten years old, I finally stopped resisting the call to salvation. As the church sang "Just As I Am," I went up front to the altar, surrendered my life to Christ, and was truly born again. I can still remember the peace that flooded my heart after making this decision. I was truly a different person afterward.

Though I had a short season of rebellion (I'm sure it didn't seem short to my parents!), I started pursuing Christ wholeheartedly when I was nineteen. It was not causal nor superficial. I ran hard after the Lord. I spent hours in prayer and the Word. I read book after book, eager to learn. I was so hungry.

Despite being born and raised in the church, despite studying relentlessly for many years, I can count on one hand the number of times I heard about the connection between the gospel and God's eternal purpose.

This is because most churches view salvation as God's ultimate intention. The messages are about getting saved. The Scriptures are read through the lens of salvation. To them, Jesus' parables and teachings are about getting saved. Salvation is the paradigm that permeates everything.

After I was saved during that alter call in fourth grade, I was "saved" again and again during many retreats, revivals, church services, rapture videos, and evangelistic skits. I was so afraid of dying and going to hell that I prayed "The Sinner's Prayer" more times than I can remember.

It finally sunk in that I was "in." But, in the modern church, once you are "saved," the emphasis then shifts to serving. We're told to serve Christ with all of our God-given talents and strengths. Attend church every time the door opens. Go on mission trips. Read the Bible. Pray. Tithe. Do the religious things we're supposed to do as Christians. Lead a Bible study. Teach Sunday School. Go into full-time ministry.

All good things, for sure. But I discovered that everything changes when our eyes are opened to God's eternal purpose. Like driving with much-needed glasses on for the first time, our worldview changes. Our view of Scripture changes. Our ideas of church change. Our perspective of salvation changes.

No longer do we view salvation as God's ultimate intention. No longer do we have a "saved to serve" paradigm. Instead, we begin to see through God's eyes. We realize that the gospel is the means to the end. But it's not *the end*. It's God's redemptive plan to restore us back to His ultimate intention.

Because salvation has been preached as God's ultimate aim for centuries, it almost seems heretical to suggest otherwise. But I'm here to suggest otherwise. *Salvation is not God's ultimate intention.* It's the means to *restore us to* His ultimate intention.

Specifically, the work of the cross restores us back to what Adam lost. And the way of the cross leads us to become God's inheritance—namely, a family of Christ-like sons for the Father, an equally yoked bride for the Son, and a temple for the Holy Spirit. We weren't saved to serve. We were saved for God Himself.

ORIGINAL INTENTION AND REDEMPTION

Think about this. If the fall had not occurred, there would be no need for the cross. Ninety-nine percent of what the church emphasizes today would be unnecessary. Adam and Eve, and subsequently, all of humanity, would have been on a trajectory toward God's ultimate intention.

The tree of life would have imparted the life of Christ into Adam and Eve, progressively transforming them into the image of the Son. Later, the implanted life of Christ would have been multiplied through Adam and Eve to the entire human race, making Adam the federal head of a new creation in full union with the eternal Son.

Unfortunately, Adam chose the forbidden fruit, delaying God's ultimate intention. Because Adam was the covenant representative of humanity, his choice affected the entire human race. His fateful decision has been imputed to us, making us sinners who chose self over Christ in the garden. His nature has also been imparted to us, making us inherently selfish and hostile to God.

The work of the cross and the way of the cross have now become an absolute necessity to restore us back to God's ultimate intention.

THE WORK OF THE CROSS AND ULTIMATE INTENTION

All that was of the Adamic race—the good and the evil—was transferred to Jesus Christ on the cross. When Jesus cried out with a loud voice, "It is finished," the self-centered antichrist nature that Adam imparted to humanity was dealt a brutal death-blow (John 19:30). Sin, self, and death went with Jesus into the grave, never to rise again.[1]

What the "last Adam" accomplished on the cross is the only solution for the first Adam's transgression in the garden.

In Adam all are sinners, but in Christ all are righteous. In Adam all are condemned, but in Christ all are justified. In Adam all will die, but in Christ all have eternal life.

Jesus' death on the cross dealt with the old creation in Adam once and for all. His finished work has paved a way for mankind to be restored to God's original intention. *This is the work of the cross.*

The work of the cross determines our legal position, for in Christ we are constituted righteous, crucified, dead, buried, resurrected, ascended, and enthroned.[2] This means we are the righteousness of God in Christ and have died to sin, self, and the Law through our union with our Savior's crucifixion and resurrection.[3] This legal position is imputed to us through faith in Jesus' finished work of the cross.

Connecting this to God's eternal purpose, it's *the work of the cross* that restores us to the place where Adam would have been if he had not eaten from the tree of knowledge and had, instead, eaten from the tree of life.

The Way of the Cross and Ultimate Intention

The *way* of the cross, on the other hand, is what the Holy Spirit is finishing in us as He works to harmonize our living condition with our legal position. It is *the way of the cross* that actualizes the finished work of the cross in our daily experience.

More than having a position of righteousness, we are to *become* righteous in how we live. More than being positionally crucified, buried, and resurrected, we are to allow the Holy Spirit to conform us to the death of Christ so that we might also experience His resurrection life.

Connecting this to God's eternal purpose, it's *the way of the cross* that moves us from receiving the imparted life of Christ to the fullness of Christ, enabling us to become a Christ-like son for the Father, a prepared bride for the Son, and a temple for the Holy Spirit to possess.

THE WORK OF THE CROSS AND THE WAY OF THE CROSS

Because of the fall, both the work of the cross and the way of the cross are essential for God's eternal purpose to be fulfilled.

The work of the cross is a constituted position based upon covenant, while the way of the cross is life-based, empowering us to live by the life of Another—the very life of God's Son who lives in us.

The work of the cross is what Jesus finished for us, while the way of the cross is what the Holy Spirit is finishing in us.

The work of the cross determines our legal position, while the way of the cross establishes our living condition.

The work of the cross restores us to where Adam would have been if he had eaten from the tree of life, while the way of the cross is how we move from the imparted life of Christ toward the fullness of Christ and God's ultimate intention.

As we develop an eternal-purpose worldview, we will see the work of the cross and the way of the cross as the necessary means to God's ultimate end—a family of Christ-like sons for the Father, an equally yoked bride for the Son, and a temple for the Holy Spirit.

CHAPTER 15

It Is Finished

When Adam ate the forbidden fruit, guilt, shame, and condemnation entered the psyche of the human race. This cord of three strands became an impenetrable barrier between God and humanity.

The Lord called out to his beloved, "Adam, where are you?"

Ashamed, Adam answered, "I was afraid because I was naked; so I hid myself" (Gen. 3:10).

Instead of running to God, Adam ran from God. Shame blanketed him, hindering the fellowship he once enjoyed with the Lord.

God's eternal purpose to bring humanity into the unceasing fellowship, love, and intimacy that the Father and the Son have enjoyed for all eternity hit a major roadblock.

Reproach, humiliation, and disgrace tormented Adam's soul. Stomach-churning guilt flooded his conscience. Adam could no longer approach the Lord without mental anguish. Fig leaves concealed the real Adam. Shame became his constant companion. Guilt tormented his once-innocent soul. Condemnation taunted him relentlessly.

And walking with God in the cool of the day was a thing of the past.

For thousands of years since, humanity has been trying to get back to the garden. Deep inside, we know that we were made to walk with God. We were created for fellowship with the Almighty. And to quote Augustine, "Our hearts are restless, until they can find rest in you."[1]

Yet, throughout history, mankind has never escaped the vexing taunts of accusation, whispering, "You are a sinner. You are evil. You can never approach a holy God."

Though humanity tried to cover this haunting feeling with the blood of bulls, goats, lambs, and rams, we have never fully escaped the torment. We have never fully broken free from the shame eating away at our souls. Throughout history, this has led to a downward spiral of sinning, feeling ashamed for our sin, trying to appease our guilty conscience with religious works, failing, being tormented by condemnation, and then sinning again. This unending cycle has plagued humanity since Eden.

Guilt, shame, and condemnation are great enemies of God's eternal purpose. Until these enemies are defeated, the Lord can never bring humanity into the fellowship of the Trinity. As long as this cord of three strands still stands, the Lord can never have the intimate fellowship with us that He's always wanted.

That's why the finished work of the cross is so critical. What Jesus finished for us on the cross destroys the power of guilt, shame, and condemnation. When Jesus cried out on the cross, "It is finished," He unraveled this cord of three strands, removing the barrier separating us from intimate fellowship with the Lord (John 19:30).

The finished work of the cross restores us to where Adam would have been if he had eaten from the tree of life. The finished work of the cross also prepares us for the deeper journey toward God's ultimate intention, whereby we become God's inheritance and representations of the Man, Christ Jesus. Before we start this deep and challenging journey, however, we need to know all that Christ did for us on the cross. This is a vast subject, but to keep it simple, here are the six most important truths.

1. The blood of Jesus satisfies God.

For centuries, the Hebrews tried to rid their guilty consciences of shame and condemnation. They sacrificed goats, bulls, and heifers year after year. Yet, they were still haunted by guilt, shame, and condemnation. Deep down, they knew that animal sacrifices were not enough (Heb. 9:9).

When Jesus—the eternal, uncreated, fully divine Son of God—became a Man and died on the cross, His perfect blood fully satisfied God. Through Jesus' work on the cross, God satisfied Himself by substituting Himself for us. Jesus died as our substitute, and His sacrifice completely satisfied the Father.

The blood Jesus shed on the cross has thoroughly atoned for our sins. The writer of Hebrews stated,

> For if the blood of goats and bulls and the ashes of a heifer sprinkling those who have been defiled sanctify for the cleansing of the flesh, how much more will the blood of Christ, who through the eternal Spirit offered Himself without blemish to God, cleanse your conscience from dead works to serve the living God. (Heb. 9:13-14)

As our substitute, Jesus sacrificed Himself by shedding His blood, and His perfect blood thoroughly cleanses our conscience from guilt, shame, and condemnation.

Perhaps you have a deep, dark past. Maybe you have been entangled in sexual sin. Or you suffered abuse for years, struggle with an addiction, or are suffocating under the weight of anxiety and depression. Maybe you hate yourself and wish you had never been born. Whatever you wrestle with, to quote Louie Giglio, "Don't let the enemy define you by your scars when Jesus wants to define you by His."[2]

Let the perfect blood of Jesus Christ, that was shed for your atonement and redemption, cleanse your conscience from guilt, shame, condemnation, rejection, and emotional pain. As Watchmen Nee said, "The blood has satisfied God; it must satisfy us also. It has . . . value that is manward in the cleansing of our conscience."[3]

Don't be defined by what was done *to you* or *by you*, but by what was done *for you*. Let Jesus' finished work establish your identity. Let His precious blood cleanse you thoroughly of all the shame you have carried. Let His precious blood wash you clean of guilt and the scars from your past.

When the devil's accusations rail against you, shouting in your ear, "You are a hopeless hypocrite; you will never amount to anything; you are a sinner; you will never please God," raise up the only weapon that can defeat Him—the precious blood of Jesus Christ.

Instead of allowing the devil to accuse you, take a stand against him. Say out loud to the enemy, "You are a liar. The blood of Jesus Christ has defeated you and has fully cleansed me. Depart from me devil! You have no authority over me."

It is by the blood of Christ alone that we overcome the accuser and his relentless accusations against us (Rev. 12:10).

In summary, the blood of Jesus Christ is at the heart of the atonement, providing forgiveness of sins, justification, redemption, reconciliation, access to the presence of God, a cleansed conscience, and victory over the devil's accusations.[4] It's the shed blood of Jesus Christ that restores us to God's ultimate intention of eternal fellowship with the Father, the Son, and the Holy Spirit.

2.   What is true of Christ is imputed to us.

In biblical times, whenever a covenant was cut between two parties, a covenant representative was always selected on behalf of each group. These representatives entered the covenant on behalf of everyone in their party and would bind the entire group to the expectations of the agreement. Everyone who belonged to a particular party was considered to be "in" its representative, so that everything the representative did and agreed to in the covenant ceremony would be transferred or imputed to each member of the group. This can be summarized by the phrase *imputation by representation.*

Literally, the word *impute* means to attribute or ascribe to a person; to assign as a characteristic; to credit to one's account; or to reckon something as belonging to someone.

Legally, to impute is to place responsibility or blame on one person for acts committed by another because of a particular relationship. For example, a child's negligence in driving a car without a license may be imputed to the parent. Did the parent drive the car without a license? No. But in a court of law, because of the parent's relationship to the child, the child's offense is imputed to the parent, so that the parent is treated by the judge as if they drove without a license.

As our covenant representative in the New Covenant, what is

true of Christ is imputed to us. As a result, we are reckoned to be righteous, crucified, dead, buried, resurrected, ascended, and enthroned.[5]

Because we are in Christ, who is our covenant representative, we are righteous and dead to sin, to self, and to the Law.[6] We are seated with Christ in heavenly places and are overcomers.[7] This is our legal position because of the finished work of the cross and is the basis for all of God's dealings with us. Paul details this concept of imputation in Romans 4-7.

At first, the concepts of imputation by representation, constituted righteousness, and our legal position sound too theological to have practical benefit. But nothing could be further from the truth.

When we are having a terrible day, mired in sin, guilt, shame, and condemnation, if we will run *to* God rather than *from* God, things will begin to change. If we will simply repent, confess our sins, and begin to agree with who we are in Christ, the fog will dissipate.

We are not hopeless hypocrites; we are the righteousness of God in Jesus Christ (2 Cor. 5:21). We are not defeated and overcome; we are more than conquerors through Him (Rom. 8:37). Sin is not our master; we have died to sin through the crucifixion of Christ (Rom. 6:2). We might feel overwhelmed, but we are seated with Christ in heavenly places, far above every power and principality (Eph. 1:21; 2:6). We are not under the heavy burden of the Law; we died to the external commandments and are joined to Christ, so that we might bear fruit for God (Rom. 7:4).

Agreeing with these truths and confessing them on a regular basis will lift you out of a funk and awaken faith in your soul.

I've discovered that agreeing with my legal position in Christ is a catalyst that activates the reality of it in my heart, mind, emotions, desires, and choices. Faith in my legal position opens my heart so that the Holy Spirit can begin to make it real in my experience. This is how victorious living begins. This is how we start down the road toward God's ultimate intention.

3. We are justified by faith.

Because the righteousness of Christ has been imputed to us, we are justified by faith in the finished work of the cross. Paul said, "The free gift [the gift of imputed righteousness] arose from many transgressions resulting in justification" (Rom. 5:16, emphasis mine).

Justification is a judicial pronouncement that one is innocent in a matter and is therefore acquitted from every charge, accusation, and punishment.

Think of justification as the opposite of condemnation. When a judge pronounces condemnation, the condemned is deemed guilty of a crime and is sentenced to some form of punishment, whether time in jail, the revoking of a driver's license, or community service. Justification, on the other hand, means that a judge reviewed a case carefully, found the accused innocent, pronounced a verdict of not guilty, and withheld any form of punishment.

Justification is different from pardon. Whereas pardon removes a penalty or debt, justification goes a step further and bestows a righteous status. Pardon says to the guilty, "You may go free; you have been released from the penalty that your sin deserves." Justification, on the other hand, says, "You may go free, for you are righteous in the matter in which you were accused."

Pardon is the remission of punishment, though guilty; justification is the declaration that no ground for punishment exists. Thus, justification involves two components: The declaration of righteousness and the remittal of punishment.

Justification not only differs from pardon but also from sanctification. To justify is to declare or to pronounce righteous, not to make righteous. Sanctification is to make righteous. Put a little differently, justification gives us a new status, while sanctification gives us a new nature. Every justified believer has been regenerated and is now progressing down the road of sanctification.

Simply put, justification makes us as if we had never sinned. *Justification restores us to where Adam would have been if he had not eaten the forbidden fruit.*

When the 16th-century leaders of the Reformation received a fresh revelation of justification by faith, it launched a history-making, nation-shaking movement that literally turned the world upside down. Likewise, when our personal revelation of justification by faith penetrates into our hearts, minds, and emotions, it radically alters our relationship with Christ and leads us back to God's ultimate intention.

4. **The Holy Spirit dwells in our spirits the moment we are born again.**

Without the indwelling Spirit, there is no born-again experience, no salvation, no eternal life. Paul made this clear when he said, "If anyone does not have the Spirit of Christ, he does not belong to Him" (Rom. 8:9). He also exhorted the Corinthians to examine themselves to see if they were truly in the faith. The litmus test of salvation is that "Jesus Christ is in you—unless you fail the test" (2 Cor. 13:5).

Because of the indwelling Spirit, you have "Christ in you" (Col 1:27). In our spirits, we have God's glory, rivers of living water, resurrection life, creative power, divine enablement, truth, help in times of need, the anointing enabling us to do God's will, the life and virtue of Christ, the wisdom and knowledge to solve problems and make sound decisions, and the kingdom of God.[8]

When we are born again, it's as if we had eaten from the tree of life. The life of Christ is implanted within our spirits through the Holy Spirit. Thus, the finished work of the cross restores us to where Adam would have been had he eaten from the tree of life, for we now have the "life-giving" Spirit and the "Spirit of life in Christ Jesus" dwelling within (1 Cor. 15:45; Rom. 8:2).

5. **We are new creations in Christ.**

Over five-hundred years before Christ was born, Ezekiel prophesied what would transpire in the New Covenant. He stated, "I will give you a new heart and put a new spirit within you; and I will remove the heart of stone from your flesh and give you a heart of flesh. I will put My Spirit within you and cause you to walk in My statutes, and you will be careful to observe My ordinances" (Ezek.

36:26-27).

God promised to do these four things in the New Covenant: 1) Give us a new heart that is soft and pliable; 2) put a new spirit within us; 3) remove our heart of stone; and 4) put His Spirit within us. This is what it means to be a new creation in Christ.

When Adam ate from the tree of knowledge, death entered his spirit. Even though it took hundreds of years for death to work itself fully into his body, Adam's spirit died instantly. That is why everything changed immediately after he ate the forbidden fruit. Though Adam—and every one in Adam—still have a spirit, their spirit is dead to God. Their spirit can no longer communicate with God unless their spirit is born again.

Because of the finished work of the cross and the indwelling Holy Spirit, your spirit has been raised from the dead. Paul said, "Though the body is dead because of sin, yet the spirit is alive because of righteousness" (Rom. 8:10).

If you are born again, let me tell you the good news about your new spirit. Your new spirit is now: One with the Holy Spirit; a partaker of the divine nature; righteous, holy, and complete; and re-created in the image and likeness of God.[9] Not only that, but when you were born again, you were given a new heart that was cleansed from sin and is now being prepared and molded for the Spirit of Christ to dwell in fully.[10]

The finished work of the cross and the indwelling Holy Spirit have made us fundamentally new creations. We are not mere men and women, like those of the Adamic race. We are a new creation with a righteous spirit, a new heart that has been cleansed from sin, and we have the same Spirit who raised Jesus from the dead dwelling inside of us.[11] When we have a revelation of what it means to be new creations in Christ, everything changes!

The finished work of the cross resurrects our spirits and restores us to the place where Adam would have been if he had eaten from the tree of life.

6. We are children of God and the betrothed bride of Christ.

When we are born of the Spirit, we become children of God with the Son's very own spiritual DNA implanted into our spirits.[12]

We now have Christ's spiritual genetics as part of our innate spiritual nature, making us children of God. John said, "See how great a love the Father has bestowed on us, that we would be called children of God" (1 John 3:1).

Not only has the finished work of the cross transformed us into God's very own children, but we are also betrothed to Christ as His bride. All who have said "yes" to Christ's finished work on the cross have participated in a betrothal ceremony with Jesus, the Bridegroom God (2 Cor. 11:2).

Just as an ancient Jewish betrothal was a legally binding commitment—requiring a certificate of divorce if the couple wanted to separate before the actual marriage ceremony—we have been joined to Christ as His bride by the new birth.

Ancient Jews considered the betrothal ceremony as an act of purchasing or acquiring a wife for the purpose of marriage. When Jesus died for us on the cross, not only was He paying the penalty for our sins, but He was also purchasing us as a bride for Himself. When we were born again, we became Jesus' very own possession. We became His bride bound to Him by betrothal.[13]

TRANSFORMED FROM GLORY TO GLORY

Because the finished work of the cross is such glorious news, it's easy to see why many believers never move beyond this into God's ultimate intention. They camp out at the work of the cross and never progress into the *way* of the cross.

The work of the cross is essential, but God's plan is to move us from "glory to glory"— from the glory of the cross to the glory of all that He established in the eternal blueprint (2 Cor. 3:18). If you are hungry and thirsty for more, there's only one path toward God's ultimate intention, and that's *the way of the cross.*

The way of the cross leads us from the initial impartation of Christ's life into the fullness of Christ's life that transforms us into God's inheritance. Don't stop at the empty tomb and call yourself complete; keep pressing into glory.

CHAPTER 16

THE WAY OF THE CROSS

The Lord warned Adam not to eat from the tree of knowledge. His command thundered within Adam's soul: "In the *day* that you eat from it you will surely die" (Gen. 2:17, emphasis mine). The Almighty vowed that Adam would die on the very *day* he ate. Yet Adam lived to be 930 (Gen. 5:5). How do we explain this?

The answer is simple. Adam, like all humanity after him, was created with a spirit, soul, and body (1 Thess. 5:23). When Adam ate the forbidden fruit, death entered his spirit. Even though it took hundreds of years for death to work itself fully into his body, Adam's spirit died instantly. That is why his eyes were opened immediately to his nakedness (Gen. 3:7). Adam became self-aware in the blink of an eye.

Internally, when Adam's spirit died, his soul was coupled together with his body. Adam's mind, will, and emotions were joined together with his mortal senses of taste, touch, sight, sound, and smell. Paul referred to this coupling together of the soul and body as the flesh (Gal. 5:19-21).

Though Lucifer is a liar, he wasn't lying about the tree of knowledge. He told the truth when he said you "shall be as gods" (Gen. 3:5, KJV). When Adam ate the forbidden fruit, self-deification entered the human race. The self-life was awakened in Adam. Self-awareness, self-consciousness, self-righteousness, self-focus, self-reliance, self-centeredness, self-rule, and self-will defined Adam's psyche. By the way, you can thank Adam for all the selfies and selfie-sticks that permeate our culture today. Promoting self is not new to the human race.

In God's eyes, everyone born is in Adam. We are not only sinners because Adam's sin was imputed to us, but also because Adam's nature was imparted to us. As Jesus said, "That which is born of the flesh is flesh" (John 3:6).

The tree of the knowledge of good and evil released death into our spirits and has awakened self-love in our souls, making us independent gods who do what is right in our own eyes. Because of the fall, we are inherently selfish, prideful, narcissistic, fixated on our self-image, rebellious, independent, and lawless.

Like we saw in the last chapter, when we put our faith in Jesus' finished work on the cross and are born again, the Holy Spirit resurrects our spirits and joins our spirits to Him. Through the Spirit's regenerating work, our spirits are instantly conformed to the image of Christ (Eph. 4:24). The work in our spirits is complete. In God's eyes, we are in Christ and no longer in Adam.

Now the Holy Spirit's work is almost entirely in our souls. Until we meet Jesus face-to-face, the Spirit is working relentlessly to deliver our souls completely from the Adamic nature.

The soul, comprised of the mind, the will, and the emotions, was not transformed by our born-again experience. Even though we are in Christ and Christ is in us, our souls are still Adamic in nature. Our souls are still dominated by self-rule, self-will, and self-importance. We still want to do what is right in our own eyes.

Because of this, the Holy Spirit is jealous to conform our proud, independent, and selfish nature inherited from Adam into the humble, meek, and selfless nature of Christ. This work in our souls will take a lifetime and can only be accomplished through *the way of the cross*. Paul referred to this as working out your salvation (Phil. 2:12).

Contrasted to the work of the cross, the way of the cross is what the Holy Spirit is finishing in us as He aligns our living condition with our legal position. The way of the cross is how we move from the finished work of the cross into God's eternal purpose.

Whereas the work of the cross affected our spirits, the way of the cross deals with our souls. Specifically, our self-life in our souls. There are six important realities about the way of the cross that help us better understand how to move toward the fullness of Christ, enabling us to become God's inheritance.

1. The way of the cross sanctifies our souls.

Paul revealed that we *have been saved*, we are *being saved*, and that we *will be saved* (Eph. 2:5,8; 1 Cor. 1:18; 2 Cor. 2:15; Rom. 5:9; 1 Cor. 3:15). Salvation is a process of justification, sanctification, and glorification.

Justification relates to our spirits and occurs the moment we are born again. Sanctification relates to our hearts, souls, and bodies, taking a lifetime to conform us into the image of Christ. Glorification relates to our bodies and will occur instantly at the resurrection of the dead.

Whereas the work of the cross relates to the salvation of our spirits through justification, the way of the cross relates to our souls being saved through the slow (and often painful!) process of sanctification.

Unlike justification, sanctification is not something that can be imputed or reckoned to us. Sanctification is the result of us being consecrated (set apart for God). This is a gradual process in our hearts, souls, and bodies that occurs as we obey the Word of God in the power of the Holy Spirit.

Whereas justification is instant, imputed to us, and gives us a new standing before God, sanctification takes a lifetime and is the result of works, obedience, and faithfulness, ultimately transforming our character.

The sanctification of our souls, through the way of the cross, is essential if we want to be conformed to the image of Christ, filled with the fullness of Christ, and set apart as God's unique possession. The way of the cross actualizes God's ultimate intention in our lives.

2. The way of the cross saves our souls.

Jesus said, "If anyone wishes to come after Me, he must deny himself, and take up his cross and follow Me. For whoever wishes to save his *life* will lose it; but whoever loses his *life* for My sake will find it" (Matt. 16:24-25, emphasis mine).

The Greek word for *life* is *psychē* and means *soul*—the mind, the will, and the emotions. Jesus was basically saying, "Whoever wishes to save his soul will lose it; but whoever loses his soul for My sake will find it." Jesus is not describing the finished work of the cross, but the *way* of the cross. Or, as some have called it, the cross-life.

The work of the cross is how our spirits are saved; the *way* of the cross is how our souls are saved. All that we inherited from Adam, still residing in our souls, must be experientially crucified. All of the selfishness, self-focus, pride, independence, rebellion, and lawlessness must die. Only the Holy Spirit can do this by applying the cross to our minds, will, and emotions.

The way of the cross is Christianity 101. It's how our souls are transformed. Paul said, "I die daily" (1 Cor. 15:31). Jesus exhorted us to take up our "cross daily" (Luke 9:23).

Embracing the cross in our souls day after day, where we ask for and allow the Holy Spirit to crucify our self-life and resurrect us in a greater union with Christ, is how our souls are delivered from the effects of the fall. It's how we are transformed from the nature of Lucifer, which was grafted into the Adamic race through the tree of knowledge, into the image of the Lamb.

The way of the cross is how our souls are progressively filled with the fullness of Christ. It's how our souls are transfigured from being a lover of self, filled with pride, independence, and rebellion, into a lover of Christ who is humble, meek, and obedient. The way of the cross is how our souls are conformed into the image of Jesus Christ.

With this in mind, Jesus was basically saying, "If you take up your cross, deny yourself, and refuse to live for what you want when you want it—choosing instead to follow Me no matter the challenge, no matter the discomfort, and no matter the cost—then this will lead to the salvation of your soul."

The way of the cross is how we move from the initial impartation of Christ's life into the fullness of Christ's life and becoming God's own possession. The salvation of the soul, through the way of the cross, is essential for God's ultimate intention to be realized in each of us.

3. **The way of the cross aligns our living condition with our legal position.**

Like we saw in the last chapter, we are righteous, crucified, buried, resurrected, ascended, and enthroned in Christ.[1] This is our legal position because Christ is our representative in the New Covenant.

Though meditating upon our legal position is powerful and transformative, the Holy Spirit is jealous for more. He wants to align our living condition with our legal position. He yearns for us to experience the resurrection life of Christ daily.

You see, it is not enough to be positionally righteous yet still struggle with sin. The Holy Spirit wants us to live righteously and to overcome sin. It is not enough to be positionally crucified with Christ yet still live for ourselves. The Holy Spirit wants to crucify every form of selfishness in us. It is not enough for us to be positionally resurrected yet still wallow around in death. The Holy Spirit wants us to live by the same power that raised Jesus from the dead.

Our living condition is how much we actually *experience* of our legal position, which is freely available to us *if we want it.*

Though Christ has finished the work once and for all on the cross, the results in our experience are ongoing. This was true for Paul, who continued to grow into who he already was by the initial implanting of the Spirit into his spirit.

For example, at the beginning of his ministry, Paul said, "I have been crucified with Christ" (Gal. 2:20). This statement expressed the truth of his legal position. Many years later, Paul wanted to know "the power of His resurrection and the fellowship of His sufferings, being conformed to His death; in order that I may attain to the resurrection from the dead" (Phil. 3:10). This statement expressed Paul's desire to be aligned in his living condition.

Paul also said, "For you have died and your life is hidden with Christ in God" (Col. 3:3). This is our legal position in Christ through the finished work of the cross. Though powerful, it is not enough to overcome the inherent selfishness in our unrenewed souls and unredeemed bodies. That is why Paul also said two verses later, "Put to death your members which are on the earth: fornication, uncleanness, passion, evil desire, and covetousness, which is idolatry" (Col. 3:5, NKJV).

"You have died" is our legal position. "Put to death" is our living condition.

Much of the Christian journey is becoming what we already are. We have died therefore we must die. We are righteous therefore we must live righteously. We have been crucified therefore we need to be conformed to Christ's death. We have been resurrected therefore we must live by His resurrection life.

If we will ask for and allow the Holy Spirit to actualize the finished work of the cross in our daily experience, we can have the fullness of Christ in our hearts and souls. We can be conformed into the image of Christ. And we can become the Lord's inheritance, His own unique possession, which is His ultimate intention.

4.   The cross works to release the fullness of the Spirit within us.

When we are born again, the Holy Spirit comes inside of us and takes up residence in our spirits (1 Cor. 6:17). But He does not want to remain solely there. He jealously desires to be released in fullness into our hearts and souls, as well. For this to happen, the cross must first work like a flint knife to circumcise our hearts, cutting away the sin and selfishness that hardens us and stifles the full release of the Spirit.

Solomon said that your heart, which connects your spirit to your soul, is the "spring" from which all "the issues of life" flow (Prov. 4:23, NKJV). Your heart is the channel that governs the measure of the Spirit that is released outward into your soul and body.

Within your heart lie your deepest emotions, desires, beliefs, intentions, motives, thoughts, hopes, attitudes, convictions, and affections. If your heart is pure, then the Holy Spirit's life can flow freely from your spirit into your heart and then outward to your soul. However, if your heart is filled with lust, pride, anger, bitterness, doubt, unbelief, jealousy, envy, criticism, or judgment, then the life of the Spirit will be suppressed and stifled. This is why we desperately need the cross to circumcise our hearts, preparing us to be the Spirit's dwelling place.

Not only do our hearts need to be circumcised, but the cross must also work in our souls. Specifically, we need the cross to break the hard, outer shell of the self-life that keeps God's life restrained and subdued within us. We need the cross to completely break our self-will and independence so that God's life in our spirits can be fully released into our minds, will, and emotions.

Jesus said, "Unless a grain of wheat falls into the earth and dies, it remains alone; but if it dies, it bears much fruit" (John 12:24). Referring to this verse, Watchman Nee explains that there is life in the grain of wheat, but a hard, outer shell restricts this life from being released.[2] Until the outer shell is split open and broken, the wheat cannot sprout and grow. The issue is not whether there is life within the wheat, but whether or not the outer shell is broken so that the inherent life can be released.

Jesus continued, saying, "He who loves his life loses it, and he who hates his life in this world will keep it to life eternal" (John 12:25). Again, the Greek word for *life* is *psychē* and means *the soul*. Jesus revealed that our hard, prideful, and selfish souls suppress the life of the Spirit within us. The only remedy is for the cross to break our souls so that the life of the Spirit can be fully released within us.

As your heart is circumcised by the cross and your soul is broken by the cross, Christ's life in your spirit is released like a mighty, rushing river into your heart and soul. This is how you move closer to toward God's ultimate intention in your life.

5. The cross works so that we live by Christ's indwelling life.

As previously stated, the way of the cross aligns our living condition to our legal position. This is determined by the measure of Christ's life released into our hearts and souls. More specifically, it's determined by the measure of Christ living in us rather than by us living. Like John the Baptist said, "He must increase, but I must decrease" (John 3:30).

Paul said, "I have been crucified with Christ; and it is no longer I who live, but Christ lives in me; and the life which I now live in the flesh I live by faith in the Son of God, who loved me and gave

Himself up for me" (Gal. 2:20).

The Christian life is the exchanged life, where we learn to live by the life of Another, the very life of the Son of God in us.

Jesus came to give us His life, and He wants His life to fill us in fullness (John 10:10). Though Christ dwells in the spirit of every born-again believer, most Christians are either ignorant of this truth or they're too selfish to let Christ live fully in them. As a result, the dead-raising, universe-creating life of the Spirit is suppressed by self-life. The indestructible life of Christ lies dormant within.

If we want God's ultimate intention to be realized in our lives, then the way of the cross is essential. We must let the cross work in our souls until Christ is living and not us.

Galatians 2:20 describes the exchanged life, where we learn to exchange our self-life for the indwelling life of Christ. We exchange our selfishness for Christ's love and let the Spirit of Christ be love in us. We exchange our pride for Christ's humility and let the Spirit of Christ be humility in us. We exchange our anxiety and gloom for Christ's peace and joy and let the Spirit of Christ be peace and joy in us. We exchange our doubt and unbelief for Christ's faith and let the Spirit of Christ be faith in us.

Paul described this exchanged life when he exhorted us to "put on the Lord Jesus Christ" and to "put on a heart of compassion, kindness, humility, gentleness and patience" (Rom. 13:14; Col. 3:12). Because these attributes of Christ already dwell within our spirits since He dwells there, you don't need to ask God to give you more love, peace, and joy. Instead, ask for and allow the cross to crucify your self-life so that Christ's love, peace, and joy can be released into your soul, becoming the love, peace, and joy that you live by.

As the cross works in our self-life and we learn to live by the indwelling life of Christ, we put ourselves on the road toward God's ultimate intention that He established before the foundation of the world.

6. The cross transforms us into God's inheritance.

Though we become children of God the moment we're born

again, we're far from being mature, Christ-like sons who are ready to rule and reign with Jesus. That is why the way of the cross is so essential. As you allow the cross to work in your heart and soul, you are progressively transformed from an immature child into a Christ-like son fit for the throne, having the character that can handle the responsibility of being a coheir with Christ.[3]

To understand how the cross works to transform us into mature sons, notice what Paul said in Romans 8:13-14: "If by the Spirit you are putting to death the deeds of the body, you will live. For all who are being led by the Spirit of God, these are sons of God." The Greek word for *sons* is *huios* and can used to distinguish a mature son from an immature child.[4] More specifically, *huios* can be used to differentiate a mature son, who is ready to share in the inheritance of his father, from an immature child who is unfit for such a weighty responsibility.

The first part of Paul's statement—when he said "if by the Spirit you are putting to death the deeds of the body"—reveals how the Holy Spirit applies the cross to our daily experience. The second part of Paul's statement—"all who are being led by the Spirit of God, these are sons of God"—reveals the connection between the cross-life and becoming a mature son of God who can handle the weighty responsibility of heirship.

The same principle applies to our preparation as the bride of Christ. Though we were betrothed to Christ when we were born again, new birth does not automatically make us ready as an equally yoked bride for Jesus. This takes years of focused preparation as we invite and allow the cross to work in our self-life. This is how our self-centered nature is put to death and how we are transformed into passionate lovers of Christ and Spirit-reliant followers of the Lamb.

Revelation 19:7 states that the bride has made herself ready. But it doesn't say *how* the bride made herself ready. When you consider this verse in context to the book of Revelation, especially Revelation 2-3, it becomes clear that the bride makes herself ready by overcoming what Jesus listed in Revelation 2-3. For example, overcoming losing your first love, lukewarmness, apathy, Jezebel, etc.

With that in mind, notice what Revelation 12:11 states about those who overcome. John said, "And they overcame him because of the blood of the Lamb and because of the word of their testimony, and they did not love their life even when faced with death" (Rev. 12:11). Once again, the word for *life* is *psychē* and means *soul*—or the self-life.

One of the hallmark traits of the bride who makes herself ready is that she will not love her self-life. She will be a living martyr, whether or not she becomes a physical martyr. She will welcome the cross deeply into her soul. She will be known in heaven as loving Christ more than she loved herself.

The way of the cross transforms us into mature sons of God fit for the throne. The way of the cross also transforms us into an equally yoked bride fit to marry Jesus Christ. Thus, the way of the cross is essential to move us from the finished work of the cross into God's ultimate intention, where we have Christ's indwelling life released within us in fullness.

CHAPTER 17

Fullness of Life

Jesus said, "I came that they may have life, and have it abundantly" (John 10:10). Jesus came to put His life within us, not just in a small measure, but with such abundance that it saturates and permeates our entire being.

Nevertheless, there's a common mistake that numerous preachers, teachers, and authors make when expounding upon this verse. They apply it to us having our best life now instead of what Jesus intended.

Here's a common example. They say, "Jesus came to give us an abundant life. Jesus wants you to fulfill your destiny. Jesus wants to make your dreams come true. Jesus wants to bless you and prosper you. King's kids should have the best house, the best cars, the best clothes, and live their best life now."

Let me be clear: Jesus did not come to give us an abundant life. He came to give us *His life* in abundance. Not our here-and-now life lived to the maximum. This false teaching is rooted in the tree of the knowledge of good and evil. It is inherently selfish. The focus is entirely upon self rather than Christ.

Am I against God blessing and prospering us? Not at all. I love when the Lord blesses my finances and prospers the work of my hands. But I am against taking a verse and twisting it in a self-centered way.

Can you see the difference between the false prosperity gospel and the true gospel? The prosperity gospel puts self as the ultimate recipient of God's greatest blessings and the object of God's intentions. The true gospel puts Christ at the center of all things. We don't exist to receive Christ's material blessings. We exist to receive Christ's life.

ABUNDANT LIFE

Jesus came to implant His life within us. But God will never be satisfied with Christ's life remaining dormant and suppressed in our spirits. God wants more than Christ's life to remain in seed form. He yearns for the life of Christ to blossom and mature in us until we "have it abundantly."

The Greek word for *abundantly* means "superabundant (in quantity) . . . by implication, excessive."[1] According to *Thayer's Greek Lexicon*, it means "exceeding some number or measure or rank or need."[2] Jesus wants His life in us to be "over and above, more than is necessary, superior, extraordinary, surpassing."[3]

Jesus came so that His life could be released in us in fullness—without limits, without hindrances, and without measure.

One of God's primary purposes for this age is to have a corporate son possessed by the fullness of Christ's indwelling life.

THE FULLNESS OF CHRIST

As previously stated, God's eternal purpose is the main theme of the book of Ephesians. You see this clearly when you carefully read Chapter 1. With this in mind, Paul used a variation of the phrase "the fullness of Christ" three times in this book. This underscores God's ultimate intention for His Son's life to be released in fullness within us.

Let's look at these three passages to see the connection between the fullness of Christ and God's ultimate intention.

First, Paul wrote, "And He put all things in subjection under His feet, and gave Him as head over all things to the church, which is His body, *the fullness of Him who fills all in all*" (Eph. 1:22-23, emphasis mine). This verse reveals God's eternal plan to release the fullness of Christ corporately in and through the church.

Two chapters later, Paul said, "To know the love of Christ which surpasses knowledge, that you may be *filled up to all the fullness of God*" (Eph. 3:19, emphasis mine). Looking closely at the context, this verse reveals God's eternal plan to release the fullness of

Christ individually in and through the living stones that comprise the church.

Finally, Paul wrote, "Until we all attain to the unity of the faith, and of the knowledge of the Son of God, to a mature man, to the measure of the stature which belongs to *the fullness of Christ*" (Eph. 4:13, emphasis mine). Once again, this verse reveals God's eternal plan to release the fullness of Christ corporately in and through His body.

In summary, God's original intention is for His Son's life to fill humanity in fullness. This ageless purpose, established before the foundation of the world, entails both an individual and corporate dimension.

Individually, God yearns for the seed of Christ in our spirits to continually increase until we have rivers of living water flowing into our hearts, souls, and bodies. A river of life so mighty that it can't be forded, shining light and releasing life to the dark and desperate world around us.

Corporately, as the fullness of Christ fills individual living stones and these stones are fit together by the Lord, then God will finally have what He's always been after—a place where He can dwell with His people. Not just visit but inhabit. Paul had this timeless goal in mind when he said, "In whom the whole building, being fitted together, is growing into a holy temple in the Lord, in whom you also are being built together into a dwelling of God in the Spirit" (Eph. 2:21-22). This spiritual house, comprised of living stones, is "His body, the fullness of Him who fills all in all" (1 Pet. 2:5; Eph. 1:23).

In short, the fullness of Christ is God's ultimate intention for us individually and corporately. Amazingly, Paul reveals that the fullness of Christ can be experienced this side of heaven. We should believe, expect, pursue, and experience the fullness of Christ in this age!

Obviously, the fullness of Christ is a relative term related to our spiritual capacity in this life to contain Him, for even the present heaven and earth cannot contain the fullness of Christ (Rev. 20:11). So, when Paul refers to the fullness of Christ in this age, it is fullness related to our present capacity to receive Him without bursting at the seams.

So, how do we move from Christ's "seed-life" planted within us at salvation to an overflow of His life that can hardly be contained? That question can be answered in seven truths, which we'll explore here and in the next chapter.

1. We need a revelation of the indwelling Spirit.

If we want to experience the fullness of Christ's life, we must first have a revelation of His Spirit within us. Tragically, many believers don't have a personal revelation of "Christ in you." They might have head-knowledge of this truth, but they lack life-changing revelation. As a result, they never think twice about Christ dwelling in them. They have no expectancy of their hearts becoming His permanent habitation. This unbelief limits the fullness of Christ from filling their hearts and souls. Paul encountered a similar experience at the church in Corinth.

The Corinthian church, focused on signs and wonders, became fascinated by speaking in tongues, miracles, prophecy, and the other gifts of the Spirit. They were very familiar with the outpouring of the Spirit but were largely ignorant of the *indwelling* Spirit.

Paul accused the Corinthians of being unspiritual, men of the flesh, infants in Christ, full of jealousy, envy, and strife, and babes who could only drink spiritual milk, unable to handle solid food (1 Cor. 3:1-4). The real zinger was that they behaved "like mere men" (1 Cor. 3:3, NKJV).

These believers had the living God dwelling inside of them, yet they acted as if they were average Corinthians off the street. Though new creations in Christ, they behaved like they were still of the old creation.

What was their problem? They lacked a personal revelation of the indwelling Spirit. They lived in the flesh because they did not know *who* lived inside of them. They were familiar with the external manifestations of the Spirit but ignorant of the internal residence of the Spirit. This is why Paul said to them, "Do you not know that you are a temple of God and that the Spirit of God dwells in you?" (1 Cor. 3:16).

The fullness of Christ is impossible until we can answer Paul's question: "Do you not know . . . that the Spirit of God dwells in you?"

Do you know this? Do you have a personal revelation of this truth? Do you truly know that the same God who created the universe, impregnated the virgin Mary with the eternal Son, and raised Jesus Christ from the dead dwells in you?

I'm not talking about giving a Sunday-School answer, quoting a Scripture, or nodding your head in agreement. I am asking: Do you have a life-changing, personal revelation that God the Holy Spirit dwells in you?

The fullness of Christ is impossible until we have a personal revelation of the indwelling life of Christ.

The trouble with the Corinthians—and with most of us—was they lacked a life-changing revelation of Christ *in you*. They didn't realize the greatness of the One who dwelled in their spirits. The same problem exists today. Much of the church is acting like mere men because we lack a personal revelation of the indwelling Spirit. Because we can't discern Him with our five senses, rationalize His internal presence with our minds, or feel Him with our emotions, we are unaware of our spirit-to-Spirit union with Him.

The indwelling Spirit is not some theory or doctrine that theologians and pastors discuss and debate. It is the blessed reality of every born-again believer. When we have a personal revelation that God the Father and God the Son have made their home in our spirits through the Holy Spirit, it changes everything. When we know *that we know* that the Spirit of God dwells within us, we will become spiritual men and women who fellowship with the Holy Spirit regularly and walk in the Spirit daily.

If you are born again, but lack the revelation of Christ *in you*, I encourage you to pray for a revelation of this truth regularly. Ask the Father to open your spiritual eyes to "the surpassing greatness of His power [in] us who believe" (Eph. 1:19).[4] Since God's power only operates in "us who believe," faith is the key that unlocks the resurrection power of the Spirit within us. Faith unleashes the indwelling Spirit's presence into our hearts, souls, and bodies, enabling His life to fill us fully.

2. We need to allow the indwelling Spirit to increase within us.

The moment we were born again, we were "sealed . . . with the Holy Spirit," who was given "as a pledge of our inheritance" (Eph. 1:13-14). The Greek word for "pledge" means "part of the purchase-money . . . given in advance as security for the rest."[5] In other words, "pledge" is much like our modern-day concept of a down payment.

Anyone who has purchased a house knows how a down payment works. If you purchase a house for $250,000, your down payment might be $25,000, and your mortgage will be $225,000 plus interest. The down payment is a pledge that you will pay the full amount over the next ten to thirty years.

In the same way, the measure of the Holy Spirit that we receive at new birth is in seed form, not fullness. Nevertheless, the Holy Spirit wants to increase within us until we have the Spirit without measure, fully released in our hearts, souls, and bodies.

Just as we make mortgage payments every month until we have fully repaid a loan, the measure of the Spirit within us is meant to increase continually unto fullness. Don't settle for anything less than the fullness of Christ in you.

Paul said that we have "the first fruits of the Spirit" and we "groan within ourselves" for more (Rom. 8:23). Any farmer will tell you that the first fruits pale in comparison to the full harvest. Though we are eternally grateful for the first fruits of the Spirit, like Paul, we should never settle until we have the fullness of the Spirit dwelling in our hearts, permeating our souls, and controlling our bodies. As we allow the Spirit to increase within us, then we begin to tap into the abundant life Christ promised.

3. Allow the indwelling Spirit to dwell in your heart.

God is a heart God. He doesn't look at outward appearances but at the heart (1 Sam. 16:7). The Spirit yearns to make your heart His home. He wants to be King in your heart. He desires to establish His kingdom there, to allow the indwelling Spirit to come fully and live His life there.

Speaking to born-again believers who had the indwelling Spirit, Paul said, "So that Christ may dwell in your hearts through faith" (Eph. 3:17). Pay attention to the conditional language in this statement. Christ does not dwell in our hearts automatically when we are born again.

I know that contradicts what we learned as children: *Just ask Jesus to come into your heart.* I'll admit this is the language we used with our daughter when she was young, too. I mean, when you have a five-year-old, how can you possibly explain the difference between the spirit and the heart? But there *are* differences. Hebrews 4:12 makes that clear.

To keep it simple, your spirit is the deepest part of your being and the place where the Holy Spirit dwells. It's the part of you that connects directly to God. We have fellowship and communion with the Holy Spirit in our spirits.

Your heart, on the other hand, is the channel that connects your spirit to your soul. Your heart has elements of spirit and elements of soul, yet it's distinct from both. It is the source of your deepest beliefs, thoughts, desires, motives, and actions (Prov. 4:27; Matt. 15:19). As the heart goes, so goes your life.

God's great goal is to conquer our hearts and dwell there continually. The Lord aims to make our hearts His permanent habitation. This was Paul's burden for the Ephesians in his great prayer in Chapter 3. Paul wanted the life of Christ in their spirits to have a permanent dwelling place in their hearts.

The word for *dwell* in Ephesians 3:17 means "to settle down in a dwelling, to dwell fixedly in a place."[6] In Colossians 1:19, this Greek word is used to describe "the totality of the attributes and power of the Godhead in Christ."[7] The noun form of this word means a "habitation."[8] In fact, according to *Strong's*, this word means "to house permanently."[9]

The ramifications of this are astounding! Paul's prayer is nothing less than the Spirit of Christ making a permanent home in our hearts, dwelling in fullness. This is far more than an occasional visitation. Christ wants to make our hearts His permanent habitation.

But there's a great enemy. And it's not the devil. It's our flesh. It's the five senses of our bodies coupled together with the mind, will, and emotions of our souls. Unless we diligently watch over our hearts, it's likely that pride, lust, doubt, unbelief, greed, jealousy, envy, judgment, or criticism will subtly creep in and defile our hearts. This is why we need the indwelling Spirit to purify our hearts, so that Christ can dwell there without rival. No matter how much He loves us, Christ will not compete with our other lovers, gods, and idols, including the idol of self.

The Holy Spirit jealously yearns to excavate our hearts from all defilement of the flesh and replace it with the fullness of Christ's uncreated life. Don't allow anything of the fallen nature to fill your heart, keeping Christ's life in your spirit suppressed and imprisoned. Let the Spirit dig deep into your heart and make it the permanent dwelling place of Christ in fullness.

After we purify our hearts from defilement, we need a strong spirit if we want Christ to "dwell in [our] hearts through faith" (Eph. 3:17, emphasis mine). Paul prayed for the Ephesians to "be strengthened with power through His Spirit in the inner man, so that Christ may dwell in your hearts through faith" (Eph. 3:16). Paul knew that their "inner man," a term that includes the human spirit, had to be strengthened with the Holy Spirit's power before Christ could dwell uncontested in their hearts. Undoubtedly, Paul was building on his prayer from Ephesians 1:19, where he prayed that the Ephesians would have a revelation of "the surpassing greatness of His power [in] us who believe."[10]

The surpassing greatness of the Spirit's power in us, according to Paul, raised Jesus from the dead, translated Him from earth to heaven, and seated Him at the right hand of God, far above all rule, authority, and power (Eph. 1:20-21). Simply put, the Holy Spirit in us is the dead-raising, Christ-ascending, King-enthroning power that enables us to live as new creations.

The logic is simple: If the Holy Spirit raised Jesus from the dead and translated Him to the Father's right hand far above all rule and authority, then that same power will enable us to live from our new spirits. That same power will enable Christ to dwell fully in our hearts.

4.   Christ dwelling in our hearts enables us to abide in Christ.

There's a vital connection between Paul's prayer in Ephesians 3 with Jesus' teaching about the abiding life from John 15. As you will see, abiding in Christ depends upon the Spirit of Christ making His home in our hearts.

Jesus said, "Abide in Me, and I in you" (John 15:4). Notice that abiding is, again, a conditional invitation. We determine whether or not we abide in Christ. If you're born of the Spirit, what's not conditional is "I in you"—or as Paul put it, "Christ in you, the hope of glory" (Col. 1:27).

The moment we were born again, Christ came to dwell in our spirits, making the abiding life possible. John confirmed this when he said, "By this we know that we abide in Him and He in us, be-cause He has given us of His Spirit" (1 John 4:13). We don't abide in Christ by trying to connect with Jesus in heaven. We abide in Christ through His indwelling Spirit. In Jesus' own words, "I in you" is the key to the abiding life.

Since the word *abide* is not frequently used in our culture, let's take a second to define it. According to *Strong's*, abide means "to stay" and refers to staying "in a given place, state, relation or expec-tancy."[11] When referring to a place, this word can mean "to stay at home."[12] Thus, *abide* has a similar meaning as *dwell,* which we just saw in Ephesians 3:17. In fact, the KJV translates this word as *dwell* fifteen times.

This underscores the connection between Ephesians 3:17 and John 15. Simply put, the key to the abiding life is allowing Christ to first make His home in our hearts. When our hearts become Christ's perpetual dwelling place through a cleansed heart and a strong spirit, the abiding life becomes possible.

With this in mind, let's look at how the abiding life revolves around connection. Jesus said, "I am the vine, you are the branch-es" (John 15:5). The vine is the life-source that supplies sap to the branches so that fruit can be produced. The vine doesn't produce fruit. The branches do, but only if they are connected to the vine.

Otherwise, the branches are useless.

As new creations in Christ, our Spirit-to-spirit connection to Christ is like branches connected to a vine. Paul said, "But the one who joins himself to the Lord is one spirit with Him" (1 Cor. 6:17). Our spiritual union with the Holy Spirit makes the abiding life possible. The key is learning how to live from the life-source of the Holy Spirit, drawing His life from our spirits outward into our hearts, souls, and bodies.

The abiding life is also how we progress into the fullness of the Spirit, moving from "fruit" to "more fruit" to "much fruit" to "fruit that remains" (John 15:4, 2, 5, 8, 16). This fruit is the byproduct of our union with the Holy Spirit and consists of both the fruit of the Spirit and Spirit-empowered works. As we learn to draw from the life-source of the Spirit, the nature of Christ is progressively formed in us. Christ's very own love, joy, peace, patience, kindness, goodness, faithfulness, meekness, and self-control begin to characterize our lives (Gal. 5:22-23).

In summary, abiding in Christ begins with our Spirit-to-spirit connection with the Holy Spirit. As we lean in to our union with the Holy Spirit and draw from His life, then Christ will make His home in our hearts, living His life through us. Like a branch drawing sap from the vine to produce fruit, the fruit of the Spirit will be produced in us in an ever-increasing measure, until we have the fullness of the Spirit without any limitations.

CHAPTER 18

INCREASING FULLNESS

Jesus came to implant His life within us. A life so abundant that it's without limits, hindrances, or measure. God wants Christ's life to blossom and mature in us until we have His life overflowing like a river to the dark and desperate world around us.

This is God's eternal purpose.

As we saw in the last chapter, there are seven ways we move from the implanted life of Christ to the fullness of Christ's life. We've already looked at four. Now let's look at the remaining three.

5. Don't put confidence in the flesh.

Philippians 3 is one of the greatest chapters in the Bible. Paul wrote this a few years before his death, after serving faithfully for over twenty-five years. At the time, Paul was perhaps the most seasoned man of God in history. He had preached the gospel in many nations, led multitudes of Jews and Gentiles to Christ, and planted numerous churches. Paul had encountered the risen and glorified Christ multiple times, had been taken to heaven where he received unprecedented revelation, and he bore the marks of suffering in his body. After writing much of the New Testament, Paul came to the end of his earthly life and realized there was so much more of Christ available to him. Despite his remarkable resume, Paul was fully aware that he hadn't experienced Christ in fullness.

Paul said, "I count all things to be loss . . . and count them but rubbish so that I may gain Christ" (Phil. 3:8). Notice that Paul wanted to gain more of Christ. How? By not putting any "confidence in the flesh" (Phil. 3:4).

"Confidence in the flesh" is a feeling of self-assurance that arises when we glory in our abilities, qualities, talents, or characteristics. It is pride in who we are and what we have achieved.

Before encountering the risen Christ, Paul had taken pride in his Jewish roots. After all, he was "circumcised the eighth day, of the nation of Israel, of the tribe of Benjamin, a Hebrew of Hebrews" (Phil. 3:5). When it came to the Law, Paul was a Pharisee. When it came to zeal for his Jewish roots, he persecuted the church. When it came to obedience to the Law, he was blameless (Phil. 3:5-6).

Paul's Jewish lineage had been his source of confidence and had shaped his identity.

For us, the possibilities of putting our confidence in the flesh are endless. We can take pride in our salaries, job titles, business connections, and the number of people we influence. We can take pride in our physical appearances, houses, cars, vacations, friends, heritage, nationality, success, fame, or children. We can take pride in the size of our churches, how many Facebook fans and Twitter followers we have, how many best-selling books and albums we've released, and in being a sought-after conference speaker. We can take pride in our knowledge of the Scripture, denominational affiliation, how many people we've led to Christ, or in knowing famous Christians. We can even take pride in our lack of pride! The list is endless.

But here's the point: Pride in who we are and what we have achieved blocks us from gaining more of Christ. Our pride, rather than Jesus' life, takes up residence in our hearts and souls.

Knowing this, Paul said, "But whatever things were gain to me, those things I have counted as loss for the sake of Christ" (Phil. 3:7).

Paul's Jewish roots were a constant source of temptation. If Paul took pride in this, it would hinder the fullness of Christ in his soul. After comparing the two, Paul counted his Jewish heritage as "rubbish so that I may gain Christ" (Phil. 3:8). Rubbish is a nice way to translate what he actually said. *Dung.* As in cow manure, horse poop, the excrement of animals.

When Paul realized how easily pride could creep in and hinder the fullness of Christ in his soul, he considered his Jewish lineage to be no better than animal excrement.

Where are you putting "confidence in the flesh"? Are you tempted to take pride in some achievement and keep Christ suppressed in your spirit? Are you taking pride in your scriptural knowledge, evangelistic success, the size of your church, or the famous people you know—and thus imprisoning Christ by your self-focus? Do you need to shed the very religion of Christianity to gain more of Christ?

Carefully considering the language Paul used in this passage, where he talked of losing and gaining, it's likely he was referring to Jesus' teaching about the salvation of the soul (Matt. 16:24-26).

Jesus described a person who gained the whole world but forfeited his soul. Paul reversed this and spoke of gaining Christ by losing what was important to his soul. Paul wanted to deny pride from creeping into his soul so that he could progressively gain more of Christ in his mind, will, and emotions.

Here's how it works as born-again believers. Our souls will either be filled with ourselves or with Christ. There is not room for both. If self increases in your soul, Christ decreases. But if you deny yourself, you will gain more of Christ in your soul. Like John the Baptist said, "He must increase, but I must decrease" (John 3:30). As those with the indwelling life of Christ in our spirits, we decide who fills our souls: self or Christ.

If we want God's ultimate intention actualized in our lives, then the way of the cross is essential. By allowing the cross to work in our self-life, putting to death everything that would lead to pride, we will gain more of Christ. As the cross breaks the hard, outer shell of our self-life, crucifying our self-centered nature, the indwelling life of Christ is released in greater measures from our spirits into our hearts and souls. This is how the fullness of Christ's life permeates our minds, will, and emotions.

6. Seek intimacy with Christ, which leads to greater fullness.

Paul wanted to know Christ so that he could gain Christ. Continuing with his theme of losing to gain, Paul said, "I count all things to be loss in view of the surpassing value of *knowing Christ Jesus my Lord*, for whom I have suffered the loss of all things, and count them but rubbish *so that I may gain Christ*" (Phil. 3:8, emphasis mine).

When Paul contrasted knowing Christ to pride in his Jewish roots, there was no comparison. He said knowing Christ was of "surpassing value." The same is true with us. Knowing Christ experientially transcends every area where we could glory in our achievements. There's simply nothing like knowing Christ. He is of "infinite value" (Phil. 3:8, NLT).

For those born of the Spirit, knowing Christ doesn't require a trip to heaven, a vision, a dream, a trance, or some other supernatural experience. Each of us can know Him internally, for the Holy Spirit dwells in our spirits. Gaining more of Christ hinges upon knowing Him deeply.

Paul said, "You were called into fellowship with His Son, Jesus Christ our Lord" (1 Cor. 1:9). How do we have fellowship with Jesus who lives in heaven? Through "the fellowship of the Holy Spirit" who dwells within us (2 Cor. 13:14).

Intimacy with Christ is internal. Knowing Christ is internal.

In the parable of the ten virgins, which could also be termed "the parable of the ten Christians," Jesus revealed that five born-again believers were wise and had extra oil while the other five were foolish and had a limited supply of oil.[1] Simply put, the five wise virgins had the Holy Spirit in abundance and this kept the fire of their first love burning through the midnight hour.

What distinguished the wise from the foolish? How did the wise get extra oil to keep their lamps burning through the dark hour? We can find the answer in Jesus' response to the foolish virgins. Jesus told them, "I do not know you. Watch therefore, for you know neither the day nor the hour in which the Son of Man is coming" (Matt. 25:12-13, NKJV).

Jesus didn't say to the foolish, "I never knew you," as He did to the lawless in the Sermon on the Mount—who were likely never born of the Spirit (Matt. 7:23). The issue for the foolish virgins was this: They didn't pursue an intimate relationship with Christ in the secret place. As a result, they forfeited the extra oil required to keep their lamps burning.

The parable of the ten virgins is not about saved versus unsaved.

It's about knowing Christ in the secret place and gaining more of Christ through intimacy with Him. The wise virgins had extra oil because they paid the price. They embraced the cross in their self-life in order to know Christ in the secret place (Matt. 25:9-10). This allowed the Holy Spirit to increase in them from an initial deposit to an overflow, from seed to fullness, from a drop of oil to an abundance. This parable shows that internal intimacy with Christ is how we move from the implanted life of Christ to the fullness of Christ, from self-life to the abundant life Christ promised.

7.   Christ increases in us as we obey the Word.

God's eternal purpose is to transform the church into a "a mature man" (Eph. 4:13). Simply defined, this is "the measure of . . . the fullness of Christ" (Eph. 4:13). This means maturity and the fullness of Christ go hand-in-hand. Put another way, the measure of Christ that fills us determines our maturity.

The Greek word for *mature* is *teleios* and means "complete" in "labor, growth, [and] mental and moral character."[2] Other meanings are "having reached its end, finished, mature" and is used especially "of persons, primarily of physical development" as in a "full-grown, mature" son.[3]

God's ultimate intention is to transform us from immature children to mature sons. He wants to conform us into a mature representation of the Man, Christ Jesus (Rom. 8:29). God will never be satisfied with Christ being in us in seed form. He is jealous for Christ to increase in us unto full stature.

After revealing God's eternal purpose to place "Christ in you," Paul said, "That we may present every man complete in Christ" (Col. 1:28). The Greek word for *complete* is also *teleios*—the same word Paul used in Ephesians 4:13 to describe the mature man. The idea is clear. God's ultimate intention is to place Christ in us and for us to then mature into a complete representation of Him, conformed into Christ's likeness and nature.

Spiritual maturity is Christ-likeness. Whereas physical maturity comes through time and intellectual maturity comes by learning, spiritual maturity can only come from obedience. Unfortunately, there is no shortcut to spiritual maturity. It can't be rushed, imputed, or imparted. It's not the result of time, age, scriptural knowledge, or ministry success.

Spiritual maturity is developed slowly by sustained obedience to God's Word by the enabling power of the indwelling Spirit.

Think about an apple seed growing into an apple tree. You can't just throw a few apple seeds into the ground, wait a few months, and then have an apple tree that yields juicy apples. There is a cultivation process that takes time. This involves germination, planting, grafting, and waiting. Finally, after much patience, the apple seed has matured in to a fruitful apple tree.

The same is true with spiritual maturity. It takes time preparing your heart, removing the obstructions that hinder growth, planting the Word into your heart, and letting the Word take root before you see any fruit. Jesus taught this in the parable of the sower.

In Luke's version of this parable, Jesus revealed God's aim to bring forth "fruit to maturity" (Luke 8:14). What is the fruit brought to maturity? The answer is found in the seed, which Jesus said is "the word of God" (Luke 8:11).

The Word of God, whether the written word we read from the Bible, a message that we listen to, or one that the Holy Spirit speaks to us personally, is a verbal or written expression of Jesus, who is the eternal Word. Every truth of the Word is like a seed containing an attribute of Christ in an embryonic state. The seed of God's Word contains Christ-like attributes that have the potential to make your heart and soul Christ-like. The seed of God's Word contains Jesus' spiritual DNA, having the inherent power to transform us into His image and likeness.

If we will cultivate our hearts, making room for the seed to germinate, the implanted Word will slowly transform us into a mature representation of Christ. This underscores the importance of listening to and reading the Word of God on a consistent basis. Planting God's Word into our hearts regularly is essential for spiritual maturity. There is no shortcut. If we will develop this discipline, we will eventually bring forth "fruit to maturity" (Luke 8:14).

The Greek word for *maturity* is *telesphoreō*, and it's like a brother to the word *teleios*—the word Paul used for *maturity* in Ephesians 4:13 and Colossians 1:28. This shows the connection between God's eternal purpose, spiritual maturity, planting the Word in our hearts, and Christ-likeness developed in our souls.

Influenced by the parable of the sower, James said that the Word of God implanted "is able to save your souls" (James 1:21). The Word of God by itself, because of its inherent power and ability, is able to transform our souls into the image and likeness of Christ. That means we should stop trying harder to become better people and start planting more of the Word into our hearts. Do less, meditate on His Word more. Stop striving in your own strength to improve yourself and spend more time cultivating heart-beliefs fully aligned with God's Word.

Though it's liberating to know of the inherent power of God's Word to transform us, we still have work to do. In this day and age, our hearts are easily influenced by worry, anxiety, distractions, riches, pleasures, technology, and hundreds of other things. But here's the good news. If we will clear the clutter from our hearts and discipline ourselves to meditate upon God's Word, then God's Word itself will do the hard work of transforming our souls into the image and likeness of Christ. If we do our part, then God's Word will do the rest. Eventually, we will see a bountiful harvest of Christ-likeness produced within us because of the inherent power in God's Word.

For our souls to be conformed to the image and likeness of Christ, there's no substitute for consistently planting His Word into our hearts. Don't repeat the shortcomings of those who only focus on the Spirit and not the Word or vice-versa. It's impossible for us to be conformed into the image and likeness of Christ apart from the Spirit *and* the Word, in conjunction. It takes both for us to have Christ's fullness.

A meticulous study of the parable of the sower in Matthew 13, Mark 4, and Luke 8 reveals seven keys to faith, full obedience, and Christ-likeness through the implanted Word of God. These are: 1) hearing the Word, 2) understanding the Word, 3) agreeing with the Word, 4) owning the Word, 5) overcoming by the Word, 6) valuing the Word, and 7) doing the Word.

Implementing these seven principles in our lives aligns our hearts with God's truth, resulting in full obedience and our souls becoming Christ-like and mature. A regular lifestyle of planting God's Word into our hearts and patiently waiting for the seeds to germinate will eventually yield a garden of Christ-likeness. In due time, Christ's love, humility, meekness, joy, peace, faithfulness, boldness, love for righteousness, and hatred of lawlessness will spring forth from our hearts.

Though planting the Word in our hearts is critical, we will never be transformed into Christ's image apart from obedience. That is why James, immediately following his exhortation to plant the Word into our hearts, said, "But prove yourselves doers of the word, and not merely hearers who delude themselves" (James 1:22). Doing the Word is how we mature into Christ's image and likeness.

Spiritual maturity can only be realized through sustained obedience.

God's Inheritance in the Saints

Stepping back, let's absorb what we've learned. The gospel restores us to God's eternal purpose. Specifically, Jesus' finished *work on the cross* brings us back to where Adam would have been if he had eaten from the tree of life. And the *way of the cross* is how we move from the implanted life of Christ to the fullness of Christ and the actualization of God's ultimate intention for us.

Now that we understand how the work of the cross and the way of the cross lead us toward God's eternal purpose, our focus in Parts 5-7 will be on God's inheritance in the saints. Namely, we will look at what God desires in a people. The Father wants a family of Christ-like sons who share in the inheritance of Christ. The Son desires an equally yoked bride to whom He can be the source of love and she will then reciprocate His love back. And the Spirit yearns for a temple that He can fill, a house in which He can dwell, and a body that He can possess.

PART 5

The Father's Inheritance
in the Saints

Before the foundation of the world, the Father decided that He would conform men and women into the image of His Son and thus have a family of sons patterned after His beloved Son. Part 5 focuses on God's predetermined plan to adopt us as His sons (Eph. 1:5).

CHAPTER 19

ADOPTED AS SONS

Just prior to His ascension, Jesus commissioned the disciples to go "even to the remotest part of the earth" (Acts 1:8). Busia, Kenya, certainly falls into this category for me. In this city in Western Kenya, located along the border to Uganda, the Lord gave me a revelation that changed my life.

Eating dinner with one of our Lifeschool leaders, Paul Musungu, there are two things that I clearly recall. First, I remember Paul eating a whole tilapia. Unlike Americans, Africans like to eat the whole fish, including the eyeballs. I was fascinated that anyone could eat something that was staring at them.

The second thing I will never forget was our dinner conversation. As Paul expounded upon adoption in the first century, my eyes were opened—almost as wide as Paul's fish. For the first time, I understood adoption during the time in which the New Testament was penned. This was a paradigm shift. It was an entirely new way of thinking about biblical adoption.

Because of my analytical, prove-it-to-me nature, I began researching first-century adoption when I returned home from Africa. Searching the internet for hours, I discovered the scholarly book *Paul in the Greco-Roman World*. This book confirmed what I learned over dinner. First-century adoption was vastly different than twenty-first century adoption.[1]

GRECO-ROMAN ADOPTION IN THE FIRST-CENTURY

In our day, parents adopt a child because they can't have children, they want to help a child whose birth parents can't raise them, or they want to rescue a child from abuse. Modern-day adoption involves parents taking a baby or young child into their home, loving them as their own, and giving them a much better life.

Adoption in the Greco-Roman world was vastly different. Due to short life expectancies and high infant death rates, many families teetered on the brink of extinction. Adoption became popular because it helped minimize this unwanted trend. For example, if a man was growing older and didn't have an adequate heir, the family would adopt an adult son who could receive and steward the inheritance when the father died. The adopted son would use the inheritance to take care of surviving family members, such as the wife and the other children.

So, there was an inherent, important connection between adoption and inheritance in the Greco-Roman world. James Walters writes, "Because the fundamental motive for adoption was the continuation of the [family], a Greco-Roman father thought first about his estate and what to do about his inheritance, and only secondarily about adoption" (emphasis mine).[2]

In many situations, it was essential for a family to bring in an adult son from another family, treat them like a natural-born son, place them as the legal heir over the inheritance, and give them the responsibility to take care of the surviving family. The adopted son would effectively step into the father's shoes, assuming all of his former responsibilities.

THE GROOMING PROCESS

Whether a Greco-Roman father brought a son into the family from the outside or designated his natural-born child as heir, the inheritor would go through a grooming process. This prepared him for the weighty responsibility of heirship.

The heir was first placed under the tutelage of a guardian. Depending on the heir's maturity, the guardian would take him through various stages of growth, education, discipline, and character development. The heir was trained in the ways, purposes, and character of the father.

Since over one-third of Roman children lost their fathers before puberty and another third lost their fathers before the age of twenty-five, this training was essential to avoid a squandered inheritance.[3] Though Roman law stipulated that a child could assume the inheritance at age fourteen, the father had the right to extend the training longer, if he deemed it necessary.[4]

Paul alluded to this custom when he wrote, "Now I say, as long as the heir is a child, he does not differ at all from a slave although he is owner of everything, but he is under guardians and managers until the date set by the father" (Gal. 4:1-2).

"The date set by the father" was related to the son's maturity. The child had to become a mature son before the father deemed him ready to inherit. But when "the date set by the father" arrived, the adoption was finalized, and the mature son was placed into his father's inheritance as the legal heir (Gal. 4:5).

Here's the main point: Adoption placed a mature, responsible, and well-groomed son as the legal heir of the family inheritance. The Greek word translated *adoption as sons* confirms this (Eph. 1:5). This word means "the placing as a son" or son placement.[5] Thus, son placement gave the mature son the full rights of sonship and the legal right to steward his father's inheritance.

Greco-Roman Adoption Summarized

Greco-Roman adoption had three phases.

1. *Placement into the family*
   If the father didn't have an heir, he would bring an adult son into the family from outside the family.[6]

2. *Preparation for the inheritance*
   The designated heir, whether natural-born or from outside the family, would be placed under a child trainer, who would groom him for heirship through intense training.

3. *Placement into the inheritance*
   When the designated heir was fully trained and prepared, the father would place him as the legal heir of the inheritance, giving

him the full rights of sonship.

A FAMILY OF CHRIST-LIKE SONS

With this cultural background in mind, notice what Paul said at the beginning of Ephesians. He wrote, "He predestined us to adoption as sons through Jesus Christ to Himself" (Eph. 1:5).

Like most, I interpreted Ephesians 1:5, and other similar passages, through the lens of twenty-first century adoption. I believed that our adoption as sons only meant that God the Father brought us, who were orphans and fatherless, into His family and adopted us as His own beloved child. Because I lacked knowledge of Greco-Roman adoption, my understanding of biblical adoption was limited.

But to truly understand this verse, we have to go back to the first-century. To arrive at truth, we can't interpret this through the lens of our own modern-day customs.

TRANSLATING "ADOPTION AS SONS"

The three words *adoption as sons* in Ephesians 1:5 are represented by only one word in the Greek, *huiothesia*. This word is comprised of *huios* and *tithēmi*. *Huios* means "a son" and *tithēmi* means "to set, put, place."[7] Putting these two words together, we get the definition we saw a moment ago, "the placing as a son."[8]

According to the *Theological Dictionary of the New Testament*, *huiothesia* "might refer either to the act or to the result."[9] The *act* of adoption refers to the adoption process, including placement into the family and preparation for the inheritance. The *result* of adoption refers to placement into the inheritance, when a mature, well-groomed son becomes the legal heir of the father's inheritance.

So, both the act of adoption and the result of adoption are important in Paul's writings. Understanding both will help us see the full picture of our adoption as sons.

"Children of God" Versus "Sons of God"

There's another nuance that must be understood. The New Testament authors sometimes differentiated between "children of God" and "sons of God" by using the Greek words *teknon* and *huios*.

If a New Testament writer wanted to refer to a child as a son or a daughter, they could use either *teknon* or *huios*. However, when a writer wanted to emphasize the honor, respect, worthiness, rank, position, Christ-likeness, or moral qualities that distinguished a mature believer, they would always use *huios* rather than *teknon*. As is always the case, context determines how a verse should be interpreted.

Let's look at an example of how *teknon* was used first. Paul said, "The Spirit Himself testifies with our spirit that we are children of God" (Rom. 8:16). *Teknon* is the Greek word for "children" and means "offspring" or "children."[10] Simply put, we become the *teknon* of God at new birth, when the indwelling Spirit implants the nature of the Son into our spirits.

Now let's consider *huios*. Paul said, "For all who are being led by the Spirit of God, these are sons of God" (Rom. 8:14). *Huios* is the Greek word for "sons" and was sometimes used to distinguish mature sons from children.

According to *Vine's Expository Dictionary of New Testament Words*, *teknon* conveys "the fact of birth" whereas *huios* "stresses the dignity and character of the relationship."[11]

Commenting on Romans 8:14, *Vine's* states, "The difference between believers as 'children of God' [teknon] and as 'sons of God' [huios] is brought out in Rom. 8:14-21. The Spirit bears witness with their spirit that they are 'children of God,' [teknon] and, as such, they are His heirs and joint-heirs with Christ. This stresses the fact of their spiritual birth (Rom. 8:16, 17). On the other hand, 'as many as are led by the Spirit of God, these are sons of God,' [huios] i.e., 'these and no other.' Their conduct gives evidence of the dignity of their relationship and their likeness to His character."[12]

In short, Paul distinguished between those *born* of the Spirit and those *led* by the Spirit. Those born of the Spirit are *teknon*, which describes all true believers in Jesus Christ. But the *teknon* who are led by the Spirit embrace the cross and allow the Holy Spirit to crucify their flesh. These *teknon* are also the *huios* of God. They are the mature sons of God.

Another example is in the Sermon on the Mount. Jesus said, "Love your enemies and pray for those who persecute you, so that you may be sons [huios] of your Father who is in heaven" (Matt. 5:44-45, emphasis mine). When Jesus said "of your Father," it's already assumed that born-again believers are God's children. What's not automatic is our response to persecution. That's why Jesus said "so that you may be sons"—so that you may be *huios,* maturing into Christ's image in a greater way.

Commenting on this verse, *Vine's* states, "The disciples were to do these things, not in order that they might become children of God, but that, being children (note 'your Father' throughout), they might make the fact manifest in their character, might 'become sons.'"[13] As *teknon* who consistently respond to persecution in a Christ-like way, we demonstrate that we are becoming *huios* who exhibit Christ's nature and character. We give evidence that we are becoming God's mature sons.

Several other passages in the New Testament use *huios* to stress maturity. For example, in the parable of the wheat and the tares, *huios* is used to describe mature wheat and tares during the end-time harvest. The wheat symbolizes the mature sons of the kingdom while the tares represent the mature sons of the evil one. The point is clear: God's *teknon* will mature into *huios* at the end of the age. The same, however, could be said of the devil's children.

When referring to Jesus, the eternal Son of God, the New Testament writers used *huios* over 240 times. *Teknon* was used only once, when Luke described the twelve-year old Jesus during Passover (Luke 2:48). We also see instances of *huios* stressing maturity in Hebrews 12:6-8 and Revelation 21:7.

In summary, *teknon* describes how we become God's children at new birth by receiving the indwelling Spirit, who gives us new spirits with the nature of Jesus Christ.[14] *Huios*, on the other hand, describes how the *teknon* of God mature into Christ-like sons by the Holy Spirit applying the cross to our self-life and by forming Christ's nature in our hearts and souls. A *teknon* is one who is born of God, while a *huios* is one who is instructed by God. A *teknon* has God's nature in their spirit in seed form, while a *huios* has God's character fully developed in their soul.

In taking us from *teknon* to *huios*, God wants to take us from immaturity to maturity. That doesn't mean, however, that we are no longer a *teknon*. No matter how mature we become, we will always be a *teknon* because we have God's nature and are born of the Spirit.

Another important point is that becoming a *huios* is a lifelong process, for as long as we live in a body of sin, we will battle the flesh (Rom. 7:18). So, becoming a *huios* doesn't make us gods, nor does it make us perfect. Becoming a *huios* is about us becoming Christlike in our hearts and souls. It's not about absolute perfection but maturity.

Putting It All Together

Now that we understand Greco-Roman adoption, the three phases of first-century adoption, the meaning of *huiothesia*, *teknon*, and *huios*, and that *huiothesia* refers to both the act *and* result of adoption, let's put it all together.

Just like Greco-Roman adoption, our adoption as sons involves three phases.

1. *Placement into God's family*

This is the initial act of adoption. Every born-again believer experiences this *individually* when we are adopted into God's family from the outside. This takes place when we make individual decisions to accept Jesus Christ as our Lord and Savior.

Paul described this in Galatians 3-4, using Greco-Roman adoption as a metaphor to explain our son placement into Abraham's inheritance. Abraham is the father who has an inheritance (3:8-9; 18; 29). His inheritance is the indwelling Holy Spirit (3:14). The

Law is our child trainer showing us our need for Jesus Christ (3:23-25; 4:1-2). The date set by the father, when our child training is complete, was Jesus' first coming (Gal. 4:4). And our son placement into Abraham's inheritance as a legal heir is when we receive the indwelling Spirit the moment we're born again (4:5-7).

God took us from outside of His family and adopted us as His very own. He placed us as sons into Abraham's inheritance, giving us the legal right to receive the promise of the indwelling Spirit. In the words of Paul, "Because you are sons, God has sent forth the Spirit of His Son into our hearts, crying, 'Abba! Father!' Therefore you are no longer a slave, but a son; and if a son, then an heir through God" (Gal. 4:5-7).

2. *Preparation for Christ's inheritance*
After we are adopted as God's child and are born of the Spirit as a *teknon*, the Father begins His grooming process. We are placed under the governmental hand of the Holy Spirit, who becomes our personal child trainer. The Holy Spirit's goal is to conform us into the image of Jesus Christ. He wants us to become a mature *huios*. T. Austin Sparks referred to this grooming process as "the school of sonship unto adoption."[15]

This child training process is detailed in Hebrews 12:5-17 and Revelation 2-3. In fact, the Greek word translated *chastening* means "to train children" (Heb. 12:7; Rev. 3:19).[16]

As our child trainer, the Holy Spirit disciplines, corrects, crucifies, circumcises, and instructs us. He works relentlessly to conform us to the pattern Son of God, taking us through various stages of growth, education, discipline, and character development. He trains us in the ways, purposes, and nature of our heavenly Father, preparing us to reign from the throne. The Spirit forms Christ in us, developing His meekness, humility, and sacrificial love. This prepares us to handle our inheritance of eternal intimacy, authority, and glory without squandering it with immature and irresponsible behavior.

3. Placement into Christ's inheritance

When the Holy Spirit's child training work is complete—when we have been conformed into the image of Christ individually, and the body of Christ has become "a mature man" corporately—then we will be placed into Christ's inheritance at His second coming (Eph. 4:13; Rev. 20:4-6).

Whereas the *initial* act of adoption is *individual,* the final *result* of our adoption is *corporate.* That is, all who have "suffered" with Christ under the Holy Spirit's child training will be placed as a corporate son into Christ's inheritance (Rom. 8:17). The final phase of our adoption as sons will be experienced together. This process is almost identical to our marriage to Jesus Christ.

We are betrothed to Christ individually when we're born again. We then prepare ourselves while the Bridegroom is away. And finally, if we make ourselves ready, we will be part of the corporate bride at the marriage supper of the Lamb. In short, we are betrothed *individually,* but we're married *corporately.* The same is true of our adoption.

We are adopted into God's family individually, but we are placed as sons into Christ's inheritance corporately. This final phase of our adoption is what Paul had in mind when he said, "Having the first fruits of the Spirit, even we ourselves groan within ourselves, waiting eagerly for our adoption as sons, the redemption of our body" (Rom. 8:23).

Notice carefully that Paul was "*waiting eagerly* for our adoption as sons." This clearly means that our adoption is not finalized yet. We must wait eagerly until "the redemption of our body," which takes place at the first resurrection when Jesus returns (Rev. 20:4-6).

T. Austin Sparks referred to this phase of adoption as "graduation from the school of sonship . . . to the throne."[17] We are destined as a corporate son to rule and reign with the Lamb from the throne (Rev. 3:20). What a beautiful eternal plan!

One final note before moving on. This final phase of adoption gave the son a new status and position in the family. But it didn't make him more loved or cherished than when he was a child. When a father placed his son as heir over the inheritance, this didn't mean the father loved him more than his other children. Instead, it was an endorsement that a child had become of age, had grown into a mature man, and had the necessary character to oversee the father's household affairs.

This is like our son placement into Christ's eternal inheritance. This doesn't make God love us more. It doesn't make us the favorite son of the kingdom. Rather, it means we have the character of Christ forged into our souls, able to handle the weighty responsibilities of sonship. It means we can rule and reign without squandering our inheritance through immature decisions. Because of this, the Father will give us a new status and the full rights of sonship throughout the eternal ages.

THE FATHER WILL HAVE A FAMILY OF CHRIST-LIKE SONS

Ephesians 1:5 reveals God's eternal purpose, which was determined in the heavenly council of the Godhead before time and creation, to have a family of Christ-like sons who will rule and reign with Jesus for the endless ages of eternity. God will accomplish this purpose through the three phases of adoption.

Understanding your role in the three phases of adoption is crucial to being prepared as a mature son, who will be placed into Christ's eternal inheritance. As we'll explore next, it all begins with being placed into God's family.

CHAPTER 20

PLACED INTO GOD'S FAMILY

At the pinnacle of Ephesians 1, a majestic chapter revealing God's eternal purpose, Paul prayed that we would know "the riches of the glory of His inheritance in the saints" (Eph. 1:18). This is not *our* inheritance in Christ, a popular theme in the church today. Rather, it's God's inheritance in a people He completely possesses. Paul unveiled this eternal mystery hidden in God for thousands of years. He uncovered God's timeless passion to have a people for Himself.

This is far greater than millions of people who've been saved. God aims to fully possess us (Eph. 1:14; 1 Peter 2:9). He wants our entire being governed by the Holy Spirit. He wants our thoughts, emotions, desires, motives, inclinations, and actions brought under the Lamb's dominion. The Lord wants "a people for His own possession" (Titus 2:14).

Frank Viola, in his book *Insurgence*, wrote,

> God is after a people whom He can possess completely. . . . It is my opinion that the Lord has never had a large group of people who were completely His own. And I seriously doubt He ever will.[1]

When Paul spoke of God's inheritance in the saints, he had in mind a people who had become "God's own possession" (Eph. 1:14). A people who had progressed beyond initial salvation to being fully possessed by the Spirit of God, making them completely His. The indwelling Spirit reigning without rival in their spirits, hearts, souls, and bodies. A people who "follow the Lamb wherever He goes" (Rev. 14:4).

Let's spend some time now looking at the Father's inheritance in the saints. Specifically, let's look at what it means to be a Christ-like son.

The Father's Eternal Dream

As the Father looked upon His Son in eternity past, beholding the excellencies of His beauty and communing with Him deeply, He dreamed of a corporate son.[2] Millions of men and women who were just like His Son, joined together in an unbreakable union. This new creation would be a complete and mature representation of His Son. They would share the same intimacy, oneness, and unbroken fellowship that the Father and the Son enjoyed throughout eternity past.

The Father's love, affection, and passion for His beloved Son would be lavished upon His corporate son, the very body of Christ. This privileged creation would be invited into the circle of the Trinity, sharing in the unbreakable union that has bound the Father and the Son together by the Spirit for the eternal ages. Forever, the Father's family of sons, together with the beloved Son, would receive the Father's affection, experience His joy, and drink from His pleasures.

Paul communicated the Father's eternal dream when he said, "He also predestined [us] to become conformed to the image of His Son, so that He would be the firstborn among many brethren" (Rom. 8:29, emphasis mine). As stated in Chapter 2, the Greek word translated *predestined* conveys a predetermined blueprint. So, Paul was basically saying, "God established a blueprint before the foundation of the world and therefore determined before time and creation to conform us into the image of Christ."

The Father's eternal dream is for those *in* Christ to become a mature representation *of* Christ. The Father yearns for a family of sons patterned after His beloved Son. The Father wants to mold us into a people who embody Christ's humility, meekness, obedience, selflessness, and sacrificial love. He wants to extract pride, presumption, and self-rule from our hearts and souls. He will not relent until the Lamb's nature is established fully within us, until the Father's great passion to "bring many sons to glory" is achieved (Heb. 2:10).

God accomplishes this eternal plan through the process of adoption. As we saw in the last chapter, this involves placement into God's family, preparation for Christ's eternal inheritance, and finally, when we are fully prepared, placement into Christ's inheritance.

Now, let's talk about the initial phase of adoption, *placement into God's family*, looking at four truths that give us greater insight into this glorious reality.

1. God is our Father.

We were outsiders who were fatherless, unloved, rejected, and wandering aimlessly. In our wayward condition, the Father saw us, chose us, loved us, sought us out, revealed Christ to us, and brought us into His family. In His great love for us, the Father adopted us and made us His very own children.

But we are not just God's children through adoption. We are also His children by new birth. John said, "But as many as received Him, to them He gave the right to become children of God, even to those who believe in His name, who were born, not of blood nor of the will of the flesh nor of the will of man, but of God" (John 1:12-13).

If we are "born . . . of God" through the inward work of the Spirit, we have "become children of God." We are the *teknon* of God. That means we have God's seed in us. Christ's spiritual DNA has permeated our spirits. Amazingly, Almighty God has become our Father.

The moment we were born again, the Spirit of the Son came into our spirits, resurrected our spirits from death, and infused us with the life of Christ. Now having the "spirit of adoption," the down payment of the Holy Spirit for our future adoption as sons, "We cry out, 'Abba! Father!'" (Rom. 8:15).

In biblical days, slaves were forbidden to call the family head "Abba."[3] This was because "Abba" was a personal name, a family word that suggested a familiar, comfortable, intimate relationship of a child to their father. By combining "Abba" with "Father," it expressed "the love and intelligent confidence" in a child's relationship with their father.[4]

Jesus said "Abba! Father!" once, when He was suffering in the Garden of Gethsemane. This demonstrates how Jesus used this phrase to connect with His Father at a deeper level in His pain and suffering.

To "cry out" to God "Abba! Father!" suggests an intimate, personal, heart-to-heart connection between a beloved child and their heavenly Father. We have this privilege because God is our Father through adoption and new birth.

2. Our Father loves us deeply.

It's impossible to articulate the depth of the Father's boundless, passionate, affectionate, and ardent love for His beloved Son. Throughout eternity past, perhaps for billions and billions of years, the Son was the sole object of the Father's affection and love.

Jesus said to His Father, "You loved Me before the foundation of the world" (John 17:24). This was not a love of duty or obligation. It was a love of deep delight, ecstatic joy, and overflowing pleasure. Clearly, the Father's infinite happiness was rooted in the enjoyment of His Son.

When the eternal Son walked the earth in human flesh, the Father shouted down from heaven twice, reminding Jesus how He felt about Him. At His baptism and during His transfiguration, the Father proclaimed, "This is My beloved Son, in whom I am well-pleased" (Matt. 3:17; 17:5).

Now consider this staggering reality. The Father loves *you* with the same love He has for His Son. Jesus made this clear in John 17:23, when He said, "You . . . loved them, even as You have loved Me." This is a circuit-blowing, mind-exploding truth.

The Father loves us just as much as He loves Jesus.

That's why Isaiah said, "But the Lord was pleased to crush Him, putting Him to grief" (Isa. 53:10). Why? So that "the good pleasure of the LORD will prosper in His hand" through the Son's "offspring" (Isa. 53:10). That is, the Father was pleased to crush His Son so that we could become His adopted sons and His born-again children—ultimately becoming His heirs, fulfilling His eternal dream for a family of Christ-like sons according to His good pleasure.

"See how great a love the Father has bestowed on us," wrote John, "that we would be called children of God" (1 John 3:1). The

Father's love for us is so great He made us His very own children, infused with His spiritual DNA and born of the Spirit of His eternal Son.

Feel the Father's love for you, precious child of God, in Paul's statements at the end of Romans 8. Do you feel buried under a weight of condemnation, guilt, shame, and accusation? Then realize: "Who will bring a charge against God's elect? God is the one who justifies; who is the one who condemns?" (Rom. 8:33-34).

Do you feel like God has abandoned you, that the heavens are closed, or that spiritual warfare is so intense that you can barely breathe? Then know that "neither death, nor life, nor angels, nor principalities, nor things present, nor things to come, nor powers, nor height, nor depth, nor any other created thing, will be able to separate us from the love of God, which is in Christ Jesus our Lord" (Rom. 8:35-39).

Do you feel like everyone is against you, that you are lonely with no friends or family who support you? Then look up to heaven and rejoice because "if God is for us, who is against us?" (Rom. 8:31).

The Father's deep love and affection for you, dearly beloved child of God, breaks the power of fear, rejection, shame, guilt, and condemnation.

When the Holy Spirit came to dwell in your spirit, it was not a "spirit of slavery leading to fear again" (Rom. 8:15). It was the Spirit of sonship, prompting us to cry out with intimate love and affection, "Abba! Father!"

Let this penetrate into your heart: God's love for you is accepting, affectionate, healing, refreshing, and joyful. The Father loves you just like He loves Jesus. The Father's love for you is perfect.

John said, "There is no fear in love" (1 John 4:18). Though some might be afraid of their earthly father because of verbal or physical abuse, the Father's "perfect love casts out fear" (1 John 4:18). This doesn't mean God's love casts out the fear of God, for this is healthy, leads to holiness, and draws us closer to His heart. Rather, the Father's perfect love breaks the fear of rejection that torments and paralyzes. His love shatters intimidation and panic. His love quiets us and gives us rest.

If the Father loves us like He loves Jesus, then as His dearly beloved child, we can rest in His perfect love, letting His affection wash over us in waves of healing that bring wholeness to our war-tattered souls.

If you are born of the Spirit, then you have a Father in heaven who is good, loves you deeply, and is jealous for you to fulfill your destiny in Christ.

Regardless of your relationship with your earthly father, your heavenly Father will never forsake, abandon, or reject you. Though He will discipline you, sometimes severely with scourgings intended to break your stubbornness, He is always motivated by love.

You can trust that your heavenly Father wants what is best for you, even if that means short-term suffering and pain. His ultimate plan is beautiful, breathtaking, and beyond comprehension.

3.   God is a good Father.

Not only is God loving, but He is also *good*. If you ask Him for bread He will not give you a rock (Matt. 7:9). If you ask Him for a fish He won't give you a snake (Matt. 7:10). Your heavenly Father is good and wants the best for you.

What is His best? It's far greater than your "best life now"—a life of luxury with admirable houses, cars, clothes, and vacations. Surely God has more for you than earthly prosperity, healing, favor, influence, and other worldly treasures, which "moths and vermin destroy, and where thieves break in and steal" (Matt. 6:19, NIV).

Though God blesses us with these things, God is good, not primarily by what He does for us, but by what He does *in* us. God is good because He recalibrates and rewires us from the inside out, fully aligning us with His eternal purpose. God is good because He will not relent until we are fully aligned with His ultimate intention. God is good because, in the eternal council of the Godhead, He looked ahead into our day and time, saw us, loved us, and personally invited us into His purpose for the ages.

As Paul meditated upon this invitation, he wrote that it was "according to the kind intention of His will," which in the Greek means the "good pleasure" of His will.[5]

God's "will" is His eternal purpose, and His eternal purpose is good beyond comprehension and joyful beyond words.

God's goodness is demonstrated by His loving invitation to us, offering us a deep, intimate, personal, eternal relationship with Him.

God's goodness is rooted in His eternal purpose to bring us into the circle of the Trinity, inviting us to enjoy the Father, the Son, and the Holy Spirit in fullness in the new city Jerusalem (Rev. 22:1-5).

God is not good because He blesses us; God is good because He gives us Himself.

4. We have the Son's spiritual DNA in our spirits.

The moment we were born again, our spirits were made alive, infused with the righteousness of Christ, and joined inseparably to the Holy Spirit (Rom. 8:10; 1 Cor. 6:17). When we were born of the Spirit, we became children of God with the Son's very own spiritual DNA implanted into our spirits.

Paul said that "we have become united with Him" (Rom. 6:5). The Greek word for *united* means "implanted by birth or nature, of joint origin, innate, congenital."[6] If we take each of these definitions and substitute them into this verse, here is what it means. At new birth,

- We have Christ's nature implanted into us.

- We are of joint origin with Christ.

- We have Christ's nature as part of our innate spiritual nature.

- We have Christ's spiritual heredity and spiritual genetics inherently within our spirits.

When we were born of the Spirit, we became recipients of a genetic transmission that is spiritual in nature. We are now partakers of Christ's very own spiritual DNA. At new birth, Christ's traits and characteristics were implanted into our spirits by the indwelling Spirit. We are now "partakers of the divine nature" in Christ (2 Peter 1:4).

Amazingly, your born-again spirit is like Jesus in righteousness and holiness (Eph. 4:24). Through your spirit-to-Spirit union with the Holy Spirit, you now have Christ's spiritual genetics as part of your innate spiritual nature.

John said, "As He is, so also are we in this world" (1 John 4:17). John didn't say that we *will be* like Him; he said that we *are* like Him.

This is a such powerful revelation that has the potential to transform your entire life. Think about this for a moment.

In your spirit, you are like Jesus. Christ's indestructible life, righteousness, holiness, and divine nature has been engrafted into your spirit, making you a partaker of His divine nature.

Imagine for a moment that the DNA of Steve Jobs or Bill Gates was implanted within you. You would have the genetics of a multi-millionaire genius in seed form. As you matured, your ability to innovate, create, envision, market, and run a large corporation would increase. Before long, you would likely become a millionaire from the revolutionary ideas that naturally came into your mind.

As born-again Christians, we have something far superior than the DNA of Steve Jobs or Bill Gates. We have Christ's very own nature engrafted into our spirits. All of His traits, characteristics, and nature, including His love, righteousness, humility, and meekness, have been engrafted into our spirits. As a child of God, you have the nature of Christ in your spirit in seed form because He dwells there. This is almost too good to be true!

Peter said, "For you have been born again not of seed which is perishable but imperishable, that is, through the living and enduring word of God" (1 Peter 1:23). A seed has all the innate qualities of its parent plant. In fact, a seed is actually a plant within a shell, created in the image of what formed it. With this in mind, Peter said that the seed planted within us is the Word of God.

Who is the Word of God? It's Christ, the eternal Son (John 1:1). This means the incorruptible seed planted within us at new birth is Christ. Since Christ is in us, all that makes Christ who He is was implanted within our spirits in seed form, making us God's very own children.

Final Thoughts

Being placed into God's family means that we have God as our Father through adoption and new birth, we are deeply loved by our Father, our Father is good, and we have the spiritual DNA of the Son in our own spirits.

Once this work is complete and we are placed firmly into God's family, the Father begins His lifelong work of preparing us for Christ's eternal inheritance. We will look at this in the next chapter.

CHAPTER 21

Prepared for Christ's Inheritance

After we are adopted as God's children and born of the Spirit as *teknon*, the Father begins His grooming process. We are placed under the governmental hand of the Holy Spirit, who becomes our personal child trainer. The Holy Spirit's goal is to conform us into the image of Jesus Christ. He wants to mature us into a *huios*.

T. Austin Sparks referred to this grooming process as "the school of sonship unto adoption."[1] Writing about this grooming process, Sparks stated,

> The purpose of sonship . . . is to bring us into a place of spiritual responsibility. God never puts responsibilities upon "official people," but upon sons. Therefore, He has to train us as children in order to develop sonship in us, to bring us there where we can take responsibilities for God.
>
> He seeks to bring us to a state of spiritual maturity, to full growth. This cannot be done in some Bible school, or by putting people "into the ministry." . . . God's school is something very different from mere scholarly activity. . . .
>
> God is seeking to develop a state in us where He can trust us. When God is dealing with us, there is behind it a wonderful assurance that He is going to put His trust in us. He is bringing us into a position of trust. We do not just want to be servants, bits of a machine, but sons who have become one with the Father, and in whose hands He can put spiritual responsibilities.
>
> When we truly recognize this, we begin to understand why God is dealing with us as He does. But because God is in it we know that the end is sure. He will bring His children through.[2]

God develops sonship in us so that He can trust us with royal responsibilities. He prepares us to handle our inheritance of eternal intimacy, authority, and glory without squandering it with immature and irresponsible behavior.

For the rest of this chapter, let's look at this grooming process in more detail. This is the second phase of adoption, *preparation for Christ's inheritance.* Let's look at five truths of this intense preparation process as God develops sonship within us.

1. The Holy Spirit is our child trainer.

Referring to Greco-Roman adoption, Paul said, "Now I say, as long as the heir is a child, he does not differ at all from a slave although he is owner of everything, but he is under guardians and managers until the date set by the father" (Gal. 4:1-2).

The immature child is the heir and owner of everything. But he doesn't yet have the moral responsibility and character to properly steward the inheritance. Given too soon, the weight and pressure of overseeing the family inheritance would surely result in ruin. The father's wealth, stored up for years, would be squandered in a few short months. The father has no other choice but to place the child under a guardian "until the date set by the father." This date corresponds with the son's maturity, when the son is finally ready to handle the weighty responsibility of being heir.

As God's children, this is what it's like for sonship to be developed within us. The moment we're born again, though we have Christ's nature in us in seed form, we are not able to handle our inheritance. It would utterly ruin us because we are so self-absorbed.

Think about it like this. My ten-year old daughter is destined to drive when she turns sixteen. Though Anna has many great qualities, she doesn't yet have the maturity and character to handle the responsibility of driving. If I gave her the keys when she was ten, she would wreck the car in minutes.

Since we are not born again into a mature state, we must be placed under the tutelage of the Holy Spirit, our guardian who trains us for reigning. We see a glimpse of this in Hebrews 12:7, which states, "If you endure chastening [discipline], God deals with you as with sons [huios]" (NKJV, emphasis mine). The Greek word for *chastening* is *paideia* and it means "the whole training and education of children," including "the cultivation of mind and morals" and "employs for this purpose . . . commands and admonitions . . . reproof and punishment."[3]

The Holy Spirit is our child trainer, who uses discipline, correction, and instruction to transform us into a *huios* of God. He develops sonship in us through crucifixion, circumcision, and intense training. He works relentlessly to change us from immature, selfish children into mature, Christ-like sons. He educates us in the ways, purposes, and nature of our heavenly Father, preparing us to reign from the throne.

When God disciplines us, He is not an angry Father, inflicting punishment for our imperfections and sins. Rather, He is a loving Father who cares deeply about us becoming His mature, Christ-like sons.

The Father disciplines us, through the Holy Spirit, so that we can share in the inheritance of the eternal Son.

With God's eternal purpose in view, suffering and brokenness, as a component of the Holy Spirit's child training, reveals God's goodness toward us. This might sound like a paradox to some, but it's the absolute truth. How can this possibly be? Because the Father will do whatever it takes for us to become His inheritance. In His great desire to be in an intimate relationship with us, the Father will not leave us as immature, selfish, and rebellious children who would squander our inheritance in Him. The Father's goodness motivates Him to break our stubborn pride and to remove every rival that blocks Christ's fullness from being released within us.

2.   The Father's goal is to conform us into the image of Christ.

The Father is not content with the implanted life of Christ remaining in seed form within us. His ultimate intention is to conform us into the image of His Son.

From the eternal council of the Godhead, an invitation has been extended to those in Christ to *become* a representation of the Man Christ Jesus. Far more important than what we do for God is who we *become* to Him.

Francis Frangipane said, "Too often, as Christians, we define ourselves by what we do for God rather than what we *become* to Him. What pleases the Father most is not what proceeds from our hands but what rises from our hearts."[4]

We are called to *become* Christ-like, conformed into His image. Paul said, "He also predestined [us] to become conformed to the image of His Son" (Rom. 8:29, emphasis mine). ·

This does not make us deity or gods. Nor does it mean that we will attain spotless perfection this side of heaven. What it does mean, however, is that the indwelling Spirit of Christ will conform our hearts and souls into the nature and character of Jesus Christ. This is about maturity, not pristine perfection. We have everything we need to become a mature representation of the Man Christ Jesus in this life.

In the Sermon on the Mount, Jesus said, "Therefore you are to be perfect, as your heavenly Father is perfect" (Matt. 5:48). Based upon this verse, some have advocated absolute perfection. But here's the issue. The Greek word translated *perfect* is often misunderstood. This word is *teleios* and it can mean "brought to its end, finished, wanting nothing necessary to completeness, full grown, mature."[5] The idea is that we can become a mature representation of Jesus Christ, but not a perfect one, at least not in this life.

If the Lord had absolute perfection in mind, we could never have a bad thought, speak an unwholesome word, or act with an impure motive. We could never judge or criticize. We could never do *anything* wrong. If you know someone who has achieved perfection in this life, let me know because I would love to meet them.

If we look honestly at our lives, each of us are a work in progress. We are rough drafts that are ever being refined by the Holy Spirit.

Bottom line: we are called to maturity, not perfection.

On the other hand, we can't lower the standard that the Father established in the eternal council. We are called to be conformed into the image of Christ, and this work begins the moment we're born again.

I realize that conformity into the image and likeness of Christ likely sounds idealistic and unattainable. But thankfully, it's not by power nor by might but by His Spirit (Zech. 4:6). I have complete confidence in the Holy Spirit's resurrection power to transform us into the likeness of Jesus Christ in fullness and to do it this side of heaven.

If the Father predetermined to conform us into the image of the Man Christ Jesus, then He will supply us with all the ability and power for that to happen. We just need to believe it and trust Him to do it.

Terry Bennett wrote about this in his book, *Within the Circle of the Throne*, stating,

> God's full measured life inside of us. . . . That simply means that the Son of God has come fully into a people and they no longer live because Christ alone lives in them. That is what it means in its simplest form. . . . Humanity has a singular destiny unlike any other creation. It is called to union of life with the Spirit of God. We are called to no longer live for ourselves in any capacity. . . . Self-life is meant to be dealt a deadly blow by a greater life, a greater promise, a greater purpose, a greater intention.[6]

We can have full union with the indwelling Spirit in this life. This is meant to be the normal Christian life. This is what the Lord has always intended.

Though only a few have experienced this type of union throughout history, I don't believe it will end that way. The Lord will release an end-time work of the Holy Spirit to bring His church into the fullness of Christ. When this happens, the Father will have a people who are a mature representation of Jesus. This is our destiny, for the Father's great eternal dream has always been to have a family of Christ-like sons.

3.   The Father works according to the pattern of the Son.

The Father develops sonship within us by forming Christ's nature and character in our hearts and souls. The Father adheres to the pattern of the Son as He sands away our pride and chisels off our rebellion. The pattern of the Son, which the Father follows in His work within us, is vividly illustrated in the Sermon on the Mount.

When Jesus preached the Sermon on the Mount, He was revealing what His heart is like. He was unveiling His character and nature to the world. The Sermon on the Mount is one of the greatest illustrations of Christ-likeness in Scripture.

Walking through this three-chapter message in Matthew 5-7, we see that Jesus has a pure, meek, merciful, and peace-loving heart that endures persecution with love for His enemies (Matt. 5:3-12).

Jesus has a heart that is free from lust, anger, and bitterness (Matt. 5:17-32). When Jesus says that He will do something, His yes means yes and His no means no (Matt. 5:33-37).

While on earth, Jesus never practiced His righteousness or performed in His ministry so that people would praise, affirm, and celebrate Him and His accomplishments (Matt. 6:1-21). There was no itch of pride in the Lord's heart. His desire was to please His Father and no one else.

During His thirty-three years on earth, Jesus lived for eternity, refusing to store up temporary treasures (Matt. 6:19-21). His allegiance was to the Father, not to money (Matt. 6:24). Because His trust was fully in His Father, Jesus didn't worry about how His needs would be met (Matt. 6:25-34). He lived in moment-by-moment trust in the Father's ability to provide for Him. Rather than having anxiety about the future, Jesus lived to advance the kingdom of God, trusting His Father to give Him everything He needed day-by-day (Matt. 6:33).

As He taught in Matthew 7:1-5, Jesus never judges a person or situation with unrighteous judgment. His perception is never clouded by pride, jealousy, envy, comparison, coveting, selfishness, accusation, or cold love. Instead, Jesus judges every person, situation, and circumstance with righteous judgment.

Jesus' call to obey His words in the Sermon on the Mount is really an invitation to become like Him (Matt. 7:24-25). Jesus' words in this sermon reveal His character and nature like no other place in Scripture.

As the Spirit works to form Christ within us, He always works according to the pattern of the Son, which is laid out beautifully for us in the Sermon on the Mount. The Holy Spirit, our child-trainer, wants to shape our deepest desires, motives, thoughts, choices, emotions, and actions according to Christ' nature, which is gloriously detailed in Matthew 5-7.

When this Spirit-led work is complete within His people, the Father will have a corporate son who has been conformed into the image and likeness of Christ.

4. The cross develops sonship within us.

As mentioned previously, the way of the cross transforms us from immature children into Christ-like sons, fit for the throne. As the Holy Spirit trains us for reigning, the cross is His chosen instrument to forge the character of Christ within us.

The cross breaks our stubborn pride and wayward rebellion. The cross slays our selfishness and independence. This is mandatory if want to rule and reign with Him.

We can never have true kingdom authority when our hearts and souls have alignment with the kingdom of darkness. Therefore, the Holy Spirit works persistently and relentlessly to instill the character capable of being a coheir with Christ.

Paul said, "If by the Spirit you are putting to death the deeds of the body, you will live. For all who are being led by the Spirit of God, these are sons of God" (Rom. 8:13-14).

Notice the first part of Paul's statement: "If by the Spirit you are putting to death the deeds of the body." This reveals the Holy Spirit's work in applying the cross to our daily experience.

Now take note of the second part of Paul's statement: "all who are being led by the Spirit of God, these are sons of God." This reveals the connection between the cross-life and becoming a mature son of God, able to handle the weighty responsibility of heirship.

Clearly, the way of the cross is instrumental in our transformation to a *huios* of God. The way of the cross is how sonship is developed within us.

5. Suffering helps train us for reigning.

Paul said, "The Spirit Himself testifies with our spirit that we are children [*teknon*] of God, and if children, heirs also, heirs of God and fellow heirs with Christ, if indeed we suffer with Him so that we may also be glorified with Him" (Rom. 8:16-17, emphasis mine). As God's children (*teknon*), we are in line to be "co-heirs with Christ" (Rom. 8:17, NIV).

Unfortunately, many stop reading at this point. They don't want to hear about the "s-word"—*suffering.*

"If indeed we suffer with Him," wrote the apostle. Suffering helps prepare us for heirship, for without the cross there is no crown; without brokenness there is no reigning with Him. Suffering with Christ helps equip us to be coheirs with Him.

As a Roman citizen, Paul likely witnessed an heir being groomed by a strict guardian. Since many guardians were slaves, they had an inherent propensity for discipline, correction, and order. This meant the young heir, under the tutelage of the guardian, had to embrace times of discipline, which resulted in a measure of suffering. This guardian was handpicked by the father to break his child of foolish, selfish, and immature ways.

Under the guardian's tutelage, the young heir felt as if he couldn't get away with anything. His mistakes were corrected and his indiscretions were disciplined. The rod was used to break his stubbornness, selfishness, and rebellion. This ensured that foolish behavior was driven out of the young heir, which could potentially cause the father's inheritance to be squandered.

During this training, the child didn't differ from the slave, even though he was owner of everything. The loving father knows his child must embrace this suffering if he is to receive the full rights of sonship.

Paul likely had this type of suffering in mind when he penned Romans 8:17.

If we want to be a coheir with Christ, then submitting to the Holy Spirit's child-training work is necessary. His loving discipline helps prepare us for the throne. And make no mistake about it—this includes suffering and brokenness. Even Jesus "learned obedience from the things which He suffered" (Heb. 5:8).

When Paul mentioned suffering in Romans 8:17, I believe he had at least three types of suffering in mind: 1) The suffering when the Lord breaks our selfish and independent ways; 2) The suffering that comes from obedience; and 3) The suffering experienced during seasons of pruning, sifting, and stripping. Let's quickly look at these three types of suffering, all of which help to prepare us for the throne.

First, we suffer when the Lord deals with our selfish and independent ways. When the Holy Spirit doesn't allow us to have our way, there is a measure of suffering. For example, the Lord might tell us to seek Him rather than spend time doing what we want. He might challenge us to attend the prayer meeting rather than watch television. Perhaps He instructs us to keep quiet rather than defend ourselves. He might tell us to give a substantial offering that prevents us from purchasing something that we desire. Maybe He tells us to leave our comfort zone and go on a mission trip.

These examples might seem minor, but when the Lord begins dealing with our self-life, there is a measure of suffering because we don't get what we want. It's like children who suffer when they don't get their way. As their will is broken, they experience temporary displeasure. The same is true with us as the Holy Spirit establishes the nature of the Lamb within us. When He breaks our independent and prideful ways, there is temporary discomfort, disruption, and displeasure.

Second, there is suffering that comes from obedience. For example, the Lord might tell us to speak a challenging word that causes others to insult, reject, persecute, or even threaten us. He might instruct us to sever ties with lifelong friends who aren't following Him wholeheartedly. He might call us to change jobs so that we have more time to be with Him and to fulfill our ministry assignment.

We suffer as a *result* of our obedience. Obeying the Lord might result in rejection and persecution; walking alone rather than being yoked to those living in compromise; or having our purchasing power reduced so that we can follow Christ.

One thing I know for certain. The more I obey Christ whole-heartedly, the more I experience spiritual warfare. Though we should always resist the devil, spiritual conflicts also bring a measure of suffering until we break through and prevail.

Third, as the Lord prepares us as His inheritance, there are seasons of pruning, sifting, and stripping. These seasons might seem like they last forever, but in the light of eternity, it's only a very short time. During these concentrated times, the Lord surgically removes pride, selfishness, independence, rebellion, and folly from our hearts and souls. As our loving Surgeon, the Lord skillfully removes what is of the Adamic nature, aligned with Lucifer and the kingdom of darkness, from our innermost thoughts, desires, and motives. His goal is to bring us fully under the dominion of the Lamb. His work continues until the kingdom of God is fully established within us. The Spirit shapes us until we have been re-constituted into the nature of the Lamb, for He is preparing us for the throne.

As anyone who has ever tasted the dealings of God knows, this is not a fun process. But it is a necessary one, if we want to rule and reign with Him.

Of course, this doesn't mean that our entire lives will be one miserable experience until we get to heaven. In my life, I have experienced both times of blessing and times of suffering. I've found that both are necessary to prepare us for ruling and reigning with Him.

When the Lord takes us through seasons of intense training and preparation, as the skillful Potter, He knows the exact amount of heat to apply to the clay to form the pot He desires.

Don't run from these types of temporary suffering, for this is preparing you to rule and reign with Him. The Spirit is dealing with your selfishness and He is developing a heart of obedience within you.

But we do have a choice whether to remain under the Spirit's discipline or to run from it. Hebrews 12:7 makes this clear. This verse states "if you endure" discipline then "God deals with you as with sons [huios]" (emphasis mine). The Greek word for *endure* means to "to stay under."[7]

Though the Lord disciplines all of His children, we choose whether to submit to His dealings or to resist His work. If we oppose His dealings, then we will remain an immature child and forfeit our high calling to be placed into the full rights of sonship. We will disqualify ourselves from ruling and reigning with Him.

There's simply no shortcut to the throne.

Just to clarify, the suffering and brokenness I'm talking about is absolutely *not* suffering a debilitating disease, being inflicted with poverty, or letting the devil destroy our lives. Not at all.

This is a deep subject far beyond the scope of this book, but if we are sick, we are to contend for healing. If we suffer lack, we are to believe God for His abundant provision. If we are attacked by the devil, we are to resist him in faith.

As we contend for these blessings and pursue a joyful, intimate relationship with the Lord, there will still be times of suffering as the Holy Spirit, our loving child-trainer, prepares us for the throne.[8]

GROWING UP

A child becomes like his father because he has his DNA. But it takes years for a child to mature into a responsible son. Likewise, we have Christ's spiritual DNA in us. We possess the potential to become a mature representation of Him, conformed into His image and likeness. But this is not automatic or guaranteed. It will only happen as we submit to the Holy Spirit's child training and embrace the way of the cross.

If we allow the Holy Spirit to break our stubborn pride and resistance, then Christ will increase within us. Eventually, when the Lord's child training is complete within His children, the Father will place His corporate son into Christ's inheritance at the second coming. Together, we will graduate from the "school of sonship" to the throne. We will look at this last phase of adoption, *placement into Christ's inheritance*, in the next chapter.

CHAPTER 22

PLACED INTO CHRIST'S INHERITANCE

If we could quiet ourselves for a moment and listen to creation, we might sense a longing, a yearning, an eager expectation.

Paul said, "For the anxious longing of the creation waits eagerly for the revealing of the sons [*huios*] of God" (Rom. 8:19, emphasis mine).

God's hidden work, as He matures His *teknon* into *huios* in obscurity and seclusion, is about to be unveiled to the world. All creation is on pins and needles to see "the revealing of the [mature] sons of God."

What the prophets foretold is at our doorstep. All creation can sense it. History and prophecy are converging. The spirit realm is stirring with activity, for the greatest move of God in history is breaking into the natural realm with unrelenting force.

The blueprint that God crafted in eternity past is alive and swirling with energy, pushing and driving toward fulfillment.

The Father will have a corporate son who is conformed into the image of Christ and nothing can stop Him. Fallen man can't hinder Him. Principalities and powers don't stand a chance. God laughs in derision at the world's elite who plot against Him.

God's ultimate intention for this age is about to be fulfilled. A mature son will be birthed who will sit upon the throne and rule the nations with a rod of iron. The birth pangs can be felt. God's children are being trained to reign.

What the Spirit has been doing in secret will be put on full display. The nations will be astonished as they behold God's corporate son, fully conformed into the image and likeness of Christ, radiating God's glory like the sun and ruling the nations with truth and justice.

GOD'S SONS REVEALED TO CREATION

Let's get the picture of what it will be like when God's sons are revealed to creation.[1] Let's fast forward in time to the end of the age.

The nations are reeling. The antichrist has decimated much of the planet. Natural disasters have wreaked havoc upon the earth, as well.

The earth's inhabitants are drunk with delusion. Much of the world has bowed their knee to the dragon and his man, the antichrist. Yet there are resistors, neither born of the Spirit nor worshipers of the dragon, who see the evil beast system and refuse to bow.

Israel is suffering terribly under the brutal regime of the lawless one. Antisemitism has reached heights never experienced before. Jews and Christians are persecuted unlike any other time in history.

People are in despair. They are hopeless, terrified, and bewildered.

In the darkest moment, light breaks in from heaven. Christ returns on a white horse and following Him are heaven's armies. Not just angels. But the bride dressed in white—the corporate son who has been resurrected and placed into Christ's inheritance.

John described it like this: "And I saw heaven opened, and behold, a white horse, and He who sat on it is called Faithful and True, and in righteousness He judges and wages war. . . . And the armies which are in heaven, clothed in fine linen, white and clean, were following Him on white horses" (Rev. 19:11, 14).[2]

Christ the head (Jesus) and Christ the body (the mature sons of God) return together to wage war against the antichrist and his ruthless regime. With irresistible force, under Jesus the commander-in-chief, this army will crush the antichrist and his evil empire.

Following this epic battle, God's sons, resurrected and radiating God's glory, will be dispatched throughout the nations with a rod of iron. They will rule cities and nations as God's government increases throughout the earth.

Together with Jesus, they will restore Israel and make Jerusalem the praise of the earth. They will break all rebellion, enforce God's Word in the nations, and release justice to the oppressed and disadvantaged.

As a result, the nations will resort to the root of Jesse, Jesus Christ, the Messiah of Israel. They will flock to Jerusalem to worship Him, seek His wisdom, and entreat Him for favor. Even the distant coastlands will bow to King Jesus.

Creation will be restored to an Edenic state, and harmony will be released within the animal kingdom.

This is why creation is longing and yearning for the revealing of God's sons. This is why creation groans with eager expectation for God's sons to be taken out of obscurity, solitude, and hiddenness and revealed for all to see.

In that day, God's glory will cover the earth like the waters cover the sea, for God's eternal purpose for the Church Age and the Kingdom Age will be fulfilled.

What started as a plan in the eternal council of the Godhead before time and creation will be fully realized. The Father will have a family of Christ-like sons who have inherited the throne. This corporate son, together with Christ, will rule the nations with a rod of iron. All things in heaven and earth will come under the headship of the Son. The only name mentioned throughout the earth will be Jesus Christ.

I can't wait for the day when God's sons are revealed to creation. It will be glorious beyond words! This is what I live for. This is why I was created and have breath in my lungs. It's also why *you* were created.

God the Father saw you in His eternal council, sought you out, and placed you into His family. He is presently training you for reigning. If you remain under the Holy Spirit's child-training rod of discipline, you will be part of the corporate son who will be placed into Christ's eternal inheritance at the end of the age.

What an amazing plan! God is so good, and His plan is absolutely stunning.

THE FATHER'S CORPORATE SON

As the Scriptures come to a close, the Father declared His ultimate intention for the church, saying, "He who overcomes will inherit these things, and I will be his God and he will be My son [*huios*]" (Rev. 21:7, emphasis mine). If you look closely, you can see that the Father was talking about our adoption as sons.

In context, "He who overcomes" refers to overcoming what Jesus listed in Revelation 2-3. This is synonymous with remaining under the Holy Spirit's child-training hand. In fact, in His message to Laodicea, Jesus said, "Those whom I love, I reprove and discipline [*paideuō* = child train]" (Rev. 3:19, emphasis mine).

If we submit to the Holy Spirit's leadership and come fully under His governmental hand, then He will empower us to overcome what Jesus stipulated in Revelation 2-3. We will overcome losing our first love, self-love, false doctrines, Jezebel, apathy, indifference, and lukewarmness.

Overcoming is how we graduate from the school of sonship, enabling us to receive our eternal inheritance. As the Father said, "He who overcomes will inherit these things."

What things do we inherit? The eternal rewards that Jesus offered in Revelation 2-3. As we have seen, these can be summarized as eternal intimacy, eternal authority, and eternal glory. Remaining under the child-trainers' governmental hand is how we overcome, and it's how our adoption as a *huios* is finalized. It's how we are placed as a son into Christ's inheritance. Like the Father said, "He who overcomes . . . will be My son."

Just to be clear, overcoming is not synonymous with justification but with sanctification. We don't overcome to get saved. We overcome because we *are* saved. We overcome because the indwelling Spirit supplies us with enabling grace. Put another way, overcoming is the same as our living condition aligned with our legal position, embracing the cross, the salvation of the soul, living the Spirit-led life, Christ-likeness, and making ourselves ready as the betrothed bride of Christ.

With this in mind, if we take what Jesus exhorted us to overcome in Revelation 2-3 and other descriptions of the overcomers in the book of Revelation, here is what the Father's family of sons will be characterized by:

- First love for Jesus—a love so deep that they love Him even more than they love themselves (Rev. 2:4-5; 12:11);

- Faithfulness to the Lamb that transforms them into living martyrs who are willing to die for their faith (Rev. 2:10);

- A love for the truth that is so consuming that all of their hearts will be in full agreement with the Word, removing all forms of compromise (Rev. 2:14-15);

- An intolerance for the ways and works of Jezebel in their sphere of authority (Rev. 2:20);

- A deep and driving hunger for God that overpowers apathy, complacency, indifference, and carelessness (Rev. 3:1-2);

- A disciplined lifestyle that helps them maintain their victory until the end (Rev. 3:11);

- A fiery passion for Jesus that consumes self-satisfaction (Rev. 3:16-19);

- A crucified self-life with hearts and souls that are fully possessed by the Spirit of God (Rev. 12:11);

- Christ-like humility, meekness, self-sacrifice, obedience, and love that overcomes the nature of the proud, independent, rebellious, self-serving, and accusatory nature of the dragon (Rev. 12:11);

- Sexual purity in their hearts, souls, and bodies (Rev. 14:4);

- Absolute obedience to the Holy Spirit that leads to following the Lamb wherever He goes (Rev. 14:4);

- Lips that only speak the truth, whose yes is yes and whose no is no (Rev. 14:5);

- Holiness and blamelessness (Rev. 14:5).[3]

This is what the Father's corporate son will look like at the end of the age.

THE PARABLE OF THE WHEAT AND THE TARES

Jesus told a parable about wheat and tares that's directly related to God's eternal purpose to have a corporate son (Matt. 13:24-30). This parable reveals what the Spirit will emphasize as we approach the end of the age. Let's take a quick look at some key parts of this parable.

First, notice that Jesus said, "The harvest is the end of the age" (Matt. 13:39). In the days leading to the second coming, the greatest harvest in history will be reaped. But what exactly will this end-time harvest look like?

If you ask most believers, they will likely describe a worldwide revival where millions of people get saved in the context of signs, wonders, and miracles. I am certainly not arguing against this, for Revelation 7:9-17 indicates that a great multitude will be saved during the Great Tribulation. But if you examine Jesus' words closely, there's an important truth that many are missing about the end-time harvest.

In this parable, Jesus teaches that the end-time harvest is the time when God's eternal purpose will be fulfilled. It's the time when the greatest number of believers in history will be transformed into the image and likeness of Christ.

Why do I say this? Because Jesus said that the wheat "are the sons of the kingdom" (Matt. 13:38). Once again, the Greek word that Jesus used for "sons" is *huios*. Based upon the context of Matthew 13:38, where we see the wheat and the tares coming to full bloom as lawlessness and righteousness reach an unprecedented level of maturity, Jesus used *huios* to emphasize a vast number of believers coming to full Christ-like maturity at the end of the age. He was looking toward God's eternal purpose to have a corporate son conformed into the image and likeness of Christ.

Jesus used *huios* to emphasize the Spirit's end-time work to produce Christ-like maturity in the hearts and souls of His people. The end-time harvest is all about God's children maturing into sons of

God, having the character to steward their eternal inheritance.

In my opinion, there has only been a remnant of the redeemed who have overcome and matured into the image of Christ throughout history. However, the good news is Jesus promised that many believers would move from immature children to Christ-like sons before He returns.

God's eternal goal is to bring "*many* sons to glory" (Heb. 2:10, emphasis mine). Before the Lord returns, many will mature, overcome, and become Christ-like sons shining forth God's glory like the sun. Though only a remnant of God's people have overcome throughout history, it will not end that way. We are on the verge of witnessing the greatest number of believers in history coming into full Christ-like maturity before the Lord returns. This is what the end-time harvest is about.

THE FINAL PHASE OF ADOPTION

When the Holy Spirit's child training work is complete and we have become "a mature man" corporately, then we will be placed into Christ's inheritance at His second coming (Eph. 4:13; Rev. 20:4-6).

Whereas the initial act of adoption is *individual*, the final result of our adoption is *corporate*. That is, all who have "suffered" with Christ under the child training of the Holy Spirit will be placed as a corporate son into Christ's inheritance (Rom. 8:17). The final phase of our adoption as sons will be experienced together.

Paul said, "Having the first fruits of the Spirit, even we ourselves groan within ourselves, waiting eagerly for our adoption as sons, the redemption of our body" (Rom. 8:23). Paul made it clear that our adoption is not finalized until "the redemption of our body," which takes place at the first resurrection when Jesus returns (Rev. 20:4-6).

Knowing that the final result of our adoption is corporate, when all of God's sons are placed together into Christ's inheritance at the first resurrection, read Revelation 20:4-6 from this perspective:

Then I saw thrones, and they sat on them, and judgment was given to them. And I saw the souls of those who had been beheaded because of their testimony of Jesus and because of the word of God, and those who had not worshiped the beast or his image, and had not received the mark on their forehead and on their hand; and they came to life and reigned with Christ for a thousand years. The rest of the dead did not come to life until the thousand years were completed. This is the first resurrection. Blessed and holy is the one who has a part in the first resurrection; over these the second death has no power, but they will be priests of God and of Christ and will reign with Him for a thousand years. (Rev. 20:4-6)

Carefully reading through this passage, you see three groups of overcomers. First, John said, "I saw thrones, and they sat on them, and judgment was given to them." From the message to the church of Laodicea, where Jesus offered the overcomers the right to sit on His throne, we know that this group represents the overcomers throughout history (Rev. 3:21).

Second, John said, "And I saw the souls of those who had been beheaded because of their testimony of Jesus and because of the word of God." This group of overcomers, which are a subset of the first group, are the martyrs throughout history who were faithful until death, just like many of the believers in the church of Smyrna (Rev. 2:10).

Third, John said, "And those who had not worshiped the beast or his image, and had not received the mark on their forehead and on their hand." Once again, this group of overcomers are a subset of the first group and refer to the saints who overcome the antichrist during the last three-and-a-half years of this age (Rev. 13:7; 15:2).

Notice that these overcomers receive the throne and the right to rule the nations at the same time. They are resurrected together at the first resurrection. Their son placement into Christ's inheritance is corporate.

T. Austin Sparks, who wrote extensively about God's eternal purpose, said, "You and I cannot inherit singly, individually: we can only inherit in a related way."[4] Expounding upon this idea, he said,

So that we are brought face to face with this matter of reaching adoption by the development of sonship in us in the School of God, I think I ought to say here that, while this does become an individual and personal matter and must be that in its application, the matter of adoption is one with that of . . . the Church . . . in view, not the individual. It is the Church which is the elect body, and it is the Church which is the elect "son," in the sense in which we are speaking of sonship now; and it is the Church which is fore-ordained unto adoption of sons, not individuals as such, although it has its individual application, and it will be with the manifestation of the sons in the corporate sense, the Church, that God reaches His full end."[5]

The final phase of our adoption, when we are placed into Christ's inheritance at the first resurrection when Jesus returns, is a corporate son placement, not just an individual one. Each of us must come into full Christ-like maturity for the Lord's eternal dream to be fulfilled.

END-TIME PROPHECY AND ETERNAL PURPOSE

As I have mentioned, I have been studying end-time prophecy extensively for over twenty years. I've read thousands of pages of commentaries and books about this subject. I've read numerous commentaries on the book of Revelation, Isaiah, and Daniel. In all my studies, I don't recall any scholar, teacher, preacher, or author connecting God's eternal purpose to the end times. Yet this is exactly what drives God's end-time agenda.

Everything about the end times is uniquely designed by God with a purpose—His eternal purpose. And the result will be the Father having what He's always yearned for—a family of Christ-like sons who will share in the eternal inheritance with His beloved Son, Jesus Christ. This is what Jesus taught in the parable of the wheat and the tares about the end-time harvest.

With this in mind, the church needs a fresh perspective of the end times, viewing it as the time when God fulfills His unique purpose for this age. Yes, God will release His wrath upon those who align themselves with Satan and the antichrist, but there is something far greater that will happen. God's sons will graduate from the school of sonship unto adoption, and their graduation will be to the throne.

YOUR TRUE DESTINY

Consider these wonderful truths for a moment:

> We are destined to be part of the Father's corporate son. We are destined to rule and reign with the Lamb from the throne. We are destined to share in the same relationship with the Father that the eternal Son has shared in for all eternity.

This is our destiny. This is God's beautiful, eternal plan that was conceived in His heart before the ages. And now this destiny is being worked out in your daily life.

The Father has placed you as His own child into His family. The Holy Spirit is now training you for reigning. And soon, when a mature man has been established throughout the nations, you will join millions of others who have allowed Christ to be formed within them. Together, we will comprise the corporate son who will be placed into Christ's eternal inheritance as our adoption as sons is finalized.

But we can never fully understand our inheritance until we first comprehend God's inheritance in us. That's why we will continue looking at God's inheritance in the saints, looking next at the Son's inheritance in us.

The Son's Inheritance in the Saints

In eternity past, the Father determined to give His Son a beloved who would love Him like the Father (John 17:26). Part 6 examines God's eternal purpose to give His Son an equally yoked bride who will partner with Him throughout the endless ages of eternity.

CHAPTER 23

The Bride of Christ

I'll never forget a conversation I had a few years ago, talking with a man about being the bride of Christ. I'll call him Dave.

Dave was tough. He was the type of guy you would want on your football team. Though I'm confident that he could beat me in arm wrestling or a boxing match, Dave had a sincere and tender heart.

During our conversation, he told me, "I've got to be honest with you. I seriously struggle with being the bride of Christ. I just can't picture myself wearing a wedding dress."

Dave continued speaking, but I zoned out. All I could see was this burly man dressed in bridal garments.

Dave kept expressing his struggle, but I had my own struggle. It took all I had not to burst out in laughter. Dave noticed my grin and began to smile himself. Soon we were truly laughing out loud.

This conversation reminded me of the struggle many have when it comes to identifying as the bride of Christ. Trust me. I don't know any men who would get excited about wearing a wedding dress.

Thankfully, this is not what being the bride of Christ is about.

If you have similar feelings, I hope the next few chapters change your paradigm of what it means to be the bride of Christ.

The Son's Inheritance in the Saints

Having just examined the Father's "inheritance in the saints," let's focus now on the Son's inheritance in the saints (Eph. 1:18).

In Ephesians 1:4, Paul unveiled God's plan "before the foundation of the world" to make us "holy and blameless before Him." This is clearly eternal-purpose language. God's ultimate intention is to make us holy, to bring us before Him, to lavish His love upon us, and to empower us to love Him in return.

With this in mind, look at what Paul said four chapters later in Ephesians 5:27: "That He might present to Himself the church in all her glory, having no spot or wrinkle or any such thing; but that she would be *holy and blameless*" (emphasis mine).

In Ephesians 1:4, Paul revealed God's eternal purpose to make us holy and blameless. In Ephesians 5:27, Paul connected this eternal purpose to "the church in all her glory" at the end of the age. Reading a few verses down, you see that the church is called to be the wife of Jesus Christ (Eph. 5:31-32).

Putting all of this together, you realize that God's eternal purpose is to give His Son an equally yoked bride as His inheritance. This is confirmed by a number of other scriptures.[1]

Paul Billheimer, in his classic book *Destined for the Throne*, writes:

> It [the Bride of Christ] is one thing and one alone: the Eternal Companion of Jesus Christ, wholly God and wholly man. The final and ultimate outcome and goal of events from eternity to eternity, the finished product of all the ages, is the spotless Bride of Christ, united with Him in wedded bliss at the marriage supper of the Lamb and seated with her heavenly Bridegroom upon the throne of the universe—ruling and reigning with Him over an ever increasing and expanding Kingdom. He entered the stream of human history for this one purpose, to claim His Beloved. . . . Creation has no other aim. History has no other goal. From before the foundation of the world until the dawn of eternal ages God has been working toward one grand event, one supreme end—the glorious wedding of His Son, the marriage supper of the Lamb.[2]

God's eternal purpose is to provide His beloved Son an equally yoked bride from the human race. Creation truly has no other aim. History truly has no other goal. God has been working since eternity past toward the glorious wedding of His Son. The Father will give Jesus a pure, spotless, holy, and worthy bride who loves Him just like the Father (John 17:26). An equally yoked bride who will partner with Jesus throughout the endless ages of eternity.

THE KINGDOM IS LIKE A WEDDING

Throughout the gospels, the kingdom of God is compared to several things. It is like a seed sown in a field, leaven that spreads imperceptibly, hidden treasure that must be discovered, a pearl of great price that has been purchased, and a king who came to settle accounts.

Central to the theme of the next few chapters, Jesus also said that "the kingdom of heaven is like . . . a wedding" (Matt. 22:2, NIV). Among the many metaphors of the kingdom, we see that the kingdom of God is like a marriage arranged by our heavenly Father for His Son.

Once you realize God's eternal purpose to provide His Son an equally yoked bride, an amazing thing happens when you read the Bible. You begin to see how frequently the Scriptures allude to weddings, brides, bridegrooms, wedding feasts, wedding attendants, and the bridal paradigm of the kingdom. The Scriptures are filled with references to the marriage that will take place between Jesus and His church. Even the order of these references speaks of their importance. Let me explain.

In God's *first* interaction with man, He provided Adam with a wife, which Paul said was a "reference to Christ and the church" (Gen. 2:18-25; Eph. 5:32).

Jesus' *first* miracle took place at a wedding in Cana when He turned water into wine (John 2:1-10). This miracle had far greater implications than just providing wine for the celebration. Jesus was making a powerful prophetic statement about His wedding at the end of the age. Just as He did in Cana, Jesus has saved His best wine for last (John 2:10). That's why, at this moment in history, the Holy Spirit is actively preparing a bride for Jesus from every tribe, tongue, people, and nation.

When Jesus was *first* introduced to the nation of Israel, John the Baptist presented Him as a Bridegroom (John 3:29). A short time later, Jesus revealed for the *first* time how his servants should minister when He referred to them as "friends of the bridegroom" (Matt. 9:15, NKJV). When Jesus corrected the seven churches of Asia Minor, His *first* message was a call to return to first love, which shows His jealous love for His bride (Rev. 2:1-7).

Now let's look at some *lasts*. In Jesus' *last* public message, He told a parable about the Father's eternal plan to have a wedding for His Son (Matt. 22:1-14). Through this parable, we see that God's eternal purpose is to prepare a suitable wife for Jesus. This *last* message to the world was critical—a wedding is coming, and we must get ready.

In one of Jesus' *last* messages to His followers, He said that "the kingdom of heaven will be comparable to ten virgins, who took their lamps and went out to meet the bridegroom" (Matt. 25:1). Once again, we see the theme of a wedding, a feast, and a marriage set in the context of Jesus' second coming.

In one of Jesus' *last* prayers, He prayed that we would be with Him forever, see His glory, be one with Him, love Him with the same love that the Father has for Him, and that He would live inside of us (John 17:22-26). This is an up-close-and-personal look at the burning desires in the heart of Jesus. He wants a bride who will see His beauty, be intimate with Him, and love Him with Spirit-empowered passion.

In the *last* book of the Bible, the book of Revelation, John is shown the marriage supper of the Lamb (Rev. 19:7-10). He sees the New Jerusalem "coming down out of heaven from God, made ready as a bride adorned for her husband" (Rev. 21:2).

In the *last* chapter of the *last* book of the Bible, we see how the bride will urge her beloved Bridegroom to return. At the end of the age, the Spirit-empowered church will cry, "Come" (Rev. 22:17). The *last* theme of the Bible is a lovesick bride—not a servant, a minister, or a soldier—crying out for her Bridegroom to return.

After examining how God revealed Himself through what He did first and what He will do last, you see how the Lord has woven His eternal purpose into the fabric of Scripture. From Genesis to

Revelation, the mystery of God's eternal plan to provide His Son with a bride is progressively revealed.

THE ROMANCE OF THE AGES

Have you ever thought about the Bible starting with a wedding and ending with a wedding? Have you ever considered Genesis beginning with the marriage of Adam and Eve and Revelation concluding with the marriage of Jesus and His church?

Much more than a history book, a book of principles and laws, or a book that gives us wisdom, the Scriptures are the ultimate romance novel between Christ and His church. If you look closely, interwoven through the pages of Scripture, in types, shadows, allegories, parables, prophecies, and ageless truths, you see the eternal romance between Jesus and His bride leaping off the pages.

Consider the book of Esther. To the natural eye, this book is a historical narrative, tracing the life of Esther, who was chosen to be queen of Persia after enduring rigorous preparation. Using her royal influence, God used Esther to spare the Jews from annihilation. But reading through the lens of God's eternal purpose, something deeper emerges. You see a prophetic picture of the bride of Christ being prepared for her King. You see a beautiful allegory of how we are made ready for our end-time and eternal partnership with Jesus.

Ruth is another example. The romance between Ruth and Boaz is a heartwarming story of tragedy turned to triumph. Ruth loses her husband in Moab and decides to return to Israel with Naomi. As the story goes, Ruth ends up marrying Boaz, who is Naomi's wealthy relative. Through their lineage come David and Jesus.

When the veil is lifted from our eyes and we see through the lens of God's eternal purpose, however, another storyline emerges. Once again, there is a type and shadow of the romance of the ages. Ruth portrays the bride of Christ, through her devotion and loyalty, maturing in bridal love. Ruth pictures our transition from the world system into the harvest fields of our heavenly Redeemer. Like Ruth, the bride of Christ will give birth to God's prophetic promises.

The Song of Solomon also unveils the romance of the ages. If you read this book with an open heart and a sensitive spirit, you can discern the heartbeat of the heavenly Bridegroom. More than a natural romance between Solomon and the Shulammite maiden, this book is an allegory of the bride of Christ and her journey into deep intimacy and partnership with Jesus.

From the opening pages, you see the Bridegroom's deep affection for His bride. Even though her heart is dark, she is lovely to Him. From the banquet hall of joyful love to the mountains of myrrh and the way of the cross, you see that God's grand mission is to set our hearts ablaze with His fire—the fire of His jealous love for His Son. Solomon's romance with the Shulammite, when seen with spiritual eyes, awakens our hearts to the ravishing love that Jesus has for us as His bride.

When the mystery of God's eternal purpose has been revealed to us, we then see the romance of the ages more clearly in the Scriptures. Through types, shadows, allegories, prophecies, and eternal truths, the bridal relationship between Jesus and His church comes into greater focus. We see that the Bible truly is the ultimate romance novel in history!

CREATION REVEALS GOD'S ETERNAL PURPOSE

Reading Genesis 1-2, you see that the creation account appears twice. In chapter one, God reveals *what* He did in creation. He created man and woman in His image. In chapter two, God reveals *why* He did it. He wanted to provide His Son an equally yoked bride. The text doesn't say that explicitly, but rather foreshadows it in the marriage of Adam and Eve.

On the sixth day, God created Adam, put him in the garden, and gave him free access to the beauty and provision of Eden. God told him to freely enjoy all of His creation except for the forbidden fruit from the tree of knowledge. He then instructed Adam to watch over the garden. To keep, cultivate, and expand it. Adam was to take dominion over the entire earth.

But one thing was missing. Adam needed a helpmate suitable for him. The Lord said, "It is not good for the man to be alone; I will make him a helper suitable for him" (Gen. 2:18). How would God do this? He put Adam into a deep sleep, took a rib from his side, and fashioned a woman from it. Eve—Adam's perfect companion who would help him take dominion over the earth—was created (Gen. 1:28). In the words of Adam, Eve was "bone of my bones, and flesh of my flesh" (Gen. 2:23).

What does Adam and Eve's marriage have to do with God's eternal purpose? Paul said that Adam was a "type" of Christ (Rom. 5:14). He also said that Eve foreshadowed the church's relationship to Christ (Eph. 5:31-32).

Just as Eve was made from Adam's side, the church came forth from Christ when the Roman soldier thrust his spear into Jesus' side. As blood and water poured forth, the blood atoned for our sins and the water pointed to the life-giving river of the indwelling Spirit. Now that Pentecost has been fulfilled and the Spirit dwells within His people, the church is "now bone of [His] bones, and flesh of [His] flesh" (Gen. 2:23, emphasis mine). More precisely, we are now spirit of His Spirit, having come forth fully from Christ's side (1 Cor. 6:17).

When we understand that Adam foreshadows Christ and Eve foreshadows His betrothed bride, we begin to see *why* the Father created the heavens and the earth. It was to provide the eternal Son with a suitable helpmate. A wife and eternal companion who would partner with Jesus to take dominion over the earth. A beloved who would advance the kingdom to all creation throughout the endless ages of eternity.

The marriage of Adam and Eve reveals God's eternal purpose to provide His Son with an equally yoked bride.

Another type and shadow, which points to our bridal relationship with Jesus Christ, is the ancient Jewish wedding system. We will look at this in the next chapter.

CHAPTER 24

THE JEWISH WEDDING SYSTEM

Jesus said, "*Then* the kingdom of heaven will be like ten virgins . . . and . . . the bridegroom."[1]

Whenever we see a *then* in Scripture, we should always seek to know *when*. So, let's ask the question: *When* will the kingdom of heaven be like ten virgins seeking the Bridegroom?

To answer this question, we need to go back one chapter and look at what the disciples asked Jesus. Specifically, they wanted to know: "What will be the sign of Your coming, and of the end of the age?" (Matt. 24:3).

Bible translators inserted a chapter break between Matthew 24 and 25, but don't let this fool you. Matthew 25 is a continuation of Jesus' conversation with His disciples, containing His response to their questions about the end times.

Most are familiar with the signs leading to the Lord's return: famines, earthquakes, wars, upheavals, offenses, apostasy, persecution, and the worship of the antichrist. But many have missed the vital connection between the disciples' question in Matthew 24 and Jesus' parables in Matthew 25.

When will the kingdom of heaven be like ten virgins seeking the Bridegroom? At the end of the age, in the days immediately preceding the Lord's return. Since we live at the end of the age, it's important to understand the parable of the ten virgins (Matt. 25:1-13). Understanding this will give us great insight into God's eternal purpose to provide Jesus with an equally yoked bride.

BACKGROUND TO THE PARABLE

To fully grasp this parable, we need to go back in history to examine Jewish wedding customs during Jesus' earthly ministry. These customs provide the context for understanding this parable.

There are five basic steps that comprise the ancient Jewish wedding system:

1. The arrangement of marriage
2. The betrothal ceremony
3. The preparation period between the betrothal and the wedding
4. The wedding ceremony
5. The wedding feast

How do these customs apply to us as the bride of Christ? Let's look at each and see.

1. The Arrangement of Marriage

The first step in the process was the arrangement, called the *Shiddukhin*.[2] This was a time of matchmaking, initiated by the fathers of the bride and groom.

Often, the couple did not know each other before the arrangement. In some cases, they would not have even seen each other before the betrothal ceremony.[3] Even so, the bride-to-be still had to give her approval before the families agreed to the marriage.[4]

Once the selection had been made, the parents prepared the *ketubah*. The *ketubah* was normally a written contract that depicted the terms and conditions of the marriage arrangement, the price to be paid by the groom, the responsibilities and obligations of both parties, and the dowry to be offered by the bride.[5]

Application

If you're a born-again believer, you are the recipient of an arranged marriage. Your heavenly Father so loved the world that He arranged a marriage between His Son and the redeemed from every nation. Now the Father has sent the matchmaker, the Holy Spirit, inviting men and women from every nation to become the bride of Jesus Christ.

After we say "yes" to this invitation, we are introduced to the *ketubah*—the marriage covenant describing the responsibilities and obligations of the bride and groom. When Jesus died on the cross to purchase us as His bride, He demonstrated and fulfilled His part of the *ketubah*. Now He waits for us to fulfill ours.

What are our responsibilities and obligations in our betrothal to Him? Jesus detailed these in the Sermon on the Mount, which can be viewed as the *ketubah* in our marriage to Him. In short, we are to take up our cross and live in obedience to His words by the enabling power of the indwelling Spirit.

2. The Betrothal Ceremony

Once the arrangement was made and the *ketubah* agreed to, the next phase was the betrothal ceremony. To prepare for this, the bride and groom were immersed in water, symbolizing a spiritual cleansing.[6]

The betrothal ceremony was considered an act of purchasing or acquiring a wife.[7] This ceremony included vows promising to get married, the exchange of rings or something else of value, and the sealing of the agreement with a cup of wine.[8] After the ceremony, there was a feast to celebrate the joyful occasion, followed by the bride and groom separating and living at their fathers' houses until the day of the wedding.[9]

After the ceremony, the couple was legally married, even though they didn't have sexual relations.[10] If the couple wanted to separate for any reason, it required a legal divorce.

Application

All who have said "yes" to Jesus Christ have participated in a betrothal ceremony. Paul said, "For I am jealous for you with a godly jealousy; for I betrothed you to one husband, so that to Christ I might present you as a pure virgin" (2 Cor. 11:2).

Our betrothal to Jesus is the romantic equivalent of *justification*. When we believed and received all that Jesus accomplished for us on the cross, the Holy Spirit saved us and came to dwell within us. At that very moment, we were justified and betrothed to Jesus

Christ as His cherished and beloved bride. The righteousness of Christ was imputed to us, and we were declared righteous in God's sight. All of our sins were forgiven and washed away, making us like pure virgins who had never sinned.

As His betrothed bride, we have also partaken in a ritual bath similar to an ancient Jewish bride. Our baptism symbolizes our spiritual cleansing, our separation to our heavenly Bridegroom, and our vow to be prepared for our future wedding.

3. The Preparation Period

The next phase was the betrothal period, a time of preparation which lasted about a year. During this phase, neither the groom nor the bride knew when the wedding would take place. Only the groom's father knew the day and the hour. He was the one who determined the specific time for the groom to go and get his bride.

During the betrothal period, the groom lived in his father's house and prepared a place for the two to live. Normally, this involved adding a room to his father's home.

While the groom was busy building, the bride prepared herself for the upcoming wedding. This typically involved three things. First, the bride was observed for her purity. This custom required at least nine months to pass. This ensured that the bride was not pregnant and it helped assure that she was a virgin.[11]

Second, the bride consecrated herself. She examined everything in her life and changed whatever was necessary in order to be ready for the holy covenant of marriage.[12] Jewish leaders began to use the term *mekadesh* (consecrated) for the act of betrothal. During the betrothal ceremony, the groom would often say to his bride that you are *mekudeshet* (consecrated) unto me.[13] The bride set herself apart from all other relationships and activities. She devoted herself completely to her groom.

Third, the bride made her own wedding garments. Ancient Jewish women did not have the luxury of going to the nearest bridal shop and purchasing a premade dress. They had to spend countless hours making their wedding garments, adorning them with the special touches to make them beautiful.[14]

Application

As the betrothed bride of Christ, we now live in the preparation period. Jesus has gone back to His Father's house to prepare a place for us. Jesus said:

> Do not let your heart be troubled; believe in God, believe also in Me. In My Father's house are many dwelling places; if it were not so, I would have told you; for I go to prepare a place for you. If I go and prepare a place for you, I will come again and receive you to Myself, that where I am, there you may be also. (John 14:2-3)

Like the bridegroom in an ancient Jewish wedding, Jesus is preparing a place for us to dwell. Contrary to popular opinion, however, Jesus is not building a mansion for us in heaven, where we will live independently from the rest of the bride of Christ. Rather, Jesus is preparing the new Jerusalem, which will be the dwelling place of the bride for all eternity (Rev. 21-22).

While Jesus prepares our eternal dwelling place, like an ancient Jewish bride, we are to wait expectantly for His return, make our own wedding garments, and consecrate ourselves exclusively to Him. We are to make ourselves ready as we anticipate our eternal destiny with our beloved Bridegroom.

Just as the betrothal is akin to justification, this preparation period is the romantic equivalent of *sanctification*.

Revelation 19:7-9 states:

> Let us rejoice and be glad and give the glory to Him, for the marriage of the Lamb has come and His bride has made herself ready. It was given to her to clothe herself in fine linen, bright and clean; for the fine linen is the righteous acts of the saints. Then he said to me, "Write, 'Blessed are those who are invited to the marriage supper of the Lamb.'" And he said to me, "These are true words of God." (Rev. 19:7-9)

Notice whose responsibility it is to make the bride ready. It doesn't say that Jesus makes his bride ready. It says, "His bride has made herself ready."

Like an ancient Jewish bride, we are responsible to consecrate ourselves and make our own wedding garments. And, much to Dave's relief, these aren't made of satin and lace. Our "garments" are the righteous acts that we do in response to our justification. These righteous acts are our numerous responses of obedience, motivated by our love for Jesus and empowered by the Holy Spirit's grace.

In making our wedding dress, the Lord will not do our part, and we certainly can't do His part. Though we are utterly dependent upon His grace, we are to pursue grace, receive grace, and live by grace so that we will be ready for our marriage to Jesus. This is what the sanctification process is all about.

4. The Wedding Ceremony

Toward the end of the yearlong betrothal period, the bride waited with great expectancy for the groom to come and take her to the wedding. Even late in the evening, the bride and her wedding party kept their oil lamps burning, just in case it was time for the wedding to take place.

The day of the ceremony was a surprise to both the bride and groom.[15] When the bridegroom was asked the date of the wedding, he could only say something like, "No man knows except my father."[16]

When the time was right, the groom's father initiated the ceremony. At the father's decree, the groom and his wedding party left his house to get his bride. As they traveled, the friends of the bridegroom shouted, "Behold, the bridegroom comes!" This was followed by the blast of shofars.

When the groom and groomsmen found the bride dressed and ready for the wedding, they traveled back together to the groom's house, where the wedding canopy or *huppah* awaited.

The wedding ceremony, or the *nissuin*, was performed under the *huppah*. The vows made during the betrothal ceremony were completed in the marriage ceremony. Once again, the wedding ceremony was sealed with a cup of wine, indicating the great joy that would accompany the festive celebration.

After the ceremony, the couple consummated their marriage with sexual relations and lived together as husband and wife from that point forward.[17]

Application

Our betrothal will soon be coming to an end, for both the Scriptures and the signs of the times make this clear. Soon, we can expect the Father to say to His Son, "Go and get Your bride, for the marriage of the Lamb has come." Then, the friends of the Bridegroom will shout, "Behold, the Bridegroom comes" (Matt. 25:6). The shofars will sound, the wedding will commence, and the bride will be with her Bridegroom forever.

Just as an ancient Jewish wedding was held under the *huppah*, it's likely to be the same in our marriage to Christ. Speaking of the Millennial Kingdom, Isaiah said, "In that day the Branch of the LORD [Jesus] will be beautiful and glorious. . . . then the LORD will create over the whole area of Mount Zion [in Jerusalem] and over her assemblies a cloud by day, even smoke, and the brightness of a flaming fire by night; *for over all the glory will be a canopy* [chuppah]" (Isa. 4:2-5, emphasis mine).

Like an ancient Jewish wedding, we too will be married to Jesus Christ under the *huppah* as the Kingdom Age commences.

5. The Wedding Feast

The wedding feast was the highlight of the wedding ceremony. It was much more extensive than what Westerners are accustomed to today. It consisted of seven full days of food, music, dancing, and celebration.[18]

The primary purpose of the wedding feast was to honor the groom. All of the guests were expected to compose poems or sing songs to him. The bride honored him by adorning herself with the beautiful garments she made during the betrothal period. The bridegroom then showcased his beautiful bride to those celebrating their holy matrimony.

After the wedding feast, the bride and groom lived together as husband and wife for the rest of their lives.

Application
Following the wedding ceremony of Jesus and His bride, there will be the most amazing wedding feast in history. John said, "Blessed are those who are invited to the marriage supper of the Lamb" (Rev. 19:9). Only the Lord knows how glorious this event will be, but I certainly want to participate in it as the wife of the Lamb.

When this glorious wedding feast is over, the wife of the Lamb will partner with Jesus for the endless ages of eternity, expanding His kingdom into all creation.

PUTTING IT ALL TOGETHER

Seen through the lens of this Jewish wedding custom, the parable of the ten virgins makes more sense. As depicted in this parable, the kingdom of heaven is like the betrothal period in an ancient Jewish wedding.

Jesus is the Bridegroom. We are His betrothed bride. Jesus paid the ultimate price to purchase us as His wife, and we now have the responsibility to give ourselves fully to Him.

The Bridegroom is away at His Father's house, preparing the new Jerusalem as our eternal dwelling place. Like an ancient Jewish bride, we are responsible to make our own wedding dress. We have an obligation to sever all allegiances with the world, consecrate ourselves fully to Him, separate from every other lover, and prepare for our upcoming marriage to the Lamb of God. Jesus, our jealous Bridegroom, will not tolerate any rivals in our hearts.

The question for us is how will we respond? Will we be like the foolish virgins who allowed their oil supply to diminish, until their lamps went out? Or will we pay the price to purchase extra oil from the dealers? Will we make Jesus our first love, our first priority in life?

There will never be an easier time to know the Lord intimately. There will never be an easier time to make ourselves ready for the greatest event in human history—the marriage supper of the Lamb.

I have discovered that knowing the Lord intimately and preparing myself for Him is easier when I understand my betrothal to Jesus Christ. This is what we'll dive into next.

CHAPTER 25

BETROTHED TO CHRIST

If you ever feel like you're waiting for more . . . like something better is right around the corner but just out of reach . . . you're experiencing the ache of this age. We are in a betrothal period, and the innate desire of our spirits is to be united with our Bridegroom. As the betrothed, however, this is an important season, and understanding our identity as the soon-to-be wife of the Lamb is paramount to our preparation.

Let's unravel six truths about this identity, which reveal our role in preparing ourselves for our Bridegroom.

1. We are pure virgins.

Paul said, "I am jealous for you with a godly jealousy; for I betrothed you to one husband, so that to Christ I might present you as a pure virgin" (2 Cor. 11:2, NASB). There's so much revelation packed into this verse that we could spend a whole chapter on it. But for the sake of time, let's focus on how our betrothal to Christ made us "a pure virgin."

When you read this verse straight from the NASB translation, it seems like betrothal comes first, and then later, through a process of sanctification, we become a "pure virgin." But when you analyze the Greek, this verse should read more like the *Young's Literal Translation* put it: "For I am zealous for you with zeal of God, for I did betroth you to one husband, a pure virgin, to present to Christ." In other words, when we were betrothed to Christ at salvation, justification made us like a "pure virgin" in His eyes.

The Greek word for *virgin* in 2 Corinthians 11:2 means "a marriageable maiden."[1] The idea is that the finished work of the cross made us eligible for marriage to Jesus Christ. But it did not make us instantly flawless. Becoming a holy and blameless bride will take a lifetime of sanctification by the Holy Spirit's enabling grace.

Perhaps the following illustration will help this sink in. Suppose there was a new invention that could restore a woman's virginity. All you had to do was take a pill and a woman's body would be just like a virgin's.

Now imagine a wealthy king who fell madly in love with a prostitute. But not just any prostitute. This prostitute had been in the business for many years and had slept with hundreds of men. No one wanted to marry her because of her sin, shame, and defilement. Her immoral lifestyle disqualified her for marriage, especially to a king. Even if the king wanted to marry her, the law of the land would prohibit him, for he is only permitted to marry a certified virgin.

When the lovesick king discovers this miracle-working pill, he's overjoyed. He can finally marry the woman of his dreams. Sure enough, after giving her the pill, the prostitute becomes a virgin. All of her sin, shame, guilt, and condemnation is instantly washed away. She is now eligible for marriage. The rest is history. The king and the virgin marry and live happily ever after.

We were like this prostitute, defiled by other lovers. We were covered from head to toe in sin, shame, guilt, and condemnation. We were enslaved to lust, corrupted by greed, and imprisoned by selfishness. In our dark and defiled condition, King Jesus fell head-over-heels in love with us. In fact, He loved us before the foundation of the world.

In the eternal councils of the Godhead, Jesus foreknew us, loved us with an unrelenting love, and began His pursuit of us. In His eyes, we were a pearl of great price, and He forsook all of His majesty and royal splendor to purchase us with His blood. Jesus endured the pain and shame of the cross by looking toward the reward of having us as His bride (Heb. 12:2).

Justification is similar to the miracle-working pill in our fictional story. The shed blood of Jesus Christ has removed our sin, shame, guilt, and condemnation. Jesus' very own righteousness has also been imputed to us, removing our adulterous past and transforming us into pure virgins who are eligible for marriage to the King.

Because of the finished work of the cross, we are no longer defined by our sin, shortcomings, failures, weaknesses, selfishness, or defilement. Christ's imputed righteousness has destroyed the power of sin and quieted the voice of condemnation and accusation. Though we are "dark" with sin, in the eyes of our beloved Bridegroom, we are "lovely" to Him (Song 1:5, NKJV). Jesus is madly in love with us, His betrothed bride.

2.   We are one with our heavenly Bridegroom.

In 1 Corinthians 6:15, Paul asked the question, "Do you not know that your bodies are members of Christ?" Two verses later, Paul said, "The one who joins himself to the Lord is one spirit with Him" (1 Cor. 6:17).

In short, we are members of Christ's body because we have been joined to Jesus Christ through our spiritual union with the Holy Spirit. Just as a baby is connected to its mother through the umbilical cord, we are connected to Jesus Christ, the head of the body in heaven, through our vital life union with the indwelling Spirit.

Now let's connect this truth to our bridal relationship with Jesus.

As Paul unveiled the mystery of the bride of Christ, he declared that "we are members of His body" (Eph. 5:30). Immediately after this statement, Paul quoted Genesis 2:24: "For this reason a man shall leave his father and his mother, and be joined to his wife; and they shall become one flesh." But Paul was not referring to earthly marriage. He was "speaking with reference to Christ and the church" (Eph. 5:32).

Here's the point: If you are born again, your union with Jesus Christ the Bridegroom already began when the Holy Spirit came to dwell within you. Thankfully, you don't have to wait until you go to heaven to experience union with Christ the Bridegroom. You have already been joined spirit-to-Spirit with Jesus Christ now.

Just as a husband and wife are joined together as one flesh, you are joined together with your heavenly Bridegroom as one spirit. Though this union will certainly increase after our marriage to Him, we can have a real, heart-satisfying, life-transforming relationship with Jesus all day every day. We can know Jesus Christ intimately through the indwelling Spirit. We can fellowship and commune with our heavenly Bridegroom at any moment. We are meant to live in this reality every day of our lives.

When this truth becomes a personal revelation, our lives will never be the same.

3. Jesus nourishes and cherishes us.

Speaking about the bride of Christ, Paul said that Jesus "nourishes and cherishes" us "because we are members of His body" (Eph. 5:29-30). Just as we take care of our bodies by eating healthy, exercising, and getting plenty of sleep, Paul said that Christ takes care of His body, His beloved bride, by nourishing and cherishing her.

The words *nourish* and *cherish* provide great insight into the tender heart of our loving Bridegroom. Nourish, in this context, means "to nourish up to maturity."[2] This word paints the picture of a loving mother longing for her baby to grow into a mature adult. The mother carefully ensures that her child gets the proper food, sleep, and rest. And as the child grows up, the mother continues nurturing her child to full maturity, providing the proper education and home environment, instilling in them a sound work ethic and the ability to distinguish between right and wrong, and equipping them to interact socially with their peers.

In the same way, Jesus is lovingly committed to our maturity. From the moment we're born again until the day we go to be with Him, Jesus' eyes are upon us, His beloved bride. He continually nourishes us to maturity, providing us with truth, revelation, loving correction, and the proper environment for growth. In His jealousy, Jesus disciplines us until we are transformed into His image.

At the same time, Jesus *cherishes* us. In the Greek, this word means "to warm, keep warm, to cherish with tender love, to foster with tender care."[3] It conveys the idea of "birds covering their young with their feathers."[4] What a heartwarming picture! In His great love for us, Jesus holds us close to His heart. He tenderly washes us with His Word so that we will be sanctified and prepared for our marriage to Him. He lovingly leads us, directing us to Himself. Jesus will do whatever it takes to protect and care for us because we are His beloved bride. Our Bridegroom's "gentleness makes" us great in Him (Psa. 18:35).

Jesus also loves to speak into our potential through His eyes of faith. Like the bridegroom in the Song of Solomon, Jesus tenderly speaks to His bride based on her budding virtues. He calls us beautiful and lovely, even though there is darkness in our hearts and souls. He lets us know that we ravish His heart, even when we stumble and fall. Jesus loves to tell us that we precious and priceless to Him.

4.   We are Jesus' beloved.

Augustine said, "If God is love, then there must be in Him a Lover, a Beloved, and a Spirit of love; for no love is conceivable without a Lover and a Beloved."[5]

In eternity past, the Father was the Lover and He poured out His passion upon His Son, the Beloved. Jesus alluded to this when He said to His Father, "You loved Me before the foundation of the world" (John 17:24).

Though the Son poured out His love back to the Father, He did not have a beloved to whom He could be the source of love. In this highly specific sense, the Son was somewhat like Adam, without a beloved of His own to unleash His love upon. The eternal Son yearned for His own beloved, but there was no "helper suitable for him" (Gen. 2:18).

So, figuratively speaking, Jesus was put into a deep sleep on the cross somewhat like Adam, and as the Roman spear pierced His side, blood and water poured forth.[6] As Adam's rib formed his bride, the blood and water formed Christ's bride. The blood cleansed us from all sin and defilement, while the water pointed to the life-giving water of the Spirit that would dwell within us, making us Christ's very own possession.

Now that the bride has come forth from Christ's side, the eternal Son is the Lover and we are His beloved. He is the source of love, and we are the recipient and the responder to His love. "We love," John wrote, "because He first loved us" (1 John 4:19). As Mike Bickle likes to say, "It takes God to love God."[7] Only to the degree that we have experienced the Lover's burning heart of love, can we, as His beloved, return that love back to Him.

Jesus said, "Just as the Father has loved Me, I have also loved you" (John 15:9). As the Father is the Lover and the Son is the Beloved in their relationship, Jesus is the Lover and we are the beloved in our relationship with Christ.

If you don't grasp anything else, please know that Jesus loves you deeply, for you are His beloved, cherished, and betrothed bride.

No matter your past or present, let this truth sink in: You are the beloved of Jesus Christ. You are the object of His affection. You are His cherished one.

5. Jesus sanctifies us with the Word.

Paul said, "Husbands, love your wives, just as Christ also loved the church and gave Himself up for her, so that He might sanctify her, having cleansed her by the washing of water with the word, that He might present to Himself the church in all her glory, having no spot or wrinkle or any such thing; but that she would be holy and blameless" (Eph. 5:25-27).

Although the bride is called to make herself ready, Jesus initiates this process of sanctification by washing us with His Word. Through the Spirit-breathed Scriptures, Jesus cleanses His bride from sin, defilement, shame, condemnation, selfishness, and strongholds. Jesus transforms the church by washing her with the water of the Word.

Jesus speaks His Word to us personally, but He also speaks to us through "friends of the Bridegroom." These are ministers whose sole purpose is to prepare the church for marriage to Jesus Christ. John the Baptist and the disciples all functioned as friends of the Bridegroom (John 3:29; Matt. 9:15). Their driving purpose was to see their best friend's bride made ready. They knew the bride of the Lamb did not belong to them, but to Jesus. Their role was to speak the Word of God over her until she was spotless, blameless, and holy.

All preachers and teachers have this same call. They are to

speak the Word to Jesus' bride in the power of the Spirit, so that she will be holy and blameless.

Whether Jesus speaks His Word to us personally or through messengers, we have to understand the three ways that Jesus secs His betrothed bride, for He will typically speak to us in one of these three ways.

First, He sees us in our legal position. That is, He sees us righteous, as overcomers, and dead to sin, to self, and to the Law. Jesus sees us in our constituted legal position because of the finished work of the cross.

One of our greatest problems is failing to see who we are through the finished work of the cross. We plead with God to do in us what He has already done. In such cases, the Lord whispers to us, "It is finished. Stop striving for what I have already done. Instead, believe that what I accomplished for you on the cross is enough."

When this becomes a personal revelation to us, our striving ceases. We rest in confidence that in Christ we are righteous, more than conquerors, and are dead to sin, self, and the Law. Because the same Spirit who raised Jesus from the dead dwells within us, we know that we can do all things through Christ who strengthens us (Phil. 4:13).

The second way that Jesus sees us is by our potential. The Lord called Abraham the father of many nations *while he was still in his barrenness.* Jesus called Peter a rock, though he was still unstable. In the same way, the Lord sees who we can become because of the indwelling Spirit. He sees our potential through His eyes of faith and calls "those things which be not as though they were" (Rom. 4:17, KJV).

Jesus sanctifies us by speaking into our potential. He knows who we can become because He knows who dwells within us. Jesus knows that we will become be a rock even though we're beset with weaknesses. Jesus knows that we will be a father of many nations even though we are barren.

The third way that Jesus sees us is in our actual condition. Our unrighteous thoughts, desires, motives, and actions are not hidden from His eyes. Revelation 2-3 makes this clear. Because of His jealous love, Jesus speaks the truth in love. Though we might prefer the truth to be sugar-coated, Jesus' words are like the thrusts of a sword that divide between soul and spirit (Heb. 4:12). Though His words are penetrating and sometimes painful, Jesus always speaks with grace. His goal is to remove everything hindering us from fulfilling our eternal destiny.

Though Jesus knows our legal position and our potential, His eyes of fire pierce through our fig leaves. There is no hiding. Jesus thrusts His sharp, two-edged sword into us, exposing the lies that we believe, holding us captive.

Does this hurt? You better believe it does! But Jesus always speaks the truth in love so that we don't sell our birthright like Esau for a "pot of stew." Read Revelation 2-3 and you'll see that Jesus doesn't mince words with us. He speaks the truth plainly so that we will overcome whatever entangles us. He speaks into our actual condition so that we will purify ourselves and make ourselves ready to be His eternal wife.

When Jesus speaks the truth to us, His grace always comes alongside, giving us the power and ability to receive and obey the truth. Yet Jesus never minimizes the truth, dilutes the truth, dances around the truth, or sugarcoats the truth because of His grace. Rather, what God's truth requires, God's grace supplies. What God's truth demands, God's grace provides. Grace never waters down the truth but empowers us to fully obey the truth with all of our hearts, minds, souls, and strength.

Whether through preachers, teachers, authors, mentors, worship leaders, prophets, or alone time in the secret place, Jesus sanctifies us with His Word by speaking to us through these three perspectives.

6.   We are to make ourselves ready.

Recall that a first-century Jewish bride was responsible for making her own wedding dress. She would spend hours creating her wedding garments, stitching them together thread by thread. As she waited for her bridegroom, she would inspect her dress carefully for stains, wrinkles, or blemishes.

Imagine if a Jewish bridegroom showed up to take his bride to the wedding and she didn't have on wedding clothes. What if she was dressed in normal attire or her wedding garments were only partially complete? The bridegroom's heart would be shattered into a thousand pieces. The love of his life demonstrated by her actions that she didn't love him like he loved her. She didn't take her marriage to him seriously.

The same will be true for us if we don't make ourselves ready. Like a bride in an ancient Jewish wedding, we are to make our own wedding dress while the bridegroom is away. Revelation 19:7-8 states, "Let us rejoice and be glad and give the glory to Him, for the marriage of the Lamb has come and His bride has made herself ready. It was given to her to clothe herself in fine linen, bright and clean; for the fine linen is the righteous acts of the saints."

Notice that the "righteous acts" are in the plural. This signifies a lifestyle of love-motivated obedience to God's Word—including the moral Law, the words of Jesus, and the writings of the apostles. These righteous acts are our numerous responses of obedience, motivated by our love for Jesus and empowered by the Holy Spirit's grace.

Our response to our justification will be our wedding clothes for all eternity. The righteous acts that we do from the gift of imputed and imparted righteousness will be our wedding garments forever.

Paul said that we are to "work out [our] salvation with fear and trembling" (Phil. 2:12, emphasis mine). This means that we work out what the Holy Spirit has already worked into us. In other words, we work *from* righteousness not *for* righteousness. We work *from* love not *for* love. We work *from* acceptance not *for* acceptance. In other words, making ourselves ready as the bride of Christ should flow out of our love for Jesus, *after* experiencing His unrelenting love for us.

Think about it for a minute. Have you ever met a bride who got ready for her wedding begrudgingly, motivated by fear, condemnation, obligation, guilt, and shame? Most brides get ready for their wedding day with incomparable joy, bliss, and an excitement that rivals little kids at Christmas. That being the case, why do we, as the bride of Christ, often make ourselves ready with dead religious works that are motivated by condemnation, guilt, and shame?

Experiencing Jesus' unrelenting love for us, as His cherished and beloved bride, is the catalyst that empowers us to make ourselves ready—not fear, condemnation, religious burdens, or man-made obligations. We want to be ready for Him simply because we love Him so much, and we want to be worthy of His heart's desire.

Revelation 19:7 states that the bride makes herself ready. Though Jesus initiates this process of sanctification, some mistakenly rely on God's sovereignty in a non-biblical way. They "trust" God to do the role that He has assigned to *us*. The Holy Spirit is "the Helper" not "the Doer." He will do His part, but He expects us to do ours, as well.

Paul said, "Just as you have always obeyed . . . work out your salvation with fear and trembling; for it is God who is at work in you, both to will and to work for His good pleasure" (Phil. 2:12-13). Here we see the division of labor in sanctification. God is already at work in us, but we are still responsible to respond to His prior work with obedience.

God has a part, and we have a part. In response to God's grace, we are called to take up our cross, put to death our flesh, obey, run, fight, press on, endure, discipline ourselves, get back up when we fall, live by the Spirit, do good works, confess our sins, repent if necessary, and persevere. All of this is our response to God's grace. As God puts new desires into our hearts, we are responsible to obey.

Jesus' Inheritance in the Saints

So, what we see is that God's eternal purpose is to provide Jesus with an inheritance in the saints, and this inheritance is an equally yoked bride, who is consecrated, devoted, pure, and passionately in love with Him (Eph. 1:18).

Every born-again believer has been betrothed to Christ as His bride. This means we are like pure virgins in His eyes, we have become one spirit with Him, and Jesus now nourishes and cherishes us in His tender love. In our relationship with Christ, Jesus is the

Lover and source of love, and we are the beloved, the recipient, and the responder to His love. To prepare us for our wedding to Him, Jesus washes us with His Word, cleansing us from sin, shame, self-ishness, and strongholds.

Seeing Jesus' great love, the question is: How will you respond? Since this age is like the betrothal period of an ancient Jewish wedding, what are you doing to prepare for your Groom? Will you make your own wedding dress, severing ties with every other lover that vies for your devotion? Will you sanctify yourself for Him alone? Or when He comes, will you be a foolish virgin, who started the sanctification process but didn't finish, leaving your wedding dress partially complete? When He comes, will He see your love for Him demonstrated by your righteous acts?

As His betrothed bride, the only response worthy of Him is to join together with the Holy Spirit and say, "Come" (Rev. 22:17).

Now that we understand the Son's inheritance in an equally yoked bride, it's time to look at the Spirit's inheritance in the saints. As we will see, the Spirit yearns for a temple that He can fill, a house in which He can dwell, and a body that He can possess and bring to maturity.

PART 7

The Spirit's Inheritance in the Saints

Before time and creation, God determined to place the Spirit of His Son into His people. Part 7 looks at the Holy Spirit's inheritance, which is a temple that He fills, a house in which He dwells, and a body that He possesses and brings to Christ-like maturity.

CHAPTER 26

A SPIRIT-FILLED TEMPLE

So far, as we have expounded upon "the glory of His inheritance in the saints," we have focused on the Father's and the Son's inheritance in His people (Eph. 1:18). As we have seen, the Father will have a family of mature, Christ-like sons who graduate from the school of sonship unto adoption and inherit eternal intimacy, eternal authority, and eternal glory. Likewise, the Son will have an equally yoked bride who will partner with Him to expand the kingdom for the endless ages of eternity.

With this in mind, we will now look at the Holy Spirit's inheritance in the saints. Namely, the Holy Spirit will have a temple that He fills, a house in which He dwells, and a body that He possesses and brings to full maturity. This can be summarized by the phrase *corporate fullness.*

As we saw in Chapters 17-18, individual fullness begins when we receive a personal revelation of the indwelling Spirit. We then experience greater measures of the Spirit as we allow Him to make His home in our hearts, abide in Christ, decrease so that Christ can increase, pursue internal intimacy, and obey the Word.

But make no mistake about it: God is not content to have a scattered group of saints who have individual fullness. His ultimate intention is for those who have experienced the full release of the Spirit to be fit together as living stones into a dwelling place of God's Spirit. This is meant to start in local churches throughout the earth, culminating in the global church experiencing corporate fullness at the end of the age.

For this to happen, there must first be individual fullness. Paul made this clear when He described the body of Christ at the end of Ephesians 1, writing, "And He put all things in subjection under His feet, and gave Him as head over all things to the church, which is His body, the fullness of Him who fills all in all" (Eph. 1:22-23).

Here's the idea: The many-membered body is intended to come into "the fullness" of Christ. Yet for this to happen, the One who is "in all" of the individual members must be the One who "fills all" of the individual members. Until the individual members of the body are filled unto fullness with the life and presence of Christ, the fullness of the body will be limited. Therefore, individual fullness must precede corporate fullness. That's why we laid the groundwork for individual fullness in Chapters 17-18. Now, in Part 7, we will look at corporate fullness.

A Temple That the Spirit Fills

Living in the twenty-first century, we don't know the full weight of being God's temple. To the Jew living in the first century, the temple was the center of culture, religion, politics, and life itself. The temple meant everything to ancient Israel. That's why Paul's statement that we are "a temple of God and that the Spirit of God dwells" in us is so profound (1 Cor. 3:16).

Do you realize what happened at your conversion? The Spirit of God came into your spirit, raised your spirit from the dead, and made you His temple. Just as the ark of the covenant contained God's glory and dwelt in the holy of holies in Solomon's temple, the very same glory of God came into your spirit the day you were born again.

Amazingly, our spirits have become the dwelling place of God in the earth! God's glory has literally taken up permanent residence within our spirits in seed form. Undoubtedly, when Paul told the Corinthians that they were a temple of the living God, he had the glory of God in mind. Inside every born-again believer resides the fiery presence of God's glory. Obviously, that doesn't mean we have the *fullness* of God's glory, which will cause heaven and earth to disintegrate when unveiled (Rev. 20:11). But it does mean that we have the first fruits of His glory—and that's significant (Eph. 1:14; Rom. 8:23).[1]

THREE PARTS OF THE TEMPLE

God's Old Covenant temple had three parts: the outer court, the holy place, and the holy of holies. Likewise, God's New Covenant temple also has three parts: the body, the soul, and the spirit (1 Thess. 5:23). Our bodies are like the outer court, visible for all to see. Our souls, with our mind, will, and emotions, are like the holy place, enlightened by the presence of God in our spirits. And the innermost place within us, behind the veil so-to-speak, lies the holy of holies. Here in our spirits, where no light has ever penetrated and the naked eye has never seen, dwells God's glory. Our spirits are the secret place of the Most High, where we meet with God and commune with Him. Our spirits are like the ark of the covenant, the container that houses God's glory.

To ancient Israel, the ark of the covenant was the place where God spoke (Exod. 25:22). It was considered an essential weapon in their military efforts against the enemy (1 Sam. 4:3). And it was the centerpiece of David's tabernacle, where worshipers ascribed glory and honor to God twenty-four hours a day, seven days a week (1 Chron. 6:31, 37).

When the ark of the covenant was placed in the temple of Dagon, the Philistine god, God's glory caused Dagon to break into pieces (1 Sam. 5:2-4). The ark of the covenant, when it was placed in the house of Obed-edom for three months, released great blessings to him and his entire household (2 Sam. 6:11-12).

Because our spirits are like the ark of the covenant that contain God's glory, we can hear God's voice, overcome the evil one, commune with God at any moment, and experience great blessings. It also means that we carry God's presence wherever we go.

When we go to the grocery store, we carry God. When we go to work, we carry God. When we go to school, we carry God. No matter what we do or where we go, we are carriers of God's presence because of the indwelling Spirit.

Let this truth sink in: We don't just carry our Bibles or even a life-changing teaching about God. We carry God Himself, for we are temples of the living God.

The Corporate Temple

Though wonderful truths, there's something far greater than individual temples, scattered and disconnected. Paul, reaching back into the eternal council, revealed that God's ultimate intention was for us to become a corporate temple.

Paul said, "So then you are no longer strangers and aliens, but you are fellow citizens with the saints, and are of God's household, having been built on the foundation of the apostles and prophets, Christ Jesus Himself being the cornerstone, in whom the whole building, being fitted together, is growing into a holy temple in the Lord, in whom you also are being built together into a dwelling of God in the Spirit" (Eph. 2:19-22).

Paul knew that individual fullness was only the beginning of God's eternal purpose. Corporate fullness was His ultimate aim.

As individual temples filled with the Spirit, the Lord intends for us to be "fitted together" and to grow "into a holy temple in the Lord." This is God's vision for every local gathering of believers. He wants every local church to become "a dwelling of God in the Spirit." Undoubtedly, Paul is not thinking outer court or holy place. He has the holy of holies in mind, the place where God's glory resides in ever-increasing measures.

The Holy of Holies

Let me ask you an honest question. Do you know of any local church where God's Spirit dwells in such fullness that it's comparable to the holy of holies? If you answered yes, let me follow up with another question. Are people who live in compromise and sin in this church falling down dead?

Here's the point: What we can get away with in the outer court and the holy place will get us killed in the holy of holies.

When God's glory rested on the church in the book of Acts, you couldn't get away with anything. If you lied, you died, just like Ananias and Sapphira (Acts 5:1-11). When a local church truly becomes a holy of holies dwelling place in the Spirit, unrepentant sinners could literally die.

Isaiah said, "Sinners in Zion are terrified; trembling has seized the godless. Who among us can live with the consuming fire? Who among us can live with continual burning? He who walks righteously and speaks with sincerity, he who rejects unjust gain and shakes his hands so that they hold no bribe; he who stops his ears from hearing about bloodshed and shuts his eyes from looking upon evil" (Isa. 33:14-15). In Scripture, Zion is the holy-of-holies dwelling place of God's glory.

When a local gathering of living stones becomes a holy-of-holies-dwelling place of God's Spirit, look out! The consuming fire of God's manifest presence will consume those living in compromise. His fire will burn those who live unrighteously, who fail to speak the truth, who gossip, and who let their eyes look upon evil.

If God's glory were to come to the church today, with the church living in such compromise, there would likely be mass casualties. Even so, God's ultimate intention is for local churches to become holy-of-holies dwelling places in the Spirit. This eternal purpose will be fulfilled before the Lord returns. The Holy Spirit will have a corporate temple that He fills with His glory at the end of the age.

The Glory of the New Covenant

As this chapter ends, I want to give you a vision for the fullness of Christ's glory in this age.[2] We have access to so much more of God's glory than we are presently experiencing. The end-time church who witnesses the return of Christ will have this glory, for Paul said that Christ will present to Himself the church in all of her glory (Eph. 5:27). As explained in a previous chapter, this is a promise for the church that applies this side of heaven.

For the Lord to have a glorious bride before He returns, we must be transformed at a deep level, from glory to glory, by the Spirit (2 Cor. 3:18). This requires God's glory in ever-increasing measures.

So, my question is: Why not us? Why not now?

Paul said emphatically that the glory Moses experienced under the Old Covenant, which caused His face to shine so brightly that the Israelites couldn't look at him, is inferior to the glory that we can experience by the Holy Spirit in the New Covenant. Paul said, "How will the ministry of the Spirit fail to be even more with glory?" (2 Cor. 3:8). He went further and said, "If the ministry of condemnation has glory, much more does the ministry of righteousness abound in glory" (2 Cor. 3:9).

Based upon Paul's language, he only tasted of this glory in the first-century, though he knew by the Spirit there was more glory for the church to experience this side of eternity (2 Cor. 3:12). I don't know about you, but this challenges me to contend for more of the Spirit's glory. If this type of glory is possible in the New Covenant, let's press in for more. Let's pursue the fullness of the Spirit in this age. Let's cry out for the greater glory of the Spirit before Jesus returns.

CHAPTER 27

GOD'S SPIRITUAL HOUSE

The Lord yearns to give us much more than sporadic visitations, seasons of revival, and various moves of the Spirit. His eternal purpose is to make the church His glorious habitation. The Spirit wants a temple that He fills and a spiritual house in which He dwells.

Peter said, "You also, as living stones, are being built up as a spiritual house for a holy priesthood, to offer up spiritual sacrifices acceptable to God through Jesus Christ" (1 Peter 2:5). The Holy Spirit's inheritance in the saints is a spiritual house built with living stones. A house where He can dwell continually in ever-increasing measures of glory.

Looking at Peter's statement, we see two important phrases that describe the Holy Spirit's inheritance. These are: "living stones" and "a spiritual house." So, how are we to become both?

LIVING STONES FIT TOGETHER

God's spiritual house is built with living stones, not dead stones. Living stones have been born of the Spirit. They have Christ's indwelling life. They have experienced a spiritual resurrection and have been joined to Christ spirit-to-Spirit.

Not only do living stones have the indwelling Spirit, they allow the Spirit to have *them*. Alive with Christ's resurrection life, living stones live in full surrender to the Spirit. They continually allow the Spirit's fullness to be released into their hearts, souls, and bodies. They are possessed by the indestructible life of Christ.

God only builds His spiritual house with living stones. He never builds it with dead stones.

Dead stones don't have Christ's indwelling life, or they keep His life suppressed through selfish and carnal living. Dead stones will never be the building blocks of God's spiritual house.

In our seeker-friendly church culture, many regular attenders aren't even born of the Spirit. Others have not submitted their lives to the government of the Lamb. For the most part, God's spiritual house can't be built in the current Christian religious system.

For that reason, the Lord is calling many living stones to leave churches that operate under the government of man, and to seek God in churches that operate outside the camp of the mainline religious system (Heb. 13:13). In this hour, there's a cry from God's heart, "Come out of her, my people" (Rev. 18:4). It's time for God's living stones to leave the Babylonian ways of the institutional church.

Those who respond to this invitation will likely go through a season of intense preparation. For some, it might even mean a season in the wilderness. During this preparation process, the Lord will shape and mold them into spiritual men and women. He will cut away the carnal and soulish mixture, fashioning them into the living stones of His spiritual house. These will be filled with the Spirit unto fullness and will be fit together with other like-minded living stones, forming God's spiritual house. A house that He will fill with His glory.

Before moving on, let me state clearly that I am not advising you to abandon the local church. I will expound upon the great need of the local church shortly. Here's what I'm suggesting: If your church is not preparing you to be the Lord's inheritance, you might want to ask the Lord if He wants to plant you in a different church. Specifically, a local church gathering where the leadership is truly under the government of the Lord Jesus Christ, the true head of the church. I'm encouraging you to find a local church where the leadership is more concerned with following the Lamb than they are with building their own kingdom. If you make this a matter of prayer, the Lord will show you what to do.

God's House Is Built with Spiritual People

When we think of God's spiritual house, we typically think of something like this: "The church is not a physical building, but it's the people who gather together." There's truth to this, but God's ultimate intention goes much deeper.

You see, God can't build His spiritual house with just any type of people. He will never build His spiritual house with carnal or soulish believers. God can only build His spiritual house with spiritual people.

In 1 Corinthians 2:14-15 and 3:1, Paul revealed three possible states of born-again believers:

> But a natural man does not accept the things of the Spirit of God, for they are foolishness to him; and he cannot understand them, because they are spiritually appraised. But he who is spiritual appraises all things, yet he himself is appraised by no one. (1 Cor. 2:14-15)

> And I, brethren, could not speak to you as to spiritual men, but as to men of flesh, as to infants in Christ. (1 Cor. 3:1)

In the first passage, the Greek word for *natural man* means "belonging to the *psuche*, soul."[1] This means that Paul was contrasting the soulish man with the spiritual man. In the second passage, Paul compared *men of flesh*—or *carnal* as the KJV translates it—with those who are spiritual. Thus, we have three possible states of born-again believers: carnal, soulish, or spiritual. These three states are determined by the part of our being which governs us. Are we led by our bodies, souls, or spirits? The good news is that we don't have to be carnal or soulish. If we yield to the Holy Spirit and let Him have His way within us, we can be spiritual men and women.

Let's take a minute and dig a little deeper into this.

THE CARNAL CHRISTIAN

A carnal Christian, though having Christ's indwelling life, is governed by the body coupled together with the soul. They are driven by what they see, hear, smell, taste, and touch and by the influence of these five senses upon the mind, will, and emotions.

Everything they do and live for is driven by the outside in. Their appetite for food, comfort, sensual desires, and worldly pleasures rules them. Though born of the Spirit, a carnal Christian lives by the dictates of their sensual appetites.

The carnal Christian will remain an infant in Christ.

THE SOULISH CHRISTIAN

The soulish Christian is governed by human reasoning, emotions, and self-preference. What they think, feel, and want drives how they live.

Soulish believers are led by what their minds calculate, logic dictates, and their thoughts speculate. They are often opinionated, obstinate, and independent.

What feels good to the soulish believer drives their actions, even if their feelings contradict God's Word. For the soulish believer, human compassion, tolerance, and empathy trump truth, righteousness, and justice. Soulish Christians are double-minded because their feelings dictate what they believe.

In addition, a soulish believer is ruled by what they want. They live by what their will insists upon having. What they want, when they want it, and how they want it drives their life.

Though born of the Spirit, the soulish Christian is hindered from knowing God in a deep way. Because God is Spirit, it's only through our spirits that we can know, experience, and encounter the Spirit of God, who communicates to us the deep things in God's heart (1 Cor. 2:10-13). The soulish Christian, living from their mind, will, and emotions, is impeded from spirit-to-Spirit communion with the Lord and is therefore limited from knowing God deeply.

The soulish Christian can accomplish many good things for God in their own strength, talent, and creativity. They can shed many tears and feel God's Spirit moving. They can be driven by human compassion and toil to help the marginalized. Nevertheless, the soulish Christian will remain an immature, unbroken child governed by what they think, feel, and want.

The Spiritual Christian

Before describing what it means to be spiritual, let me first describe what it doesn't mean.

Shouting amen during the preaching, dancing spontaneously, lifting up hands, shedding tears, blowing shofars, quoting Scripture, wearing Christian t shirts, going on mission trips, and bringing "justice" to the marginalized don't make us spiritual. Though spiritual Christians might do some of these outward acts, these do not *make us* spiritual, for nothing external can ever make us spiritual internally.

So, when I speak of the spiritual Christian, I'm referring to their state internally, not how they might demonstrate their spirituality externally. So, what does it mean to be "spiritual"?

Spiritual Christians are those who are fully submitted to the Holy Spirit. The five senses of their bodies, along with the mind, will, and emotions of their souls, are under the indwelling Spirit's control. Though still having their own thoughts, feelings, and desires, these do not control or lead them. They have learned to separate the soul from the spirit and are quick to bring all that is of the soul under the lordship of Jesus Christ. They are ruled and governed by the Holy Spirit alone.

Spiritual Christians have a personal revelation that Christ dwells within them. This revelation has transformed their lives. They have experienced Christ internally and know that He is their life-source. They have learned to live by His indwelling life.

As a result, their spirits have been strengthened as the uncontested leader. Their bodies and souls have become servants of their spirits. They live by spiritual intuition and commune with the Spirit. They know God intimately and are given revelation of the deep things in His heart.

Those who are led by the Spirit in this way are the mature sons of God (Rom. 8:14). These are the spiritual ones, the living stones whom God will use to construct His spiritual house, for they have no carnal or soulish mixture.

Spiritual Christians are not perfect, but they are ever yielding more of their self-life to the indwelling Spirit. To be completely ruled and governed by the Spirit will likely take a lifetime. But I've discovered that if we will start walking down this path, the Lord's grace will take us where we could never go. He will accomplish in us what we never dreamed was possible.

The Dividing of Soul from Spirit

Hebrews 4:12 states, "For the word of God is living and active and sharper than any two-edged sword, and piercing as far as the division of soul and spirit, of both joints and marrow, and able to judge the thoughts and intentions of the heart."

Because our souls and spirits are so tightly interwoven, only God's living and active Word can surgically expose the thoughts, emotions, and desires that are influencing our spirits. Until this sword penetrates into our hearts, we easily mistake our soulish impulses for the Spirit's leadership. We're unaware that our thoughts, emotions, and desires have been masquerading as His voice.

The Lord, from whose mouth proceeds "a sharp two-edged sword," sometimes speaks sharp and cutting words to expose the mixture of flesh and soul with the Spirit (Rev. 1:16). His aim is to transform us into spiritual people, the living stones from which He builds His spiritual house.

Under the Old Covenant, when priests offered sacrifices, they would tie an animal to an altar and split it in half with a sharp knife. The knife was so sharp that it pierced the animal to the joints and marrow, exposing the animal's internal organs for all to see. The author of Hebrews obviously had this in mind when he said, one verse later, "But all things are open and laid bare to the eyes of Him with whom we have to do" (Heb. 4:13).

In the New Covenant, we are like the sacrificial animal, the "living and holy sacrifice" that the Lord lovingly splits open, dividing our souls from our spirits with the sharp, two-edged sword of His living words (Rom. 12:1).

When the Lord's sharp and cutting words slice through our inner man, it becomes apparent how much our own thoughts, emotions, and desires are influencing us. This is one of the most loving acts our Bridegroom can do for us. This is one of the ways Jesus sanctifies His bride.

When the Lord speaks this way, it's not pleasant. I mean, how would you feel if the Lord told you, "Get behind Me, Satan. You are a stumbling block to Me" (Matt. 16:23)? Yet this is exactly what Jesus said to Peter, revealing that Peter's pride and self-interest were clouding his judgment.

Not speaking like this would have kept Peter in his prideful condition. Because Jesus loved Him with the purest love, He spoke a sharp and cutting word that laid bare Peter's heart. This enabled him to see the true condition of his heart, giving him the opportunity to be transformed more into Christ's nature and likeness.

I don't know about you, but I surely want the Lord to speak this way to me, even if it's temporally painful. I want the Lord, by His living and active Word, to open up my innermost thoughts and lay them bare to me. I want Him to unveil the deepest thoughts and intentions of my heart, so that I can yield those parts of my being more fully to the Holy Spirit. I hope you do, too.

Because of the fall, even after we've been born of the Spirit, we are so inherently selfish that we start believing that God thinks like us, feels like us, and wants what we want. Imperceptibly, our souls lead us rather than the indwelling Spirit.

Until Jesus surgically separates our souls from our spirits, it's almost impossible to discern God's leading in our spirits from what we think is God's leading in our minds, will, and emotions. When the Lord divides soul from spirit, He highlights the voices that are influencing us. We then begin to discern His voice more clearly from amongst all the noise and clutter in our souls.

This Spirit-led surgery is critical if the Lord is going to have the living stones to build His spiritual house. This work will transform us from carnal and soulish people into spiritual men and women of God.

Just to clarify, the Lord's "cutting words" are vastly different from

Satan's accusatory and condemning words. When the Lord divides soul from spirit, His words are specific, bringing hope and confidence even though challenging, and leading to true repentance and transformation. Ultimately, His words make us feel clean. Satan's condemning voice, on the other hand, results in discouragement, guilt, and shame. His false accusations produce anxiety, distress, and despondency. While Christ's words bring us back to Himself, Satan's lies keep us in the same condition, making us feel hopeless, dirty, unworthy, and isolated.

A SPIRITUAL HOUSE AND A MATURING BODY

I want to end this chapter by showing you the connection between the Lord's spiritual house and His maturing body. In Ephesians 2:21-22, Paul says, "In whom the whole *building*, being *fitted together*, is *growing* into a holy *temple* in the Lord, in whom you also are being *built together* into a dwelling of God in the Spirit" (emphasis mine). Notice the italicized words. God's building is fit together by individual living stones and is growing into a temple, a dwelling place of the Spirit.

In Ephesians 4:15-16, Paul says, "We are to *grow up* in all aspects into Him who is the head, even Christ, from whom *the whole body*, being *fitted* and *held together* by what every joint supplies . . . causes the *growth of the body* for the building up of itself in love" (emphasis mine). Again, notice the italicized words. The Lord's body grows up and matures as each individual member is fit together and contributes to the body by drawing from Christ's indwelling life.

Paul is basically describing the same thing using different metaphors. We are both a spiritual house of living stones and a body of individual members that are meant to grow up in spiritual maturity together.

In the next chapter, we will take a closer look at the body that the Spirit wants to possess and bring to Christ-like maturity.

CHAPTER 28

THE BODY OF CHRIST

When people think of the church, many envision a building, a weekly service, or music and a message. While the church can certainly gather in a building and there's usually music and a message, this is not the church.

The church is a body, not a building; an organism, not an organization.

Paul said, "He put all things in subjection under His feet, and gave Him as head over all things to the church, which is His body, the fullness of Him who fills all in all" (Eph. 1:22-23).

The *ekklēsia*, the Greek word for church, is not a place we go once a week. It's a gathering of those who have the indwelling life of Christ. As Paul said, the church "is His body"—a body that we can only belong to *if the Holy Spirit dwells within us.*

The body of Christ is "the fullness of Him who fills all in all." When the One who is "in all" of the individual members "fills all" of the individual members, then we will begin to see the fullness of Christ. This means that individual fullness precedes corporate fullness.

At the same time, the fullness of Christ can never be realized by scattered and disjointed individuals, even if they are filled with the Holy Spirit. God's eternal purpose to release the fullness of Christ will ultimately be accomplished *corporately*—not merely individually. The Lord's ultimate aim is to fill us with the fullness of the Spirit and lovingly fit us together with other like-minded living stones into a spiritual house, who gather regularly under the headship of Jesus Christ.

Don't Abandon the Local Church

Many believers, having been burned by organized religion under the government of man, despise the church. They rarely, if ever, gather together with other Christ followers who are filled with the Spirit. Isolated and independent, they seek Jesus on their own, blinded to their desperate need for Christ's corporate body.

These lone rangers will never come into the fullness of God's eternal purpose—no matter how much they love Jesus, no matter how abandoned they are, no matter how much they pray, fast, and seek God, and no matter how nice they are.

God established an immutable law in His eternal council that can never be violated. Namely, the fullness of Christ can only be experienced corporately—not merely individually (Eph. 1:22-23; Eph. 4:13). If you care about the fullness of Christ, please don't abandon the local gathering of His people who are submitted to the Holy Spirit.

The Lord's agenda for His church is so much greater than your individual agenda or your individual ministry. The day of independence and isolation must end if we're ever to see the fullness of Christ.

Jesus is coming back for a united bride, not a harem of isolated, me-and-Jesus seekers. The Lord is preparing a corporate man, a unified son, to place into His eternal inheritance—not a scattered and independent group of children doing their own thing.

If you want to see the fullness of Christ released at the end of the age, you need to understand the importance of His indwelling life expressed corporately through His unified body.

The Holy Spirit's Inheritance in the Saints

So far, as we have looked at the Holy Spirit's inheritance in the saints, we have seen that He wants a temple to fill and a spiritual house in which to dwell. Now we will look at the third aspect of His inheritance—a body to possess and bring to full maturity. There are three dimensions to this: Christ as the head of the church, the body expressing Christ's indwelling life, and the body becoming a mature man.

CHRIST IS THE HEAD OF THE CHURCH

Frank Viola said, "Before Jesus Christ entered the pages of human history, there were only two races: Jew and Gentile. But with the coming of Christ, and the church . . . there are now three races: Jew, Gentile, and the *ekklēsia* of God."[1]

Paul said, "Give no offense to Jews or to Greeks or to the church of God" (1 Cor. 10:32). Based upon this statement, early Christians referred to themselves as the "third race."[2]

The *ekklēsia* is a new creation that corporately expresses Christ's resurrection life in this world.

Though we are new creations individually, having a new spirit, a new heart, and the indwelling Spirit, the *ekklēsia* is a new creation corporately. Jesus Christ is the head and we are His body. Together, we are mutually interdependent upon one another. By our life-union with the indwelling Spirit, we as the body are connected to the head, Jesus Christ.

Just as our body needs a head for life, nourishment, and direction, as the body of Christ, we need Jesus Christ as our head in order to receive His life, nourishment, and direction. Likewise, just as our physical head needs a body to express itself, Jesus Christ in heaven depends upon His body on earth to express His life. There is a mutual interdependence between Jesus Christ—the head—and His body.

As we saw previously, God's eternal purpose is to bring everything in heaven and on the earth under the headship of Jesus Christ. This eternal initiative starts with the church.

Before the Father gathers the rebel earth under the headship of Jesus Christ during the Kingdom Age, He will first bring the body of Christ under the headship of His Son in the Church Age. This internal work is at the forefront of God's purpose for this age. He will establish the reign of the Lamb within the hearts and souls of His people. When this has been accomplished and the bride is made ready, the Church Age will end and the Kingdom Age will begin (Rev. 19:7).

This brings me to an important point. The second coming of Christ will not take place until the church has become a mature representation of the Son. Put another way, the return of Christ hinges upon the child-training work of the Holy Spirit to prepare a corporate man, a mature son who will be placed into Christ's inheritance. This preparation of the corporate man is one of the primary purposes of the Church Age.

Mike Bickle said, "While many saints are waiting to 'go up' at the rapture . . . God is waiting for the Church to 'grow up.'"[3] This echoes Paul's admonition for us to "grow up in all aspects into Him who is the head" (Eph. 4:15).

To grow up into the head requires a life of complete and absolute surrender. It means yielding fully to the Holy Spirit, so that He can transform us into spiritual people who follow the Lamb wherever He goes (Rev. 14:4). This type of growth begins when you stop trying to fit Jesus into your life and allow Christ to *become* your life.

When we grow up into Christ the head through our vital life-union with His Spirit, Jesus becomes our control center, absolute authority, spiritual nourishment, and life supply. He becomes our all in all.

THE BODY EXPRESSES CHRIST'S LIFE

Paul said, "Do you not know that your bodies are members of Christ?" (1 Cor. 6:15). Not only are we temples of the Holy Spirit, but we are also members of Christ's very own body. The church is Jesus Christ on the earth.

Because of the indwelling Spirit, we are connected to the risen Christ. We have a vital life-union with Him. We are partakers of His life. We are His body on earth joined to Christ the head, who is enthroned in heaven.

Paul made an amazing statement when he said, "For even as the body is one and yet has many members, and all the members of the body, though they are many, are one body, so also is Christ" (1 Cor. 12:12).

The body of Christ on earth *is* Christ. What a profound statement and revelation! The fullness of Christ is Christ the head in
heaven joined to Christ the body on earth. We are literally the
expression of Christ's heavenly life in the earth. Of course, that
doesn't make us gods. But we are a corporate vessel that God fills
and possesses.

When Saul (Paul) was traveling to Damascus, he had a life-
transforming, history-altering encounter with the risen Christ. As
light suddenly flashed around him, he fell to the ground and heard
the voice of Jesus say to him, "Saul, Saul, why are you persecuting
Me . . . I am Jesus whom you are persecuting" (Acts 9:4-5).

Wait. What? How could Saul possibly be persecuting Jesus,
who had ascended to heaven several years before this encounter?

From Jesus' perspective, His *ekkelsia*, His body, *is* Him. To treat
His body well is to treat Him well. Conversely, to persecute His
body is to persecute Him. The body of Christ on earth is Jesus on
earth. Together, we are the expression of His life in the earth.

This point becomes resoundingly clear in Jesus' parable of the
sheep and the goats (Matt. 25:31-46). Without getting into all the
details of this parable, we see that how we treat the Lord's brothers is how we treat Him (Matt. 25:40). If members of His body are
hungry and we feed them, we also feed the Lord. If members of His
body are thirsty and we give them something to drink, we also give
the Lord a drink. The same is true with visiting prisoners, cloth-
ing the naked, caring for the sick, and showing hospitality to the
stranger. The way we treat the body of Christ is the way we treat
Christ, for in the Lord's eyes, His body is an extension of Himself.

THE BODY WILL BECOME A MATURE MAN

Paul declared God's ultimate intention for the body of Christ, revealing that we are to become "a mature man . . . the measure of the
stature which belongs to the fullness of Christ" (Eph. 4:13). This is
a corporate calling, not an individual calling. This calling must be
answered corporately by a mature church, united as one body at
the end of the age.

Imagine a football team with the best quarterback, running

back, and wide receiver in the league. Even though they have the best three players, the rest of the team is lousy. The offensive line can't block. The defense can't stop anybody. What would be the result? This team would not win many games. The same is true with the body of Christ. Even if a few individuals are filled with the fullness of Christ, God's eternal purpose can't be accomplished apart from corporate fullness.

You see, before the Lord can return, Ephesians 4:13 must be fulfilled in the church. The Lord will have a corporate son, comprised of many individual sons, that will be filled with the fullness of Christ. He will have a mature man that has been completely transformed into a representation of Jesus Christ.

Nevertheless, this will not be sovereignly accomplished apart from our participation. We have a vital role to play. God will not fulfill our part, and we can't fulfill God's part. For the Lord to have a mature man, a corporate son, the head and the body must work together in unison.

This eternal purpose can only be realized when the individual members of the body yield fully to the indwelling Spirit, allow Christ to be their life, and then allow Him to fit them together with other members of the body.

ONE BODY

In the context of writing about the mature man, Paul said that we are to come "to the unity of the faith" (Eph. 4:13). When you understand the Greek, the unity of the faith could be translated the oneness of the faith.[4]

The oneness of faith that Paul mentioned and that Jesus prayed for is far greater than merely getting along with different tribes in the body of Christ (John 17:21, 23). It is far greater than abstaining from criticism, judgment, and gossip about those with whom we differ. It is far greater than co-laboring in city-wide projects or praying and fasting together for revival.

This oneness is not a forced unity through conformity. Nor is it a guilt-based unity, where we strive to accomplish unity in the flesh because "we should" and "we must."

The oneness of the faith is an organic and life-based work of the Holy Spirit. A oneness where each individual member is fully devoted to Christ, fully intimate with Christ, fully surrendered to Christ, fully mature in Christ, fully aligned to God's eternal purpose, and fully filled with Christ's life.

Only when the individual members of Christ's body experience this type of fullness and are fit together as living stones will Jesus have the oneness that He prayed for (John 17:21, 23). This is the oneness of faith for which He died. This is the oneness of faith that will be accomplished at the end of the age.

As we conclude this chapter, let's press into the fullness of Christ and become the inheritance that the Holy Spirit yearns for jealously. Let's willingly become the Holy Spirit's inheritance—a corporate temple that He fills, a spiritual house in which He dwells, and a body that He possesses and brings to maturity.

When the body of Christ in the nations becomes a mature man at the end of the age, the Lord will place this corporate son into Christ's eternal inheritance, which we will look at next.

PART 8

Our Inheritance in Christ

God's eternal purpose is to give His people eternal intimacy, eternal authority, and eternal glory. Jesus described this in His promises to the overcomers in Revelation 2-3. If we could grasp just a glimpse of the unimaginable intimacy, authority, and glory offered to us in Christ, it would instill fresh hope, perspective, courage, and joy into our hearts. Let's dive into our rich inheritance in Christ now.

CHAPTER 29

COHEIRS WITH CHRIST

As God's adopted children, we live in the tension of the "already but not yet." We have *already* been placed into God's family as His beloved child. We have *already* been placed into Abraham's inheritance as a legal heir and have received the indwelling Spirit (Gal. 3:14,29; 4:1-7). But our adoption has *not yet* been finalized.

As Paul voiced, "We ourselves, having the first fruits of the Spirit, even we ourselves groan within ourselves, waiting eagerly for our adoption as sons, the redemption of our body" (Rom. 8:23).

There is a groan within true believers for our adoption to be completed—for us to receive our resurrected, glorified bodies and be placed as a mature son into Christ's inheritance.

Paul expressed this tension between the already but not yet in Ephesians 1. He revealed that we have already received an inheritance but it's only a down payment for the future. He said, "We have obtained an inheritance" and we "were sealed in Him with the Holy Spirit of promise, who is given as a pledge of our inheritance" (Eph. 1:11, 13-14).

The initial act of adoption into God's family made us Abraham's heir and a partaker of the Holy Spirit. Yet as Paul stated, the final result of our adoption is future, for which we wait with intense longing and groaning. As "fellow heirs with Christ," we are in the school of sonship unto adoption, being trained by the Holy Spirit for our future son placement into Christ's inheritance.

Paul said, since we are God's *teknon* by new birth, then we are also "heirs of God and fellow heirs with Christ" (Rom. 8:17). The Greek word for *fellow heirs* means a "coheir," a "participant in common," a "joint-heir," and a "co-inheritor."[1] As God's *teknon* by new birth, we are destined to inherit with Jesus Christ.

But what does that mean? What exactly is our inheritance in Jesus Christ? What is our eternal destiny as God's adopted sons? The next few chapters will answer these questions as we look in detail at our eternal inheritance as coheirs with Christ.

THE FIRST-BORN SON'S INHERITANCE

To understand our inheritance as coheirs with Christ, we first need insight into primogeniture. Though most in the Western culture are unfamiliar with this term, primogeniture was deeply embedded in the culture of the ancient world, especially when the Bible was written.

Primogeniture is the exclusive rights of inheritance that belong to the firstborn son. These rights included a position of authority in the family (Gen. 25:23), being set apart as priest of the family (Ex. 13:2), and receiving the double portion of the father's estate (Deut. 21:17).

In the most ancient genealogies, a clear distinction was made between the firstborn son and the younger sons (Genesis 10:15; 22:21; 25:13; 35:23; 36:15). The firstborn son received special blessings (Gen. 27:19), special privileges (Gen 29:26), and special recognition (Gen. 22:21).

Though the rights of primogeniture were normally given to the oldest son, Scripture contains at least three exceptions to this rule. The oldest son could forfeit his firstborn privileges due to improper behavior (Esau and Reuben). A father (or grandfather) could reassign the firstborn privileges to a younger son (Jacob and Ephraim). And God Himself could appoint a younger son to have firstborn privileges (Isaac, Joseph, and David).

JESUS IS THE FIRSTBORN SON

The book of Hebrews reveals that Jesus Christ is the "firstborn" Son of God, the "heir of all things" (Heb. 1:2, 6).

Referring to Jesus as the "firstborn" does not deny His deity, as some have claimed throughout church history. Rather, this statement reveals that the Man Christ Jesus, fully God and fully man, will receive the fullest measure of inheritance, just as firstborn sons received in biblical times.

After declaring that the Man Christ Jesus is the firstborn Son and heir of all things, the author of Hebrews briefly referred to several Messianic prophecies (Heb. 1:5; 8-9; 13). His goal was to reveal that Jesus, as the Messiah of Israel, will inherit all of these promises.

Because the primary audience of Hebrews was Jewish and knew the Messianic Scriptures intimately, the author raced through these references to make his next point. However, we can't miss what the Spirit of God was communicating, even if the author was brief.

Through these Messianic references, the Holy Spirit wants us to know that Jesus is the fulfillment of the Davidic Covenant, and He will fulfill the Messianic prophecies of Psalm 2, Psalm 45, and Psalm 110.

As the heir of the Davidic Covenant, Jesus will sit on the throne of David and reign over the house of Jacob forever (Heb. 1:5; 2 Sam. 7:14; Luke 1:31-33; Isa. 9:7). From David's throne in Jerusalem, Jesus will rule the nations for one-thousand years during the Kingdom Age (Jer. 3:17; Zech. 14:9; Rev. 20:4).

As heir of the promises of Psalm 2, Jesus will inherit the ends of the earth as His possession, rule over the nations with a rod of iron, and shatter the rebellious in His wrath (Heb. 1:5; Ps. 2:7-12).

As heir of the promises of Psalm 45, Jesus will return to the earth with vengeance, wage war against God's enemies with force, rule the nations with His scepter of righteousness, and be married to His redeemed people who have made themselves ready (Heb. 1:8-9; Psalm 45:6-7).

As heir of the promises of Psalm 110, Jesus is a priest-king after the order of Melchizedek. Simply put, He has merged the two offices of priest and king into one and will rule the nations from Zion (Heb. 1:13; Ps. 110; Zech. 6:13).

When these Messianic prophecies are fulfilled during the Kingdom Age, God's eternal purpose to sum up everything in His Son will be accomplished in the earth (Eph. 1:10; Rev. 20:6).

As we are about to see, this is not only Christ's inheritance. It's also *our* inheritance as God's adopted sons.

THE CHURCH OF THE FIRSTBORN

After describing Jesus as the firstborn son, the heir of all things, and detailing His Messianic inheritance, the author of Hebrews said that we are "partakers of a heavenly calling" and have become "partakers of Christ" (Heb. 3:1,14).

Based upon the emphasis of Christ's inheritance in the book of Hebrews, I believe a better translation is "partakers *with* Christ." In fact, the New Living Translation communicates this idea, stating, "We will share in all that belongs to Christ." This surely relates to our calling as "heirs of God and fellow heirs with Christ" (Rom. 8:17).

The Greek word for *partakers* means "sharing in, partaking of, a partner, participant, a sharer, by implication, an associate."[2] Clearly, we are invited to share in the inheritance of Christ as "firstborn" sons (Heb. 12:23).

At the second coming of Christ, when our adoption as sons is finalized, those who submitted fully to Holy Spirit's child-training will be given a firstborn status. This will allow us to partake of the full eternal inheritance of Jesus Christ. With this in mind, it's noteworthy that the book of Hebrews mentions the "church of the firstborn," underscoring our call to share in the inheritance of Jesus Christ as firstborn sons (Heb. 12:23).

The book of Revelation also emphasizes this concept. For example, the Father says, "He who overcomes will inherit these things, and I will be his God and he will be My son [huios]" (Rev. 21:7, emphasis mine). As God's *teknon*, we are destined to be co-heirs with Christ and to "inherit these things." Yet for the moment, we are being groomed by the Holy Spirit, the child trainer who is preparing us for the throne. If we remain under His governmental hand, allowing Him to fully prepare us for placement into Christ's eternal inheritance, then, in the Father's own words, "[we] will be [His] son"—we will be His *huios*. We will be the overcomers who "will inherit these things."

Summarizing Revelation 21:7, overcoming is how we become God's *huios*. Overcoming is how we graduate from the school of sonship and receive our adoption as sons. Overcoming is how we receive a firstborn status, which determines whether or not we're placed as a legal heir into Christ's eternal inheritance.

What exactly is Christ's eternal inheritance? Jesus describes this in Revelation 2-3, when He details the eternal rewards offered to those who overcome. As we saw in Chapter 4, our inheritance can be categorized into eternal intimacy, eternal authority, and eternal glory.

God's Ultimate Intention for Us

Before detailing the specifics of eternal intimacy, authority and glory, let me first explain why Jesus' promises in Revelation 2-3 are actually God's original intention for all of His people.

To get started, it is clear that the rewards detailed in Revelation 2-3 are only given to "the overcomers." What's not as clear, however, is whether all believers are overcomers or only the believers who overcome what Jesus listed in Revelation 2-3, such as losing your first love, false teachings, Jezebel, indifference, and lukewarmness, just to name a few.

Esteemed, honorable, God-fearing, and Christ-loving men and women have held both points of view throughout church history. So, taking the time to carefully consider both points of view is critical. However, it would be too time-consuming in this book to properly consider both sides of this argument, for there are many key verses that need to be examined. There are tensions on both sides of the debate that need to be carefully resolved. For this reason, this debate is out of scope for this book.[3]

With this in mind, for the sake of simplicity and readability, when I describe the eternal intimacy, eternal authority, and eternal glory that we are destined to inherit as God's adopted sons, I use "we" and "us" rather than "overcomers," even though it's only the overcomers who will receive this inheritance. I also use "destined," not to imply that our inheritance is automatic and guaranteed, but to stress that this is God's ultimate intention for each of us.

My goal is to clearly describe God's eternal purpose for every born-again believer. It's not to debate whether or not every born-again believer is guaranteed to receive this inheritance.

As we consider the various promises made to the overcomers in Revelation 2-3, realize that these are more than rewards given to the faithful. Though true, there's something deeper that we need to understand.

What Jesus offers the overcomers is God's original intention, decreed in the eternal council of the Godhead before one act of creation. God's eternal purpose has *always been* to give His adopted sons the eternal intimacy, authority, and glory that Jesus detailed in His messages to the seven churches of Asia Minor. Seeing from this perspective changes the way we view these promises. More than a reward for faithfulness, more than a badge given to an elite set of super Christians, these promises have always been God's intention for all of His people.

As we examine the indescribable promises in Revelation 2-3, realize that these are God's predestined plan for you and me. These promises are Jesus' loving and passionate invitation to us into God's eternal purpose, which the Godhead determined in the eternal council before time and creation.

These incredible promises describe the inheritance reserved for God's *huios,* for those who have graduated from the school of sonship unto adoption. As you read through these promises in the next two chapters, let this truth awaken in your heart and soul: *You have been destined for eternal intimacy, eternal authority, and eternal glory.*

CHAPTER 30

Eternal Intimacy

Because God is supremely relational, He invites us into the same intimacy, communion, fellowship, and love that the Father and the Son shared through the Holy Spirit in eternity past. This becomes clear when we understand Jesus' promises to eat from the tree of life, to feast upon hidden manna, to receive a white stone with a new name written on it, to be adorned with white wedding garments, to have the Father's and the Son's names inscribed upon us, and to dine with Jesus (Rev. 2:7,17; Rev. 3:4-5, 12, 20).

Let's take a look at these seven stunning promises now, for this is your *ultimate* destiny!

1. Eat from the Tree of Life

God's ultimate intention is for us to eat from the tree of life for all eternity. Jesus said, "To him who overcomes, I will grant to eat of the tree of life which is in the Paradise of God" (Rev. 2:7).

As we saw in Chapters 17-18, we can experience the fullness of Christ's life in this age. Of course, that's based upon our present capacity in our unredeemed bodies. Put another way, the fullness of Christ in this age is a relative term, for if we experienced the absolute fullness of His glory in our present condition, we would burst at the seams.

Though we can experience much greater measures of Christ's life than we presently know this side of heaven, it fails to compare with the fullness of His life that will be released within us in the ages to come.

Partaking of the tree of life in heaven, which contains the Son's indestructible life, will release greater measures of Christ's life into our spirits, hearts, souls, and glorified bodies. Throughout eternity, as we partake of this tree, Christ's infinite life will increase within us. As a result, we will have the capacity to enjoy Jesus in the holy of holies at the deepest level of intimacy and love.

From personal experience, we know that the tree of the knowledge of good and evil imparted a deep selfishness into the DNA of our souls and made us profound lovers of self. It seems reasonable, therefore, that the tree of life would have a similar but opposite effect. That is, eating from the tree of life will likely impart the Father's love for Jesus into us in greater measures, fulfilling Jesus' prayer in John 17:26, which states, "That the love with which You loved Me may be in them."

In decoding this promise to eat from the tree of life, we need to understand that God's love flows out of His life. That's why eating from the tree of life will not only release Christ's life within us in greater measures; it will also impart the Father's love for His Son into our hearts and souls in greater measures, ultimately giving us the ability to love Jesus like the Father.

This interpretation makes even more sense when you consider the context of this promise, which was given to the church at Ephesus. The Lord rebuked this busy and active church for losing their first love (Rev. 2:4-5). Jesus exhorted them to make loving Him their most important pursuit. He admonished them to keep the main thing the main thing.

If we make loving Jesus our first priority in this life, then it appears that God will take our weak love and multiply it exponentially in the ages to come, giving us the capacity and the ability to fully enjoy Jesus at the deepest level of love.

When I consider what it will be like to eat from the tree of life in eternity, I imagine that this fruit will awaken dormant emotions in us for the Son of God. This will then bring us into a deeper union with God's heart, giving us the capacity to experience God's deepest pleasures continually without being overwhelmed by the intensity. As a result, this will transform us into true worshipers whose main desire is to simply worship Jesus in the fullness of His glory for all eternity.

2. The Hidden Manna

God's ultimate intention is for us to dwell in the holy of holies for all eternity, forever feasting upon the deep revelation that comes out of intimacy with the Father, the Son, and the Holy Spirit. Jesus alluded to this when He said, "To him who overcomes, to him I will give some of the hidden manna" (Rev. 2:17).

The "hidden manna" likely refers to the manna that was put into the golden pot in the ark of the covenant, where it remained perpetually in the holy of holies. Only the high priest could see the ark once a year on the Day of Atonement.

The "hidden manna" also refers to Jesus Himself, who is the true bread or manna from heaven. Jesus is the One who sustains His people by His words (John 6:48-51; Matt. 4:4).

Putting these two concepts together, eating the hidden manna is likely a metaphor that describes our eternal intimacy with the Godhead in the holy of holies. Jesus offers us immediate and permanent access to Himself, where we will feast upon His words forever in deep intimacy with Him. We are invited to enjoy rich fellowship with the Father, the Son, and the Holy Spirit in the fullness of glory.

Our fallen minds can't fathom the utterly inconceivable depths of intimacy that God invites us to enjoy. The spiritual ecstasy that we will experience as we communicate with Him at the deepest levels of love. The intrigue, enthrallment, and captivation that we will feel as He speaks to us and reveals His personality in ways we had never known. The ravishing and exquisite pleasures that will overcome our emotions as His love washes over us, in wave after wave of the Bridegroom's affection for us, His cherished bride. And the spiritual joy that we will experience as we feast upon Jesus, the hidden manna, for the endless ages to come.

Just as eating brings physical satisfaction, as hunger pains are silenced and cravings are met, Jesus as the hidden manna will satisfy our souls and enrich our resurrected bodies as we dwell in the holy of holies.

For all eternity, Jesus will be the feast on which we dine.

3. A White Stone with a New Name Written on It

God's ultimate intention is for us to enjoy an individual and corporate union with our heavenly Bridegroom. This is what Jesus implied when He said, "To him who overcomes . . . I will give him a white stone, and a new name written on the stone which no one knows but he who receives it" (Rev. 2:17).

In the Roman Empire, white stones were given to honor those who offered valiant service to the community, in battle, or who were victorious in an athletic game. Those who received the white stones were given special privileges and were admitted to special events, including the games and feasts hosted by the Roman Empire.

The white stone Jesus offers is likely an invitation to the marriage supper of the Lamb. This is greater than a one-time event. As the wife of the Lamb, we are invited to feast upon Jesus, the bread of life, for the endless ages of eternity. The corporate bride will dine with Jesus in deep eternal fellowship.

The "new name written on the stone which no one knows but he who receives it" likely reflects our unique, individual relationship with Jesus. It will characterize who we are, how we lived our lives in the secret place with Jesus while on earth, and perhaps how we will function in eternity.

In biblical days, a name was more than a label that set people apart from others. A person's name reflected their nature. A person *was* their name. When God renames us, it will personify our transformation into the nature of Christ and will reflect our new identity and eternal destiny.

In our culture, most brides receive a new last name when they get married. This is likely what Jesus had in mind when He promised to give us a new name on a white stone. When we marry Jesus as His prepared bride, we will receive a new name.

But there is more to this name than its newness and its signal of marriage. The only ones who will know their new name are God and those who receive it. This new name, which will be hidden from everyone else, points to the intimate, private, and intensely personal nature of our eternal relationship with Jesus.

The white stone with a new name written on it is our Bridegroom's unique gift to us, His cherished and beloved bride. This refers to both our corporate and individual relationship with Him for all eternity.

4. Wedding Garments

God's ultimate intention is to give us wedding garments for our marriage to Jesus, our heavenly Bridegroom. Jesus said, "He who overcomes will thus be clothed in white garments" and "will walk with Me in white, for they are worthy" (Rev. 3:4-5).

The white garments are described further in Revelation 19:7-8, when a great multitude in heaven proclaims, "Let us rejoice and be glad and give the glory to Him, for the marriage of the Lamb has come and His bride has made herself ready. It was given to her to clothe herself in fine linen, bright and clean; for the fine linen is the righteous acts of the saints."

To better understand the white garments of fine linen, recall the Jewish wedding system that we looked at previously. Remember that while the bridegroom was away preparing their house, the betrothed bride made her own wedding dress. She spent countless hours meticulously stitching her wedding dress, thread by thread. She also thoroughly inspected her dress for stains, wrinkles, or blemishes. After all, how would her bridegroom feel if he showed up to take her to the wedding and she didn't have on her wedding clothes? Or if her dress was only partially complete? Undoubtedly, it would signify that the bride had other interests and affections that were more important than him.

That's why Jewish brides were serious about this custom. They wanted to ensure that their dress was ready to put on at a moment's notice for the sudden appearance of the bridegroom.

Like the Jewish bride who made her own wedding dress, we are to work out our salvation through love-based obedience for Jesus Christ. This is how we ensure that we are ready for the sudden appearance of our Bridegroom. Only those with white garments will be allowed to participate in the marriage supper of the Lamb as the bride of Jesus Christ (Matt. 22:12).

If we will do our part to make ourselves ready, God will do His part and give us white garments of fine linen for our marriage to His beloved Son.

5. The Father's Name Written on Us

God's ultimate intention is for the Father to have a family of Christ-like sons who are His inheritance. Jesus alluded to this when He said, "He who overcomes . . . I will write on him the name of My God" (Rev. 3:12).

This verse doesn't reveal where the Father's name will be written. But if you read Revelation 22:4, it's clear that the Father's name will be written on the forehead of the overcomers.

This will brand us as the Father's inheritance and signal that we have graduated from the school of sonship unto adoption. It will testify that we remained under the child-training work of the Holy Spirit, suffering nobly, until Christ was formed in us. Those who follow the Lamb wherever He goes will receive this mark, for "they are blameless" (Rev. 14:5).

The Father's name will be written on the "mature man," the corporate son who has come into "the measure of the stature which belongs to the fullness of Christ" (Eph. 4:13). This mark declares that we have overcome, that we "will inherit these things," and that we are God's mature, Christ-like sons that He has longed for since eternity past (Rev. 21:7).

This corporate son, branded with the Father's name, will receive a firstborn status, allowing them to fully share in Christ's eternal inheritance. These mature, responsible, broken, Spirit-led sons will take part in the first resurrection, radiate God's glory like the brightness of the sun, return with Jesus at His second coming, vanquish God's enemies, judge the nations, administer God's righteousness and justice in their assigned sphere of influence, and rule the nations with a rod of iron (Rev. 20:4-6; Matt. 13:43; Rev. 17:14; Rev. 2:26-27; Rom. 8:19-22).

All creation is groaning, longing, and yearning for the revealing of the mature sons of God, the overcomers branded with the

Father's name on their foreheads. This corporate son will return with Christ at His second coming and will restore the earth to God's original intention (Rev. 17:14; Rom. 8:19-21).

6. Jesus' New Name Written on Us

God's ultimate intention is for the Son to have an equally yoked bride as His inheritance. Jesus likely had this in mind when He said, "He who overcomes . . . I will write on him . . . My new name" (Rev. 3:12).

Having the Son's name written on our foreheads brands us as Jesus' very own possession. It testifies that we are part of the corporate bride the Son has longed for since eternity past. It signals that we have become Jesus' inheritance because we made ourselves ready as His beloved, cherished bride. It demonstrates that while the Bridegroom was away, we made our own wedding dress, carefully stitching together our white garments by working out our salvation with fear and trembling (Phil. 2:12).

The Son's name will be written on the corporate bride who paid the price to purchase the oil of intimacy during the Bridegroom's delay (Matt. 25:1-13). These will burn with the Father's very own love for the Son and will have Jesus as their exceedingly great reward. These are the ones who paid the price to know the Lord intimately in the secret place and pursued Him as their first love.

All of heaven is waiting intently for the day when the corporate bride is branded with the Son's new name, marking her as His cherished inheritance. Heaven's joy and gladness about this ultimate event of the ages can't be expressed or articulated in human language (Rev. 19:7-9).

What an eternal plan that God established before the foundation of the world! We have been invited to be the bride of Jesus Christ for all eternity, to be branded as His own inheritance for the eternal ages.

7. Dining with Jesus

God's ultimate intention is for us to enjoy forever what the Godhead has forever enjoyed. Namely, we are invited into the circle of the Trinity, where we will experience the same fellowship, intimacy, and union with the Godhead that the Father, the Son, and the Holy Spirit have enjoyed for all eternity.

Jesus said, "Behold, I stand at the door and knock; if anyone hears My voice and opens the door, I will come in to him and will dine with him, and he with Me" (Rev. 3:20).

Many have used this verse as a call to salvation. But Jesus was not speaking to unbelievers; He was speaking to His church. Notice also that Jesus' knock is His voice speaking to us.

In biblical days, table fellowship was a common image for deep communion and the strong bonds of affection and companionship. Dining brought people together, where they shared intimate conversations, inside information, and secrets. In biblical times, dining was one of the most enjoyable experiences of life. Even in our day, dining is the place where we let down our guard and really connect with people. When we share a meal with someone, we usually become real and communicate with them at a heart-to-heart level.

In the same way, Jesus yearns for deep fellowship with us, both now and for all eternity. He longs for us to enjoy Him as He enjoys us. He wants us to hear His voice and talk with Him as two friends would over dinner. The Lord wants to share His intimate secrets with us. He wants to share what is on His heart.

Though we can taste of this promise now, Jesus was undoubtedly looking ahead to the marriage supper of the Lamb. The Greek word for *dine* in this verse is *deipneo*, which is derived from *deipnon*—the Greek word used in Revelation 19:9 to describe the "marriage supper of the Lamb."

When Jesus invites us to dine with Him, He is offering us the opportunity to experience deep communion, intimacy, oneness, and friendship with Him both now and throughout the eternal ages. The pleasure and privilege of eternal intimacy with Jesus is inexpressible. Nothing compares.

Intimacy Beyond Our Imagination

While now we are limited by 26 letters of the English alphabet and

finite human understanding, one day the mysteries of true intimacy with God will be made clear. "For now we see in a mirror dimly,
but then face to face; now I know in part, but then I will know fully
just as I also have been fully known" (1 Cor. 13:12).

Even more amazingly, eternal intimacy is only part of our inheritance in Christ! Let's look next at Jesus' gracious offer of eternal
authority and glory.

CHAPTER 31

ETERNAL AUTHORITY AND
ETERNAL GLORY

My daughter, Anna, went through a stage where she was enamored with princesses. I'll always cherish the memories of Anna and her friends running upstairs to put on their princess dresses and coming downstairs to model them for us.

At first, I had a hard time relating to this, in all honesty. I grew up in a house with three brothers, where all we did was play sports and talk about sports. So, having a daughter enlightened me to an entirely new perspective of life. It made me wonder: perhaps God has wired the thought of royalty, especially when linked with true love, into our hearts. It surely seems like this is every little girl's dream, right?

Likewise, I can't help but notice how many magazines at the checkout counter are plastered with the faces of the British royals. There's no denying that the world has an obsession with princes and princesses—whether Hollywood versions or tabloid caricatures.

Well, I would suggest that our earthly preoccupation with royalty is a pale, fallen reflection of our high calling in Christ. We are, in reality, destined for the throne. As God's beloved, we are offered a position of judicial responsibility and kingly oversight in the most powerful royal family in history. God's ageless plan is for us to rule and reign with Jesus for the unending ages: the ultimate union of royal authority and true love. That's infinitely better than anything Disney could create, isn't it?

God's predetermined purpose is incredible. Think about it: When Jesus returns, He wants to give us authority over the nations. He wants to use us to bring justice and righteousness into the sphere of authority entrusted to us. For the endless ages of eternity, we are called to expand God's kingdom throughout the universe, so that His government will continually increase (Isa. 9:7).

This type of eternal authority becomes clear when we understand Jesus' promises to receive the crown of life, to have authority over the nations, and to sit down with Jesus on His throne (Rev. 2:10, 26-27; Rev. 3:21).

Let's take a look at these three amazing promises now.

1. The Crown of Life

God's ultimate intention is for us to be kings who rule the universe with His Son. Jesus said, "Be faithful until death, and I will give you the crown of life" (Rev. 2:10).

The Greek word for *crown* is *stephanos* and it means "a mark of royal or exalted rank."[1] *Stephanos* was a wreath or garland given as a prize to victors in the public games.[2] The crown of life, therefore, is the crown given to the overcomers who will rule and reign with Christ.

This crown will signal our authority as kings in God's kingdom, for Jesus will give us His royalty for our loyalty. If we remain faithful until death, He will give us the victor's crown, which will testify that we were more than conquerors, demonstrated by our overcoming lifestyle.

This is not to say that we will be like gods or even close to equality with God. In fact, perhaps the greatest purpose of the overcomer's crown is for us to worship the Lord with it. Like the elders who cast their crowns before the throne and exclaim that God alone is worthy, I'm sure that we will do likewise (Rev. 4:10-11).

As the bride of Christ, we will love Jesus with such a passionate love that we will cast our crowns at His feet and say, "You are worth far more than any crown. Though we are grateful for the crown that You have given us, we are not in it for authority but for You. You are our reward, not kingdom authority. But we are honored beyond words to partner with you to expand Your kingdom because we love You."

2. Authority Over the Nations

As the equally yoked bride of Christ, God's ultimate intention is to give us authority over the nations. Jesus said, "He who over-comes, and he who keeps My deeds until the end, TO HIM I WILL GIVE AUTHORITY OVER THE NATIONS; AND HE SHALL RULE THEM WITH A ROD OF IRON, AS THE VESSELS OF THE POTTER ARE BROKEN TO PIECES, as I also have received authority from My Father" (Rev. 2:26-27).

When Christ's body has fully matured and our adoption is finalized at the end of the age, we will be given eternal authority. Our first assignment, with this newly bequeathed authority, will be to partner with Jesus to enforce God's kingdom rule throughout the earth during the Kingdom Age.

If you recall, the Kingdom Age is when God's kingdom will come to the earth in fullness. It's when Jesus will reign as King from Jerusalem for a thousand years (Zech. 14:16; Rev. 20:4). This will be a time of unprecedented peace, prosperity, righteousness, and glory (Zech. 14:9; Isa. 60). Heaven will invade earth, all of God's enemies will be defeated, and Satan will be bound for a thousand years (Rev. 20:2-3).

During this time, there will be worldwide justice, the abolition of war, unprecedented peace, fullness of joy, healing, longevity of life, the swift punishment of sin, and economic prosperity.

Jesus, who is the King of the Jews, will make Jerusalem the capital city of the kingdom of God (Isa. 2:1-4). From Jerusalem, God's kingdom will go forth in fullness into every Gentile nation in the earth.

But it will not just be Jesus alone who advances the kingdom. God's sons (male and female), who have become mature and complete representations of Christ, will be given authority over the nations.

This authority will be like a rod of iron, that with one sharp blow breaks clay pottery into hundreds of pieces. The imagery is unmistakably clear—the authority of God's sons will bring swift alignment to God's rule. Those who rebel against God's authority will suffer grave consequences.

This kingdom authority will be displayed the moment Jesus and the sons of God return to the earth. Together, they will use their rod-of-iron authority to utterly destroy the antichrist, the false prophet, all of his military, and everyone in the nations who took the mark of the beast (Rev. 17:14).

After this, they will use their authority to enforce God's rule in the earth and to deal ruthlessly with all who rebel against the Lord and His Word. Those entrusted with authority over the nations will have "authority over ten cities" or "five cities," depending upon God's determination (Luke 19:17-19). These will be literal cities, perhaps cities we know today, such as New York City, Washington, D.C., London, Sydney, or Rome.

God's sons, who have been placed into Christ's eternal inheritance, will be given authority over the nations. We will rule and reign with judicial responsibility and kingly oversight, bringing justice and righteousness into the sphere of authority entrusted to us.

3. The Throne

God's ultimate intention is to give us a seat with Jesus on His throne. Jesus said, "He who overcomes, I will grant to him to sit down with Me on My throne, as I also overcame and sat down with My Father on His throne" (Rev. 3:21).

What an amazing promise! This has to be one of the most amazing invitations in the entire Bible. Our eternal destiny is to sit down with Jesus on His throne and to rule the nations with Him forever.

Let this sink into your heart: You are destined for the throne. Jesus, the great King of the universe, has asked you to marry Him and to rule the nations in partnership with Him forever. You are called to rule and reign with Christ throughout the eternal ages. This has to be one of the most unbelievable offers in the entire Bible.

Think about it. God Himself is offering us the privileged position of ruling and reigning with Jesus Christ for all eternity. God has invited us to something far greater than being the president of the only superpower in the world. Jesus has invited us to sit down with Him on His throne and to rule the nations with a rod of iron in the Millennial Kingdom and for all eternity.

Revelation 20:4 states, "Then I saw thrones, and they sat on them, and judgment was given to them. . . . And they came to life and reigned with Christ for a thousand years." Paul said to the Corinthians, "Do you not know that the saints will judge the world?" (1 Cor. 6:2-3).

We are called to judge the nations in partnership with Jesus during the Millennial Kingdom. We are invited to be Jesus' right-hand men and women—co-rulers with Him in His kingdom.

There's even better news. This invitation extends far past the thousand-year reign of Christ on the earth. Revelation 22:5 states that we will "reign forever and ever." This literally means, when you understand the Greek, for the ages to the ages.[3] Our eternal inheritance in Jesus Christ is to partner with Him to expand God's kingdom into the vastness of creation in each unique age throughout eternity (Isa. 9:7).

ETERNAL AUTHORITY SUMMARIZED

When the Lord has fully established His government within a people during the Church Age, Jesus will return with these same people (His bride) to fully establish His government throughout the earth during the Kingdom Age.

In this age, resistance to His kingdom will be futile. The kingdom of God will penetrate into every sphere of society, including the world's systems of government, religion, economics, education, media, and business. God's mode of operation will no longer be voluntary submission, but mandated subjection. Every knee will bow and every tongue will confess that Jesus Christ is Lord, as Jesus and His bride rule the nations with a rod of iron.

ETERNAL GLORY

Now let's look at our inheritance of eternal glory. We are invited to minister to the Father and the Son as priests. We are offered the capacity to see God's face without being incinerated. We are called to experience perpetual pleasure in His presence. And we were created to radiate God's glory like the sun shining in its strength. This becomes clear when we understand Jesus' promises to become a pillar in the temple, to have the new city Jerusalem inscribed upon us, and to shine like the sun in the kingdom of our Father (Rev. 3:12; Matt. 13:43).

Let's take a look at these three glorious promises now.

1. A Pillar in God's Temple

God's ultimate intention is for us to dwell in the holy of holies in heaven's temple and to minister to Him as His priests continually. Jesus said, "He who overcomes, I will make him a pillar in the temple of My God, and he will not go out from it anymore" (Rev. 3:12). Before explaining "a pillar in the temple," let's first consider heaven's temple.[4]

When God ordered Moses to make a tabernacle, Hebrews tells us that it was modeled after the heavenly one (Heb. 8:4-5). Looking at the earthly tabernacle, we can conclude that heaven's temple has an outer court, a holy place, and the holy of holies.

Here are a few other important points to keep in mind. The Father and the Son are the temple in the new Jerusalem, the bridal city that will come onto the scene after the one-thousand-year reign of Christ on the earth (Rev. 21:22). Also, it appears there will be an earthly temple in Jerusalem during Jesus' millennial reign (Zech. 6:12-13). So, this promise applies to the present heaven, the coming temple in the Millennial Kingdom, *and* the future temple of the new Jerusalem, which is the Father and the Son.

With this in mind, let's look at what it means to be a pillar in the temple. A pillar, which bears the weight of a building, signifies stability, firmness, beauty, permanence, and importance. Putting all of this together, the promise to be a pillar in the temple likely means that we will have unlimited and permanent access to dwell in the holy of holies of the present heavenly temple, the coming Millennial temple, and the future temple of the new Jerusalem, which is the Father and the Son. This will allow us to fulfill our calling as priests-kings after the order of Melchizedek.

In the New Covenant, we have to understand that our priesthood is not of the old order of Levi, but of the new order of

Melchizedek. Simply put, since Jesus is a priest after the order of Melchizedek, then so are we (Heb. 5:10).

What does this mean? To keep it simple, the priesthood of Melchizedek combines the two offices of priest and king. Under the Levitical system, the priest and the king were two separate offices. But under the Melchizedek priesthood, these two offices have been merged together as one (Zech. 6:13). Revelation 1:6 states that Jesus "has made us kings and priests to His God and Father" (Rev. 1:6, NKJV). As priests after the order of Melchizedek, we are both priests and kings to God.

As priests, we will minister directly to the Father and the Son in their radiance, majesty, and glory. As kings, we will go forth from the holy of holies with great authority to rule the nations with a rod of iron.

2. The New City Jerusalem Written on Us

Once Jesus' millennial reign is complete, the heavenly temple will be replaced by the Father and the Son, who will become the temple of the new Jerusalem (Rev. 21:22). Jesus said, "He who overcomes . . . I will write on him . . . the name of the city of My God, the new Jerusalem, which comes down out of heaven from My God" (Rev. 3:12).

God's ultimate intention is for us to dwell with Him and in Him in the holy of holies of the new Jerusalem, where we will behold His glory, see His face, and minister directly to Him as priests for the eternal ages.

After the millennial reign of Christ, John saw "a great white throne and Him who sat on it" (Rev. 20:11, NKJV). Some say this is the Father. Others say this is the Son. I believe that this is the Son since judgment was entrusted to Him (John 5:22).

Notice what it says next. "From whose face the earth and the heaven fled away" (Rev. 20:11, NKJV). There are intense implications in this statement.

When God's glory is unveiled in a greater dimension in the face of Christ, heaven and earth will be like an animal in flight-mode, running for its life. The present heaven and earth will be unable to handle the intensity of God's glory beaming from Christ's unveiled face. That's why God must create a new heaven and a new earth that can sustain *the age of Christ's unveiled face.*

Now here is where the new Jerusalem comes into the picture. Revelation 22:3-4 states that "His bond-servants . . . will see His face, and His name will be on their foreheads" as they minister to the Lord in the new Jerusalem. Our destiny is to be a priestly bride who has the capacity in our resurrected and glorified bodies to see Christ's unveiled face and not be incinerated.

It's here, in the new Jerusalem, that we will minister to the Father and the Son through the Holy Spirit in the most intimate, face-to-face communion and fellowship imaginable. What a beautiful promise to have the new Jerusalem branded upon us!

Here's something else to consider: The new Jerusalem *is* the holy of holies of the new heaven and the new earth. Here's why I believe this.

The holy of holies in Moses' tabernacle measured 10 cubits wide, long, and high. Similarly, the holy of holies in Solomon's temple measured 20 cubits wide, long, and high. Connecting the dots, it appears that the new Jerusalem—which is also a perfect cube that measures 1,500 miles wide, long, and high—is the holy of holies of the new heaven and the new earth.

Perhaps God made the new Jerusalem, as His holy-of-holies city, the smallest He could without it bursting at the seams from the concentrated radiance of Christ's glorious and beautiful face.

The main point is that the new Jerusalem will be the permanent dwelling place of the bride after the Millennial Kingdom. God's inheritance, both the wife of the Lamb and the firstborn sons of God, will minister to Him as a priestly-bride for the eternal ages. God's bondservants, who follow the Lamb wherever He goes, will be allowed to see God's face in the deepest, most intimate places of glory.

3. Shining Like the Sun

God's ultimate intention is for us to shine like the sun in the radiance of His glory. Though this promise is not from Revelation

2-3, it's too incredible not to mention. Describing the end-time harvest where God's children come to full maturity as sons, Jesus said, "Then the righteous will shine forth as the sun in the kingdom of their Father" (Matt. 13:43, NKJV). The "righteous" are the "the sons of the kingdom" (Matt. 13:38). They are God's adopted sons who are placed into Christ's eternal inheritance at the end of the age.

If you want a glimpse of your eternal destiny, look up at the sun during a hot summer day. In a similar way, God's ultimate intention is to clothe you in such brilliant glory that you shine and radiate like the brightness of the sun.

When John saw Jesus in all of His glory, "His face was like the sun shining in its strength" (Rev. 1:16). The Father intends nothing less for His Christ-like sons. Our face is meant to shine forth like the brightness of the sun for all eternity. Oh the glory and beauty that awaits God's overcoming sons!

Describing our resurrection bodies, Paul said, "There is one glory of the sun, and another glory of the moon, and another glory of the stars; for star differs from star in glory. So also is the resurrection of the dead" (1 Cor. 15:41-42).

This verse suggests that there will be varying degrees of glory for the redeemed. Those who have fully embraced the internal work of the cross and have completely surrendered their self-life to the Holy Spirit will shine forth like the brightness of the sun. Others, who have lived with a mixture of self and God, might have the glory of the moon. And still others, who were saved and justified but lived for themselves, perhaps will have the glory of a faint star.

Though the redeemed will have varying degrees of glory in their resurrected bodies, God's ultimate intention is that all of us would shine forth like the sun. The Father jealously yearns for us to radiate His glory just like Jesus, the pattern Son of God.

GOD IS OUR INHERITANCE

Reading through the details of our eternal inheritance in Revelation 2-3, you see the consummation of God's original intention.

You see God's eternal purpose, which the Godhead determined in the eternal council, brought full circle. You see Jesus urging us with love and affection to take seriously our invitation into the circle of the Trinity. You see the Lord's desire to bring us into the fellowship of God's burning heart and to give us eternal intimacy, eternal authority, and eternal glory.

What you discover is that God Himself is our inheritance. As John Piper said, "God is the gospel."[5]

The Lord told Abram, "I am . . . your exceedingly great reward" (Gen. 15:1, NKJV). If your idea of heaven is anything less than the Man Christ Jesus, you will be sorely disappointed. We are inheriting a Man—the Man Christ Jesus. He is our exceedingly great reward. He is our inheritance. He is our prize, treasure, and crown. Not things. Not money. Not a mansion. God Himself.

The Lord told Aaron—and by implication, all the Levites—"You shall have no inheritance in their land nor own any portion among them; I am your portion and your inheritance" (Num. 18:20). The same is true with us. God is our inheritance.

We are invited to forever enjoy what the Trinity has enjoyed forever. Our inheritance is the same love, intimacy, fellowship, pleasure, and delight that the Father, the Son, and the Holy Spirit have enjoyed for the endless ages of eternity past. We are destined to inherit God as our Father, the Son as our Husband, and the Spirit as our life. We have been chosen, sought out, and pursued by a God who burns with love for us. We have been marked for the circle of the Trinity.

In closing, we are invited to become first-born sons who inherit eternal intimacy, eternal authority, and eternal glory.

Conclusion

As we come to the end of this book, I'd like to tell you a story. A "God-story," to be exact.

In 1996, the Olympics came to my lifelong city of Atlanta. It was also the year that I first met Noel Mann from Brisbane, Australia, who later became a spiritual father to me.

The first time I met Noel, I was shocked by how serious he was about the Lord. Close to sixty at the time, Noel was the most intense person I had ever met. As a young man in my twenties, I had never encountered someone who was so focused on the Lord.

From 1996 to 2012, Noel and Di (his wife) traveled back to Atlanta almost every year to minister at our church for two to three weeks at a time. The services were nothing less than a divine confrontation. The anointing on Noel's life made the powers of darkness nervous. The people under their influence reacted to Noel in unseemly ways. The meetings were powerful.

Whenever Noel ministered, it was like Elijah had come to town. Those living in compromise were called out. Those living in sin were rebuked. Those who were demonized manifested. Everyone felt the deep sting of conviction and divine upheaval.

If you drifted away during a service, he would stop his message and exhort you to wake up and pay attention. If you didn't come prepared for church, he would let you know about it in a not-so gently way. I found out quickly that you couldn't get away with anything around Noel.

Growing up in a denominational church, this was unlike anything I had ever experienced. To be honest, it took me a while to get used to his passion and focus.

Though some couldn't see it because of his intensity, Noel embodied the love of Christ unlike many people I have ever met. Whenever you saw Noel, he would give you a hug. You could literally feel God's love flow from him to you. Receiving a hug from Noel felt like you had just received an embrace from the heavenly Father.

Whenever Noel came to town, my favorite thing was spending time with him talking about the Lord. I probably learned more in our conversations than I did in our meetings. I was young in the Lord back then, so I could ask Noel questions about anything, and he always seemed to know the answer. I would receive what I thought was a life-changing revelation, and when I told Noel about it, he had received the same revelation twenty years before me.

It was a tremendous blessing being mentored by such a faithful and passionate man of God. I miss those days.

I'll never forget Noel's devotion to the Lord in the secret place. When Noel stayed at my parent's house, he would lock himself in my dad's office every day and spend about six hours praying, fellowshipping with Jesus, and meditating on the Word. That was shocking to me, as well. I couldn't imagine spending that much time with the Lord. But when Noel spoke, like the apostles of old, you could tell that he had been with Jesus.

His words were sharp and cutting. His message was straight from the Lord's heart. His exhortations cut you to the quick and led you to repentance. After every service, it felt like a true prophet had come to town. Similar to Elijah, Noel was a "troubler" to those living in compromise and sin (1 Kings 18:17).

Noel was not a famous minister. Most people will never know the name Noel Mann. But for those who did, his love for Jesus overflowed to them and impacted them for eternity.

Without those years of Noel ministering to our church and to my life, I'm convinced I would be living a nominal Christian life. Who knows? I might not even be walking with the Lord at all. Our church would probably have shut its doors, as well. And our missions ministry in Africa, Lifeschool International, would not have the impact it's having today.

One thing I know for certain: This book would not exist without Noel's influence in my life.

In the fall of 2012, when Noel was in town ministering, I heard a word from the Lord that I never wanted to hear. Angie went into the grocery store to get food for lunch, while I sat in the car. While waiting for her, I sensed that this was the last time I would ever see Noel face to face.

Then the Holy Spirit quickened Acts 20:25 to me, where Paul told the Ephesians, "And now, behold, I know that all of you, among whom I went about preaching the kingdom, will no longer see my face." I wept as the Lord spoke this to me, not wanting to believe it, hoping that I was not hearing from the Lord.

Several years went by before Noel's next trip to Atlanta was planned, but in September of 2016, it appeared that my sensing was wrong and that I would see Noel once more. Close to eighty, Noel was planning to come to Atlanta again. But this time, in addition to ministry, Noel was going to lead the ordination service as my father handed the baton to me and appointed me as the senior pastor of our church. It was to be a precious moment that I had been holding close to my heart.

The day that Noel was scheduled to leave from Australia for Atlanta, however, my mom called me as I was driving to work. Her words are forever lodged in my mind: "Noel died suddenly. He had a heart attack."

In an instant, I was crushed.

So many memories flooded my heart. So much gratitude filled my soul for all the years Noel labored in prayer and ministry so that we could come into our calling. My spiritual father had passed away, but his influence would remain with me for eternity.

A Divine Appointment in Germany

Fast forward a year to October 2017. My dad, mom, and I went to Kenzingen, Germany, to teach students at a Bible school about God's eternal purpose. We went to teach them much of the material in this book, actually.

As we were making plans for this trip, we realized that a team of intercessors from Zion Christian Ministries, the church Noel led for many years, was going to be in Germany at the same time.

Noel was a seasoned intercessor and had engaged in many spiritual battles. Often, the Lord led him and a team of intercessors to strategic places, where they confronted the powers of darkness and released the prophetic agenda of the Lord. One assignment he never finished was praying for the Reformation to be completed.

A team of intercessors from Zion Christian Ministries felt led of the Lord to carry out this prayer assignment. They would go to Wittenberg, Germany, in October 2017, the same month when all of Germany and the world celebrated the five-hundredth year of the Reformation spearheaded by Martin Luther.

It just so happened that the Lord had us there at the same time.

Think about God's providence in this. We had never been to Germany. We hadn't seen our dear friends since Noel's death. They would be in Germany the same time we were, when the whole nation celebrated the five-hundredth year of the Reformation. Only the Lord could have arranged this.

We decided to meet together in Mainz, about thirty miles from Frankfurt. I didn't think too much about this city, but later I would discover its significance.

When we saw our friends for the first time since Noel's death, several of us could barely talk because of the tears. It was such a precious moment, one of the most memorable times of my life. It was the first time we were able to celebrate Noel's life together and grieve his passing. The presence of the Lord was so tangible. I knew that heaven had orchestrated a divine appointment.

But the Lord had more in store. Little did I realize, as we were walking through the city of Mainz, that we were in the place that helped launch the Reformation. It didn't hit me until I saw a sign for the Gutenberg Museum. Then I realized we were in the city where the Gutenberg printing press was invented.

If you know anything about the Reformation, this invention was the catalyst for the writings of Martin Luther to spread throughout Germany, Switzerland, France, and other parts of Europe. Without the printing press, Martin Luther's revelation of justification by faith would have died with him. If Johannes Gutenberg didn't invent the movable type printing press, it's possible there would have been no Renaissance, no Industrial Revolution, no Technological Revolution, and no western democracy. The modern world might not exist without this critical invention.

Before the Gutenberg printing press, most books were copied

by hand through painstaking and laborious manual labor. This means that very few books were made, and only the wealthy and elite could possess these rare commodities. Because information could not be easily disseminated, most people lived in intellectual darkness.

Gutenberg's invention allowed books to be produced in greater numbers, more quickly and less expensively than ever. This led to a massive social and cultural revolution. What the internet was to our day, the Gutenberg printing press was to fifteenth- and sixteenth-century Europe.

So here we were, in Mainz, Germany, the catalyst city of the Reformation, five-hundred years after Martin Luther posted his 95 Theses that launched the Reformation. Here we were, teaching about God's eternal purpose as our dear friends carried out Noel's desire for an anointed prayer assignment directed towards the completion of the Reformation.

Then it hit me like a bolt of lightning. My eyes were opened to the Lord's sovereign orchestration. I realized we were in a moment of divine convergence.

Once the Lord had my undivided attention, I sensed the Holy Spirit impress on my heart: "Martin Luther recovered justification by faith and many other truths. But he never recovered God's eternal purpose. Before Jesus returns, I will release the last reformation that will recover God's eternal purpose and prepare the church for the coming of the Lord."

Recovering God's Eternal Purpose

The mystery that Paul unveiled in Ephesians and Colossians has become a mystery in the church again. But what would happen if we rediscovered the blueprint from eternity?

As we come to the end of this book, let's envision what the church could look like if we fully recovered God's ageless purpose.

Imagine what would happen if the church got the right starting point, before time and creation. If we experienced God's love for His Son and His love for us . . . and we then burned with the Father's love for His Son. If we became a corporate son who entered into the same relationship with the Father that Jesus has. If we discovered that the person of Christ was vastly superior to the religion called Christianity that is about Him. If we gave Jesus Christ preeminence in His house and placed Him at the center of the church again.

Imagine what would happen if we had an eternal-purpose worldview and understood that the work of the cross and the way of the cross lead us toward God's ultimate intention. If we had a true revelation of Christ in you, the hope of glory. If Christ's life was released in fullness within us, both individually and corporately. If Christ was formed in the church, and we became a corporate son—a mature and complete representation of Him. If the kingdom of God was fully established within us, and we were prepared to return with Christ to establish His kingdom throughout the earth in the age to come.

Imagine what would happen if we remained under the Holy Spirit's child-training until we were ready for the corporate adoption, a firstborn son status, and placement into Christ's eternal inheritance. If we purchased the oil of intimacy and made our own wedding dress while the Bridegroom was away. If the church was free of carnal and soulish mixture and became spiritual men and women who are the living stones of God's spiritual house, a true dwelling place of the Spirit. If we truly became God's inheritance, a people that He fully possesses.

Imagine what would happen if the church became what the Father has always looked for in a corporate son: A people who love Jesus as their first love, are faithful to the Lamb unto death, and love the truth with all of their hearts. A people who don't tolerate the ways and works of Jezebel in their sphere of authority. A people who have a deep, driving hunger for God that overpowers apathy, complacency, indifference, and carelessness. A people aflame with fiery passion for Jesus that consumes self-satisfaction. A people who embrace the crucified life, exchanging their self-life for the fullness of Christ's life. A people of the Lamb's nature, who embody Christ's humility, meekness, self-sacrifice, obedience, and love that overcomes the nature of the proud, independent, rebellious, self-serving, and accusatory nature of Lucifer. A people who walk in sexual purity in their hearts, souls, and bodies. A people who follow the Lamb wherever He goes in absolute obedience to the Holy Spirit's promptings. A people who are holy and blameless, and their words have been purified from lies, gossip, slander, accusation, and judgment.

Imagine what would happen if the church took their old wineskins to the cross and embraced an internal rewiring according to God's ultimate intention. If we made God's eternal purpose our life purpose. If we lived for God's ultimate intention and wanted to be successful in God's eyes rather than man's.

If this were to happen, we would surely see the Reformation launched by Martin Luther five-hundred years ago in Wittenberg, Germany, reach its intended completion. We would see the church finally made ready as a corporate son, a bride, and a spiritual house. God would finally have what He's always been after in a people.

Let's be the generation who recovers God's eternal purpose and does our part to hasten the Lord's return (2 Peter 3:12). Let's be the generation who helps complete the last reformation.

Will you join me, so that together we might fully recover God's eternal purpose?

END NOTES

Chapter 1

1. Ken Kessler, *Understanding Your Inheritance in Christ* (Marietta, GA: Restoration Times Publications, 2004), pp. 150-173.
2. DeVern Fromke, *Ultimate Intention* (Indianapolis, IN: Sure Foundation, 1998), p. 16.
3. Rev. 20:11
4. Of course, no one knows how long eternity extends into the past before creation, but for the sake of helping us to understand, I put billions and billions of years to make a point that we could better relate to.

Chapter 2

1. https://www.blueletterbible.org/lang/lexicon/lexicon. cfm?strongs=G3724&t=NASB, referenced on 6/2/2017.
2. Ibd.
3. Blue Letter Bible. "Dictionary and Word Search for *boulē* (Strong's 1012), *Vine's Expository Dictionary of New Testament Words*". Blue Letter Bible. 1996-2012. See https://www.blueletterbible.org/lang/lexicon/lexicon. cfm?Strongs=G1012&t=NASB, referenced on 6/2/2017.
4. Gerhard Kittle, *Theological Dictionary of the New Testament* (Grand Rapids, MI: Eerdman Publishing, 1985), p. 108.

Chapter 3

1. Philippians and Philemon are also part of *The Prison Epistles*.
2. F.F. Bruce, *The Epistles to the Colossians, to Philemon, and to the Ephesians* (Grand Rapids, MI; William B. Eerdmans Publishing Company, 1984), p. 241.
3. Ephesians 1:22; 3:10; 3:21; 5:23; 5:24; 5:25; 5:27; 5:29; and 5:32.
4. The meaning of these cryptic promises will become clear when we analyze these promises in Part 8.

Chapter 4

1. See Col. 1:16; John 14:6; Rom. 8:29; Eph. 1:5; Isa. 53:10; John 12:24; Eph. 5:22-32; Eph. 1:10.
2. As I explain in a later chapter, I believe that the new Jerusalem is the holy of holies of the new heavens and new earth.
3. https://www.austin-sparks.net/english/books/000924.html, referenced on July 24, 2018.

Chapter 6

1. This was a reference to the Great I Am that Moses encountered at the burning bush (Exod. 3:14).
2. John Piper, *The Pleasures of God* (Portland, OR: Multnomah Press, 1991), p. 38.
3. Ibid., p. 95.
4. Ibid., p. 37.
5. Ibid., p. 31.
6. Ibid., p. 24.
7. Inspired by Piper, *The Pleasures of God*, p. 27.
8. Ibid., p. 27.
9. https://www.cmalliance.org/devotions/tozer?id=1412, referenced on 7/31/2018.
10. Piper, *The Pleasures of God*, p. 31.

Chapter 7

1. Terry Bennett, *Within the Circle of the Throne* (Vanleer, TN: Messengers of Shiloh, 2018), p. 106.
2. Gerhard Kittel and Gerhard Friedrich, *Theological Dictionary of the New Testament, Abridged in One Volume* by Geoffrey W. Bromiley (Grand Rapids, MI: William B. Eerdmans Publishing, 1985), p. 273.
3. Paul E. Billheimer, *Destined for the Throne* (Fort Washington, PA: Christian Literature Crusade, 1975), pp. 25-26.
4. See http://www.samstorms.com/all-articles/post/incarnation-and-humanity, referenced on June 16, 2017.
5. Ibid.
6. Ibid.

Chapter 8

1. The Hebrew word for breath can also be translated spirit.
2. We know that the tree of the knowledge of good and evil was a "delight to the eyes" (Gen. 3:6). But the reason why I think it was likely that the tree of life was ordinary and unappealing is from studying the ways of God in Scripture. For example, Jesus could have clothed Himself with the most beautiful of human flesh and been born in the most respected city in the world. Instead, He chose to have an unattractive appearance and was born in a manger in the small city of Bethlehem amidst the stench of manure (Isa. 53:2). The Lord seems to enjoy hiding the beauty of His ways in ordinary and unappealing packaging to test our response.

Chapter 9

1. See Isaiah 4:2; 33:17-22; 9:6-7; 53-54; 42:1-4, 6-7; 49:1-8; 62:6-7.
2. See Daniel 7:13-14; Jeremiah 23:5; Haggai 2:7; Zechariah 14:9.

Chapter 10

1. See https://www.austin-sparks.net/english/books/000806.html, referenced on 8/16/2018.

2. The Greek word for "summing up" is *anakephalaioō*. This word is derived from *ana* meaning "up" and *kephale* meaning "a head." Digging a little deeper, *kephale* refers to "anything supreme, chief, or prominent," such as a "master lord." Thus, the word *anakephalaioō* refers to the gathering together of all things in heaven and earth under the headship or lordship of Christ. See Blue Letter Bible. "Dictionary and Word Search for *anakephalaioō* (Strong's G346), *Vine's Expository Dictionary of New Testament Words*". Blue Letter Bible. 1996-2012. See https://www.blueletterbible. org/lang/lexicon/lexicon.cfm?Strongs=G346&t=NASB, referenced on 8/16/2018. See also Blue Letter Bible. "Dictionary and Word Search for *kephale* (Strong's G2776), *Outline of Biblical Usage*". Blue Letter Bible. 1996-2012. See https://www. blueletterbible.org/lang/lexicon/lexicon.cfm?Strongs=G2776&t=NASB, referenced on 8/16/2018.
3. Blue Letter Bible. "Dictionary and Word Search for *aiōn* (Strong's G165), *Vine's Expository Dictionary of New Testament Words*". Blue Letter Bible. 1996-2012. See https://www.blueletterbible.org/lang/lexicon/lexicon.cfm?Strongs=G165&t=NASB, referenced on 8/16/2018.
4. Ibid.
5. http://www.TheEternalBlueprintBook.com/TEB-Resources/TheAgesInScripture. pdf
6. See the following articles: http://www.TheEternalBlueprintBook.com/TEB-Resources/WhyIDontBelieveInPreterism.pdf; http://www.TheEternalBlueprintBook. com/TEB-Resources/WhyIDontBelieveInPostmillennialism.pdf; http://www. TheEternalBlueprintBook.com/TEB-Resources/WhyIDontBelieveInAmillennialism.pdf; http://www.TheEternalBlueprintBook.com/TEB-Resources/WhyIDontBelieveInPremillennialism.pdf.

Chapter 11

1. Even if Lucifer didn't fall, I believe that God would have still put both trees in the garden because man had to choose to follow God voluntarily. Man had to make a choice between independent living or submission to Christ.
2. You can see the details of this seed preserved in Luke 3:23-38.
3. See Revelation 12:5, 7-12.

Chapter 12

1. The KJV, NKJV, ASV, YLT, WEB, and HNV translate it in some variation as "within in you" while the NLT, NIV, ESV, CSB, NASB, and RSV render it in some variation as "in your midst."
2. Biblesoft's *New Exhaustive Strong's Numbers and Concordance with Expanded Greek-Hebrew Dictionary* (Seattle, WA: Biblesoft, Inc. and International Bible Translators, Inc., 2010), s.v. "entos," referenced from OneTouch OB-2 (Seattle, WA: Biblesoft, 2016).
3. *Thayer's Greek Lexicon, Electronic Database* (Seattle, WA: Biblesoft, Inc., 2006), s.v. "entos," referenced from OneTouch OB-2 (Seattle, WA: Biblesoft, 2016).
4. *Vines Expository Dictionary of Biblical Words* (New York: Thomas Nelson Publishers, 1985), s.v. "entos," referenced from OneTouch OB-2 (Seattle, WA: Biblesoft, 2016).

5. Frank Viola, *Insurgence* (Grand Rapids, MI: Baker Books, 2018), location 190-201 in the Kindle app.
6. John 3:3-5; Luke 17:21; Matt. 10:7-8.
7. This doesn't mean they will be perfect this side of heaven, for they will not receive a resurrected and glorified body until Jesus returns (Rev. 20:6). Nevertheless, the Lord will have a glorious, holy, and blameless bride before the second coming (Eph. 5:27).
8. Inspired by Francois Fenelon. See https://jesus.org.uk/wp-content/uploads/2012/02/fenelon_progress.pdf, referenced on 2/1/2019.

Chapter 13

1. Because Israel is such a controversial subject, please see my online article *God Will Fulfill His Promises to Israel* for more information about why I believe the kingdom will be restored to Israel in the next age. See http://www.TheEternalBlueprintBook.com/TEB-Resources/GodsPromisesToIsrael.pdf
2. http://www.TheEternalBlueprintBook.com/TEB-Resources/WhyIDontBelieveIn-Preterism.pdf
3. http://www.TheEternalBlueprintBook.com/TEB-Resources/WhyIDontBelieveIn-Postmillennialism.pdf
4. http://www.TheEternalBlueprintBook.com/TEB-Resources/WhyIDontBelieveIn-Amillennialism.pdf
5. http://www.TheEternalBlueprintBook.com/TEB-Resources/WhyIDontBelieveIn-Premillennialism.pdf
6. Rev. 20:1-6; Isa. 2:1-4; 9:6-9; 11:1-16; 51:1-8; 60-62; 65:17-25; Ps. 2:6-12; 110:1-7; Matt. 5:5; 6:10; 17:11.
7. See Ps. 2:9; Isa. 2:4; 4:1; 9:3-7; 11:4-9; 12:3-6; 14:7-8; 25:8-9; 28:17; 29:17-19; 30:23-25; 32:17-18; 35:3-6; 42:1-4; 60:1-14; 61:1-2; 61:4-7, 10; 65:20, 22; 66:24; Jer. 31:8; Ezek. 36:36-38; Mic. 4:6-7; Zeph. 3:19; Zech. 14:14-19; Rev. 20:7-10.
8. See https://www.austin-sparks.net/english/books/000806.html, referenced on 8/16/2018.

Chapter 14

1. I'm referring here to what was imputed to Jesus on the cross. I'm speaking of our position in Christ. We will battle sin and self until we die.
2. 2 Cor. 5:21; Rom. 6:3-6; Col. 3:1; Eph. 2:6.
3. 2 Cor. 5:21; Rom. 6:11; Gal. 2:20; Rom. 7:4.

Chapter 15

1. https://christianhistoryinstitute.org/incontext/article/augustine, referenced on 10/2/2018.
2. https://www.facebook.com/officialLouieGiglio/posts/dont-let-the-enemy-define-you-by-your-scars-when-jesus-wants-to-define-you-by-hi/1071729973003045, referenced on 10/2/2018.
3. Watchman Nee, *The Normal Christian Life* (Fort Washington, PA: CLC Publications, 2009), location 169 in the Kindle app.
4. Matt. 26:28; Rom. 5:9; Acts 20:28; Heb. 9:12; 1 Pet. 1:19; Rev. 5:9; Col. 1:20; Eph.

2:13; Heb. 10:19; Heb. 9:14; Rev. 12:11.
5. 2 Cor. 5:21; Rom. 6:3-6; Col. 3:1; Eph. 2:6.
6. 2 Cor. 5:21; Rom. 6:11; Gal. 2:20; Rom. 7:4.
7. Eph. 2:6; Rom. 8:37.
8. 1 Cor. 3:16; John 7:38-39; Rom. 8:11; Gen. 1:2; Col. 1:15-16; John 16:13-14; John 14:16; 1 John 2:27; Gal. 5:22-23; 1 Cor. 2:16; Luke 17:20-21.
9. Eph. 2:5; 1 Cor. 6:17; 2 Peter 1:4; Rom. 8:10; Heb. 12:22-23; Eph. 4:24.
10. Eph. 3:14-19
11. 1 Cor. 3:3; Rom. 8:10; Acts 15:9; Eph. 3:17; Rom. 8:11.
12. John 1:12-13; 1 John 3:1; Rom. 8:16-17
13. In parts 5 and 6, we will talk about these two dimensions in more detail.

Chapter 16

1. 2 Cor. 5:21; Rom. 6:3-6; Col. 3:1; Eph. 2:6.
2. For more information about this, I highly recommend Watchman Nee's book *The Release of the Spirit.*
3. Rev. 3:21; 20:6; Rom. 8:17.
4. I will explain *huios* in great detail in Chapter 19.

Chapter 17

1. *Biblesoft's New Exhaustive Strong's Numbers and Concordance with Expanded Greek-Hebrew Dictionary* (Seattle, WA: Biblesoft, Inc. and International Bible Translators, Inc., 2010), s.v. "perissos," referenced from OneTouch OB-2 (Seattle, WA: Biblesoft, 2016).
2. *Thayer's Greek Lexicon, Electronic Database* (Seattle, WA: Biblesoft, Inc., 2006), s.v. "perissos," referenced from OneTouch OB-2 (Seattle, WA: Biblesoft, 2016).
3. Ibid.
4. I put "in" in this verse because I believe that's the point Paul's trying to make. In fact, the Greek word used for "toward" is *eis* and is translated "in" 138 times by the KJV. For those born of the Spirit, God's power works in our lives from the inside out, from our spirits where the Holy Spirit dwells.
5. *Biblesoft's New Exhaustive Strong's Numbers and Concordance with Expanded Greek-Hebrew Dictionary* (Seattle, WA: Biblesoft, Inc. and International Bible Translators, Inc., 2010), s.v. "arrhabon," referenced from OneTouch OB-2 (Seattle, WA: Biblesoft, 2016).
6. *Vines Expository Dictionary of Biblical Words* (New York: Thomas Nelson Publishers, 1985), s.v. "katoikizo," referenced from OneTouch OB-2 (Seattle, WA: Biblesoft, 2016).
7. Ibid.
8. Ibid.
9. *Biblesoft's New Exhaustive Strong's Numbers and Concordance with Expanded Greek-Hebrew Dictionary* (Seattle, WA: Biblesoft, Inc. and International Bible Translators, Inc., 2010), s.v. "katoikizo," referenced from OneTouch OB-2 (Seattle, WA: Biblesoft, 2016).
10. See note #4.
11. *Biblesoft's New Exhaustive Strong's Numbers and Concordance with Expanded Greek-Hebrew Dictionary* (Seattle, WA: Biblesoft, Inc. and International Bible Translators,

Inc., 2010), s.v. "meno," referenced from OneTouch OB-2 (Seattle, WA: Biblesoft, 2016).

12. *Liddell and Scott Abridged Greek Lexicon* (Seattle, WA: Biblesoft, 2014), s.v. "meno," referenced from OneTouch OB-2 (Seattle, WA: Biblesoft, 2016).

Chapter 18

1. For more information about this parable, see my online article *The Parable of the Ten Christians* here: http://www.TheEternalBlueprintBook.com/TEB-Resources/TheParableOfTheTenChristians.pdf

2. *Biblesoft's New Exhaustive Strong's Numbers and Concordance with Expanded Greek-Hebrew Dictionary* (Seattle, WA: Biblesoft, Inc. and International Bible Translators, Inc., 2010), s.v. "teleios," referenced from OneTouch OB-2 (Seattle, WA: Biblesoft, 2016).

3. *Abbott-Smith Manual Greek Lexicon of the New Testament* (Seattle, WA: Biblesoft, 2014), s.v. "teleios," referenced from OneTouch OB-2 (Seattle, WA: Biblesoft, 2016).

Chapter 19

1. J. Paul Sampley, *Paul in the Greco-Roman World* (Harrisburg, PA: Trinity Press International, 2003), pp. 42-76.

2. Ibid., p. 56.

3. Ibid., p. 54.

4. Ibid., p. 54.

5. *Biblesoft's New Exhaustive Strong's Numbers and Concordance with Expanded Greek-Hebrew Dictionary* (Seattle, WA: Biblesoft, Inc. and International Bible Translators, Inc., 2010), s.v. "huiothesia," referenced from OneTouch OB-2 (Seattle, WA: Biblesoft, 2016).

6. Sampley, *Paul in the Greco-Roman World*, p. 43.

7. *Biblesoft's New Exhaustive Strong's Numbers and Concordance with Expanded Greek-Hebrew Dictionary* (Seattle, WA: Biblesoft, Inc. and International Bible Translators, Inc., 2010), s.v. "huios," referenced from OneTouch OB-2 (Seattle, WA: Biblesoft, 2016). Also, *Thayer's Greek Lexicon, Electronic Database* (Seattle, WA: Biblesoft, Inc., 2006), s.v. "tithēmi," referenced from OneTouch OB-2 (Seattle, WA: Biblesoft, 2016).

8. *Biblesoft's New Exhaustive Strong's Numbers and Concordance with Expanded Greek-Hebrew Dictionary* (Seattle, WA: Biblesoft, Inc. and International Bible Translators, Inc., 2010), s.v. "huiothesia," referenced from OneTouch OB-2 (Seattle, WA: Biblesoft, 2016).

9. Gerhard Kittel and Gerhard Friedrich, *Theological Dictionary of the New Testament, Abridged in One Volume* by Geoffrey W. Bromiley (Grand Rapids, MI: William B. Eerdmans Publishing, 1985), p. 1215.

10. *Thayer's Greek Lexicon, Electronic Database* (Seattle, WA: Biblesoft, Inc., 2006), s.v. "teknon," referenced from OneTouch OB-2 (Seattle, WA: Biblesoft, 2016).

11. *Vines Expository Dictionary of Biblical Words* (New York: Thomas Nelson Publishers, 1985), s.v. "teknon," referenced from OneTouch OB-2 (Seattle, WA: Biblesoft, 2016).

12. *Vines Expository Dictionary of Biblical Words* (New York: Thomas Nelson Publish-

ers, 1985), s.v. "huios," referenced from OneTouch OB-2 (Seattle, WA: Biblesoft, 2016).

13. Ibid.

14. See Ephesians 4:24. Notice the past tense. Your new self, which is your new spirit, has been created in holiness and righteousness of the truth in the image of Christ.

15. T. Austin Sparks, *God's Spiritual House*. (Austin-Sparks.Net, 1942), the title of Chapter 6.

16. https://www.blueletterbible.org/lang/lexicon/lexicon.cfm?Strongs=G3811&t=NASB, Outline of Biblical Usage, referenced on 8/18/2017.

17. T. Austin Sparks, *God's Spiritual House*. (Austin-Sparks.Net, 1942), location 1204 in the Kindle app.

Chapter 20

1. Viola, *Insurgence*, location 2116 in the Kindle app.

2. God's eternal purpose is the dream of His heart. As I have already demonstrated through Scripture, the Father's eternal plan was to bring many sons to glory (Heb. 2:10). These sons will be conformed into the image of Jesus Christ (Rom. 8:29). From God's perspective, these many sons are to become a corporate son, or as Paul described, "a mature man" (Eph. 4:13).

3. *Vines Expository Dictionary of Biblical Words* (New York: Thomas Nelson Publishers, 1985), s.v. "abba," referenced from OneTouch OB-2 (Seattle, WA: Biblesoft, 2016). Also, John R.W. Stott, *The Message of Romans* (Downers Grove, IL: InterVarsity Press, 1994), p. 233.

4. *Vines Expository Dictionary of Biblical Words* (New York: Thomas Nelson Publishers, 1985), s.v. "abba," referenced from OneTouch OB-2 (Seattle, WA: Biblesoft, 2016).

5. *Vines Expository Dictionary of Biblical Words* (New York: Thomas Nelson Publishers, 1985), s.v. "eudokia," referenced from OneTouch OB-2 (Seattle, WA: Biblesoft, 2016).

6. *Thayer's Greek Lexicon, Electronic Database* (Seattle, WA: Biblesoft, Inc., 2006), s.v. "sumfutos," referenced from OneTouch OB-2 (Seattle, WA: Biblesoft, 2016). Also, see https://www.blueletterbible.org/lang/lexicon/lexicon.cfm?Strongs=G4854&t=NASB, Outline of Biblical Usage, referenced on 8/12/2017.

Chapter 21

1. T. Austin Sparks, *God's Spiritual House*. (Austin-Sparks.Net, 1942), the title of Chapter 6.

2. https://www.austin-sparks.net/english/books/002941.html, referenced on 11/2/2018.

3. https://www.blueletterbible.org/lang/lexicon/lexicon.cfm?Strongs=G3809&t=NASB, Outline of Biblical Usage, referenced on 3/5/2019.

4. https://twitter.com/FFrangipane/status/1107910853129617408, referenced on 3/25/2019 (emphasis mine).

5. https://www.blueletterbible.org/lang/lexicon/lexicon.cfm?Strongs=G5046&t=NASB, Outline of Biblical Usage, referenced on 8/12/2017.

6. Bennett, *Within the Circle of the Throne*, pp. 118-119.

7. *Biblesoft's New Exhaustive Strong's Numbers and Concordance with Expanded Greek-Hebrew Dictionary* (Seattle, WA: Biblesoft, Inc. and International Bible Translators, Inc., 2010), s.v. "hupomeno," referenced from OneTouch OB-2 (Seattle, WA: Biblesoft, 2016).

8. If you are interested in learning more about the Lord developing sonship within us, I highly recommend Bill Britton's *The Harness of the Lord*. http://www.billbritton-ministries.com/page/815337, referenced on 11/2/2018. See Chapter 2.

Chapter 22

1. What follows can be supported by the following Scriptures: Dan. 9:27; Rev. 13:4; Rev. 6:2; Matt. 24:21; Matt. 24:7; Rev. 6:12; 11:13; 16:18; 2 Thess. 2:11; Rev. 13:3-4, 8; Zech. 14:16-19; Zech. 14:2; Dan. 12:1; Rev. 13:7; Rev. 17:14; Luke 19:17-19; Rev. 2:26-27; Zech. 14:1-9; Isa. 62:6-7; Isa. 11:10; Isa. 2:2-4; Isa. 9:7; Isa. 42:4; Isa. 51:3; Isa. 11:6-9; Isa. 11:9; Hab. 2:14; Zech. 14:9.

2. Revelation 19:7 states that the bride is dressed in fine linen. Since this statement is made just a few verses before Revelation 19:14, the context suggests that the armies that follow Jesus on white horses are the bride who has made herself ready. This is further supported by Revelation 17:14, where the called, chosen, and faithful return with Jesus Christ to wage war against the antichrist and His regime.

3. Holiness and blamelessness would also apply to overcoming the deeds of the flesh that Paul mentioned in Galatians 5:19-21.

4. See https://www.austin-sparks.net/english/books/000924.html, referenced on 1/10/2019.

5. Ibid.

Chapter 23

1. See Rev. 19:7-9; Rev. 21:2; Matt. 22:1-14; Matt. 25:1-13.

2. Paul E. Billheimer, *Destined for the Throne* (Fort Washington, PA: Christian Literature Crusade, 1975), pp. 25-26.

Chapter 24

1. Matthew 25:1, ESV, emphasis mine.

2. Barney Kasdan, *God's Appointed Customs* (Baltimore, MD: Messianic Jewish Publications, 1996), pp.48.

3. Mendell Lewittes, *Jewish Marriage, Rabbinic Law, Legend, and Custom* (Northvale, New Jersey: Jason Aronson, Inc., 1994), pp. 41.

4. Kasdan, *God's Appointed Customs*, p.49.

5. Kasdan, *God's Appointed Customs*, p. 49 and Lewittes, *Jewish Marriage, Rabbinic Law, Legend*, pg. 51-56.

6. Kasdan, *God's Appointed Customs*, p. 49.

7. Lewittes, *Jewish Marriage, Rabbinic Law, Legend, and Custom*, pp. 67.

8. Kasdan, *God's Appointed Customs*, p. 50.

9. Lewittes, *Jewish Marriage, Rabbinic Law, Legend, and Custom*, pp. 73.

10. Kasdan, *God's Appointed Customs*, p. 50.

11. https://static1.squarespace.com/static/5361a40fe4b081613fd61652/t/5c5a7367ec21 2df19f91b2e6/1549431657327/Jewish+Wedding+System+%26+Bride+of+Christ+-

+mbs113m.pdf, referenced on 3/8/2019.

12. Kasdan, *God's Appointed Customs*, pp. 51.
13. Lewittes, *Jewish Marriage, Rabbinic Law, Legend, and Custom*, pp. 67
14. Lewittes, *Jewish Marriage, Rabbinic Law, Legend, and Custom*, pp. 83-84.
15. Kasdan, *God's Appointed Customs*, pp.51.
16. John Hagee, *The Final Dawn Over Jerusalem* (Nashville, TN: Thomas Nelson, Inc., 1998), pp.184.
17. Kasdan, *God's Appointed Customs*, pp.52.
18. Ibid, pp. 52.

Chapter 25

1. *Thayer's Greek Lexicon, Electronic Database* (Seattle, WA: Biblesoft, Inc., 2006), s.v. "parthenos," referenced from OneTouch OB-2 (Seattle, WA: Biblesoft, 2016).
2. *Thayer's Greek Lexicon, Electronic Database* (Seattle, WA: Biblesoft, Inc., 2006), s.v. "ektrefoo," referenced from OneTouch OB-2 (Seattle, WA: Biblesoft, 2016).
3. *Thayer's Greek Lexicon, Electronic Database* (Seattle, WA: Biblesoft, Inc., 2006), s.v. "thalpoo," referenced from OneTouch OB-2 (Seattle, WA: Biblesoft, 2016).
4. *Vines Expository Dictionary of Biblical Words* (New York: Thomas Nelson Publishers, 1985), s.v. "thalpoo," referenced from OneTouch OB-2 (Seattle, WA: Biblesoft, 2016).
5. Quoted in Frank Viola, *From Eternity to Here* (Colorado Springs, CO: David C Cook, 2009) p. 37 in the Kindle app.
6. As mentioned in Chapter 23, Adam was a "type" of Christ (Rom. 5:14). Eve also foreshadowed the church's relationship to Christ (Eph. 5:31-32).
7. See http://www.mikebickle.org.edgesuite.net/MikeBickleVOD/2016/20160401_ Loving_Jesus_First_Commandment_Established_in_First_Place_(PFJ2016).pdf, referenced on 11/20/2018.

Chapter 26

1. Some contend that we don't have God's glory, just His presence dwelling within us. But Paul clearly said that the ministry of the Spirit in the New Covenant had more glory than Moses in the Old Covenant (2 Cor. 3:6-12). And it's from this initial deposit of the Spirit's glory that we are progressively transformed into the image of Christ, from glory to glory (2 Cor. 3:18). Having an initial deposit of God's glory in our spirits doesn't mean that we will never sin or battle with the flesh. But as this glory in our spirits increases and begins to fill our hearts and souls in ever-increasing measure, then we will be transformed into Christ's image in greater degrees. This will then give us a greater ability to conquer the cravings of the flesh and walk in holiness and purity.
2. Again, this is not the fullness of God's glory that will melt the present heavens and earth with fire. I'm talking about the fullness of His glory that we can handle. I'm talking about the fullness of His glory based upon our present capacity in our unredeemed bodies.

Chapter 27

1. *Vines Expository Dictionary of Biblical Words* (New York: Thomas Nelson Publishers, 1985), s.v. "psychikos," referenced from OneTouch OB-2 (Seattle, WA: Biblesoft, 2016).

Chapter 28

1. Frank Viola, *From Eternity to Here* (Colorado Springs, CO: David C Cook, 2009), p. 265 in the Kindle app.
2. Ibid.
3. Mike Bickle, *The Book of Revelation Study Guide* (Kansas City, MO: Forerunner Books, 2009), backcover.
4. The word translated *unity* is the Greek word *henotēs*. This word is derived from the Greek word *heis*, which means "one." See https://www.blueletterbible.org/lang/lexicon/lexicon.cfm?strongs=G1520&t=NASB, referenced on 11/22/2017.

Chapter 29

1. *Biblesoft's New Exhaustive Strong's Numbers and Concordance with Expanded Greek-Hebrew Dictionary* (Seattle, WA: Biblesoft, Inc. and International Bible Translators, Inc., 2010), s.v. "sygklēronomos," referenced from OneTouch OB-2 (Seattle, WA: Biblesoft, 2016). See also *Vines Expository Dictionary of Biblical Words* (New York: Thomas Nelson Publishers, 1985), s.v. "sygklēronomos," referenced from OneTouch OB-2 (Seattle, WA: Biblesoft, 2016).
2. *Biblesoft's New Exhaustive Strong's Numbers and Concordance with Expanded Greek-Hebrew Dictionary* (Seattle, WA: Biblesoft, Inc. and International Bible Translators, Inc., 2010), s.v. "metochos," referenced from OneTouch OB-2 (Seattle, WA: Biblesoft, 2016). See also *Thayer's Greek Lexicon, Electronic Database* (Seattle, WA: Biblesoft, Inc., 2006), s.v. "metochos," referenced from OneTouch OB-2 (Seattle, WA: Biblesoft, 2016).
3. If you would like to read my view on who the overcomers are, please read my online article http://www.TheEternalBlueprintBook.com/TEB-Resources/WhoAreTheOvercomers.pdf

Chapter 31

1. *Thayer's Greek Lexicon, Electronic Database* (Seattle, WA: Biblesoft, Inc., 2006), s.v. "stephanos," referenced from OneTouch OB-2 (Seattle, WA: Biblesoft, 2016).
2. *Vines Expository Dictionary of Biblical Words* (New York: Thomas Nelson Publishers, 1985), s.v. "stephanos," referenced from OneTouch OB-2 (Seattle, WA: Biblesoft, 2016).
3. "Forever and ever" is literally "ages to ages." In fact, the Young's Literal Translation, translates this as "to the ages of the ages."
4. See Revelation 7:15; 11:19; 14:15; 14:17; 15:5; 15:6; 16:1; 16:17.
5. http://www.desiringgod.org/books/god-is-the-gospel, referenced on 8/25/2017.

About the Author

Bryan Kessler is the senior pastor of Restoration Life Church and Ministry Center in Marietta, Georgia. Since 2003, he has also served as the vice president of Lifeschool International, a global missions ministry that trains and equips pastors in Kenya, Uganda, Tanzania, Malawi, Zimbabwe, Zambia, South Africa, and DR Congo.

Bryan spends much of his time studying, writing and teaching about topics related to God's eternal purpose, the bride of Christ, the overcomers, the way of the cross, and the fullness of Christ. Bryan has been married to his wife Angie for twenty years, and they have one daughter.

Bryan worked as a full-time software programmer for two decades before becoming the senior pastor of Restoration Life in May, 2017. He holds a bachelor's degree in industrial engineering from the Georgia Institute of Technology and has been serving in ministry since 1995.

For More Information

Restoration Life Church and Ministry Center
P.O. Box 671063
Marietta, GA 30066-0136

Email: Info@RestorationLife.org

Websites: www.RestorationLife.org (church)
www.LifeschoolInternational.org (missions ministry)
www.PursuitOfChrist.org (online resources and blog)
www.TheEternalBlueprintBook.com (book website)

68484514R00194

Made in the USA
Middletown, DE
16 September 2019